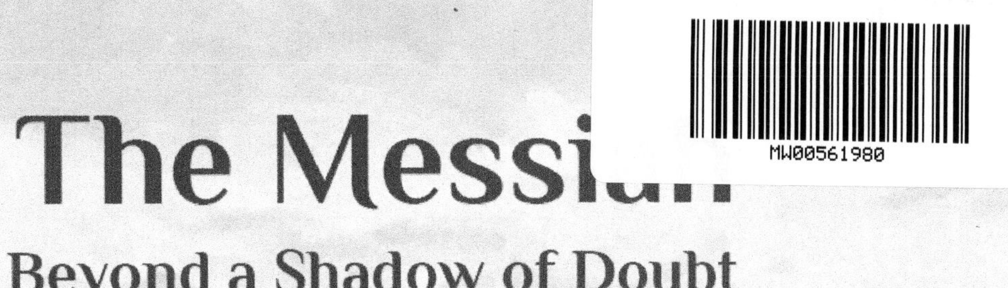

The Messiah

Beyond a Shadow of Doubt

A Study of the Messiah in the Appointed Times

by Donald McCluskey - illustrated by Kate Orr

www.TheAppointedTimes.com

Rev. 0122264-24

Contents

Sincerest thanks to those who made this work possible!

Abby, Alan, Amy, Andy, Bob, Chris, David, Elaine, Ervin, Jared, Jesse, Jill, Joan, John, Karen, Kate, Laurie, Mark, Missie, Richard, & Rob

"Employ your time in improving yourself by other men's writings so that you shall come easily by what others have labored hard for."

– Socrates

Dedicated

To Those Who Seek

Glory and Honor and Immortality

"Great are the works of the Lord.
They are studied by all who delight in them."

Psalm 111:2

Preface

Ideas are frequently evaluated by the way they have evolved or have been lived out by their followers. It is better, however, to first examine the source of a teaching with a sincere effort to understand the principles as they were first conceived by their author. When we judge something by the way it has morphed over time, we risk missing the genius and truth that was originally envisioned.

This is certainly the case with the Jewish holy days, the Lord's Appointed Times that were revealed to the people of Israel almost 3,500 years ago. Only a careful examination of Moses' original words in light of ancient Israel's culture can reveal the intended meaning of the Appointed Times. The observances of these events have changed dramatically throughout the centuries, but God's plan, which they reveal, has not.

For reasons that become obvious later in this book, much of the significance of the Appointed Times has been lost throughout the ages to the extent that their meaning is no longer recognizable. Even though this appears to be an enormous loss to the Faith, the reason is, no doubt, Providential in nature. One of the subtle themes that recurs throughout the Scriptures is that God hides knowledge, but in His mysterious way, He reveals it in His good timing.

As you read this book, you will no doubt encounter ideas and concepts that are new to you, some that differ from your current understanding, and some that make you a little bit uncomfortable. But consider this—we are going to examine the evidence from the source in the same way that an archeologist dusts an artifact and then muses on how it should be woven into the grand tapestry of a culture and history. In a similar way, we will examine evidence about the Lord's Messiah and explore the ultimate mystery of man communing with God Himself.

My purpose in writing about the Messiah is to proclaim the significance of something that has been before the eyes of mankind for millennia but for some reason has been virtually unnoticed. God's Word contains truths that are far deeper than the prose and poetry on its surface. Truth is buried within like precious treasure, and it is up to us to seek it, muse upon it, and respond accordingly. My hope is that we can unearth some of these beautiful truths together through the pages of this book. I am honored that you have chosen to walk with me on this journey through the Lord's Appointed Times and revel in the joy of God's magnificent gift to mankind—His Messiah.

Introduction – Something Unique!

The Appointed Times are one of the greatest sources of theological truth in the entire Bible—the fountainhead of many branches of theology, especially those relating to the Messiah. Our reason for writing this book is to demonstrate how the Jewish holy days make it clear, beyond a shadow of doubt, that Jesus of Nazareth is truly the Messiah. These sacred events highlight the things that are important to God, so we do not have to rely on the uncertain wisdom and insights of man in our quest for discerning His truth.

The Lord designed the Appointed Times in a curious way. Through them, He created mysterious shadows that teach about the things He was going to do, long before they were actually accomplished. Yet their meanings became obvious only after the events were fulfilled by His Messiah. Indeed, the Appointed Times are exceedingly special treasures in the Scriptures, unique in their approach and in the messages they reveal.

It would be legitimate to ask: If the Appointed Times are such a valuable source of theology, why didn't they become a significant part of church doctrine? Why didn't the apostles emphasize the relationship between these ceremonies of Moses and the Messiah? Why didn't the church fathers clarify the correlation for us? Why weren't the Jewish religious leaders overwhelmed by the obvious fulfillment and point their nation to Jesus as their Messiah?

If I may be so bold, I believe it has been the Lord's intention that the Appointed Times have been muted throughout the ages. Perhaps, in His mysterious, sovereign way, He will make it obvious to all who will see and one day remove the hardening from those who have refused to see. Perhaps this will be the generation that will see and recognize Jesus as the Messiah.

Theater Israel

The Messiah and the Appointed Times were given to Israel[1], but you should know that the nation of Israel was not created just for Israelites—it was for the world. The nation of Israel was brought into existence so everyone could observe and learn about God, about His holiness, mercy, justice, and love. Israel is a theater filled with dramas and commentary that show that no one is exempt from God's justice when His ways are violated, not even His own people—dramas about His tender mercy, love, forgiveness, and blessing for those who honor Him, and the perils and darkness for those who do not.

1 *Romans 9:4–5*

Most importantly, Israel was the chosen vehicle through which God would send His Messiah into the world. From the stories of the Bible, we learn of His plan to redeem mankind through His Messiah, who will one day take center stage in the cosmic performance and welcome His children into the ultimate paradise to enjoy the provisions and security of the only true Sovereign. Theater Israel is God's forum for revealing Himself to the world, to all mankind.

Our Direction

This book explores two primary subjects: The Messiah and The Appointed Times. You may be familiar with the concept of the Messiah, but to sharpen your understanding, we devote an entire chapter to clarify its meaning in the Scriptures. As we explore the concept of the Messiah, it is essential that we understand the reason He had to die. Why did He have to die? It is an excellent question that deserves a thoughtful, clear answer.

We will spend the remainder of our time together exploring the Appointed Times. It is strange that very few Christians have heard of the Appointed Times, since they are not a secret in the Bible. They are situated in the heart of the Law of Moses in the 23rd chapter of Leviticus, which is somewhat uncharted territory for many. You may be tempted to close this book at the mention of Leviticus, asking what book of the Bible could be drier and less relevant to New Testament believers? But I assure you, the Lord's Appointed Times reveal secrets and explain mysteries about the Messiah that are fresh and alive and able to breathe new life into your faith.

Furthermore, the Appointed Times explain the origin and meaning of important scriptural terms that are somewhat vague to many people. Terms such as Passover, The Feast of Unleavened Bread, First Fruits, Pentecost, The Day of Trumpets, the Day of Atonement, and the Feast of Booths. Understanding these holy days will enhance your overall understanding of God's Word and help you construct a comprehensive picture of His Messiah.

The Intersection

We can certainly study about the Messiah and the Appointed Times independently of each other, but it is in the intersection of these two subjects that special truths come to light that reveal connecting threads within the Scriptures. The Appointed Times are like luminous fibers in a tapestry that highlight the most important themes of God's Word and lead us to the Messiah. Through this study, you will see connections between themes in the Bible that are otherwise not obvious, thus deepening your overall understanding.

There is a third area that adds light to our study of the Messiah and the Appointed Times, which is tracking time in Israel. As the name suggests, timing is an integral part of the Appointed Times, so it follows that we should seek to understand how the ancient Israelites tracked time. A study of the ancient Jewish calendar provides valuable keys that give insight into the meaning of the Appointed Times, especially in their messianic significance. This knowledge can also add color and accuracy as we interpret other stories of the Bible, making it a useful tool for every student of the Word.

Beyond Magnificent

The message of the Appointed Times is the message of the Lord. Through these ceremonies, He has intimated truths that are important to Him, and they should be of supreme importance to each of us. The concept of the Messiah is beyond magnificent, yet my words are wholly inadequate to convey this message with the grandeur that it deserves. I pray that the Spirit of Christ will move in your heart to consider this message so that you will know the hope of His calling and the riches of the glory of His inheritance for those who believe.

Four Goals

This book has four underlying goals:

The First is to demonstrate, beyond a shadow of doubt, that Jesus is truly the Messiah.

The Second is to show how God's desire and plan for saving mankind was orchestrated from the very beginning of time—His Messiah and salvation were not simply a bandage that was applied after the fall of man.

The Third is to fortify believers in their faith in Jesus. As we study the Messiah in the Appointed Times, believers' confidence and trust in God's Word and in Jesus as the Messiah will be strengthened.

The Fourth is to give hope, not simply in the forgiveness of the Messiah, but that we will one day be liberated from the futility of living mortal lives in a world that is laced with grief. For we will, one day, be raised from the dead to live forever as immortals in paradise, at peace with God—a hope like no other—a hope that can sustain believers in their darkest hours in this life.

How to Read This Book

The subject of the Messiah in the Appointed Times is one of the most fascinating studies in all the Scriptures. In order to make the message understandable to as many people as possible, I have included some information that will help those who may not be as versed in the Scriptures or the stories of the Bible. For the reader who already has this knowledge, I ask for your patience, as we occasionally review some fundamental stories and concepts, especially in Chapter 4, which provides a historical background of the Appointed Times. The review information may be useful to all readers, and at the very least it will help to clarify our usage of terms.

For the reader who is less familiar with the Bible, I hope that you persevere in understanding this material—it is certainly worth the effort. This book provides valuable aids, including a rich set of endnotes, information about the Hebrew calendar, a glossary, background information from the Talmud, Quick Facts tables about each Appointed Time, and an explanation of the synoptic gospels. I am confident that you will be able to grasp this information with a little effort, so this book has been designed to assist you in your journey.

Footnotes

You will notice many footnotes in the text, which provide additional information about the subject at hand, including biblical and extra-biblical references. Significant effort has been applied to documenting points from many sources, so you can see where and how they were derived—you do not have to take my word as the only source of information. The footnotes include biblical references, Jewish writings, and historical and scientific documents. As much as possible, the oldest, most reliable sources have been used.

Understanding the Ancient Calendar

As mentioned earlier, understanding how the ancient Israelites tracked time is one of the keys to understanding how the Appointed Times relate to key events of Jesus' ministry. If we were to study the Appointed Times by our modern calendar, we would likely miss the message and the intricate timing that the Lord built into the time signature of the Messiah.

But rather than explaining those concepts in line with the main flow of this book, I have provided all of the timing information that you will need (and more) in a compendium called *Tracking Time in Israel*, which has been included in its entirety at the end of this book. In many places, the reader is directed to a specific section of the compendium that explains the immediate subject at hand. The compendium is a valuable tool that can shed light on many stories of the Bible, and especially on the Appointed Times.

Glossary

A comprehensive glossary has been included, which explains many of the important words and terms that are used in this book.

The Talmud

The Talmud is an authoritative body of Jewish literature that provides commentary on the Law of Moses, usually in very practical ways, that the Jewish rabbis interpreted and implemented the commands of Moses. Even though the Jewish faith highly esteems the writings of the Talmud, they do not consider it to be inspired or inerrant, as are the writings of Moses, the Psalms, and the Prophets.

> *The Talmud (Hebrew for "study") is one of the central works of the Jewish people. It is the record of rabbinic teachings that spans a period of about six hundred years, beginning in the first century C.E. and continuing through the sixth and seventh centuries C.E. The rabbinic teachings of the Talmud explain in great detail how the commandments of the Torah are to be carried out.*[2]

I have cited many passages from the Talmud that explain the Jewish understanding and implementation of the Appointed Times. In most cases, references have been provided so readers can verify my words. This does not, however, suggest that I am adopting the teachings and perspectives of the Talmud—only that it is a rich source of information that can add light to our study.

2 *(Isaacs 2003) – Introduction, Page ix*

Quick Facts about Each Appointed Time

Each Appointed Time chapter references a Quick Facts table that lists the high-level details of the event. This information gives a bird's-eye view of the Appointed Time and helps the reader relate it to the bigger picture of God's plan.

The Synoptic Gospels

As you read this book, you should be aware of the phenomenon that the look and feel of the first three gospels, Matthew, Mark and Luke, differ from that of the gospel of John. Matthew, Mark, and Luke are referred to as the synoptic gospels, since they appear to be very similar to each other in their verbiage, content, and perspectives, they are said to look alike. Thus, they are referred to as the syn (i.e., same or similar) optic (i.e., look) gospels.

For example, the synoptic gospels contain many parables that Jesus taught—some are even recorded in all three synoptic gospels. On the other hand, none of the parables from the synoptic gospels are recorded in John. One of the more challenging differences is found in the way that all four gospels describe the timing of the events that occurred during the week of Jesus' crucifixion.

A superficial study of the four gospels could lead a person to conclude that contradictions exist between accounts of the synoptic gospels versus that of John. Thus, it is very important to be aware that this *apparent* discrepancy exists, since it could otherwise cloud our understanding of Jesus' fulfillment of the Appointed Times. In *Chapter 10 – Abib 14 – The Lord's Passover*, we spend a fair amount of time exploring how the differences between the synoptic gospels and John should be understood in order to see how all four gospels harmonize beautifully with each other.

The Genuine Article

Finally, you will notice that I focus on the original words of Moses regarding the Appointed Times. Indeed, the observances of the various festivals and holy days were changed throughout the centuries by kings and by the Jewish oral law. But the mysteries of the Messiah are most clearly seen in the Lord's original words to Moses—the shadows of the festivals, new moon, and Sabbath days. You will find, therefore, that this book does not focus on the subsequent changes to the Appointed Times that evolved in the years that followed the death of Moses—we will focus only on the Appointed Times as they were originally conveyed to him.

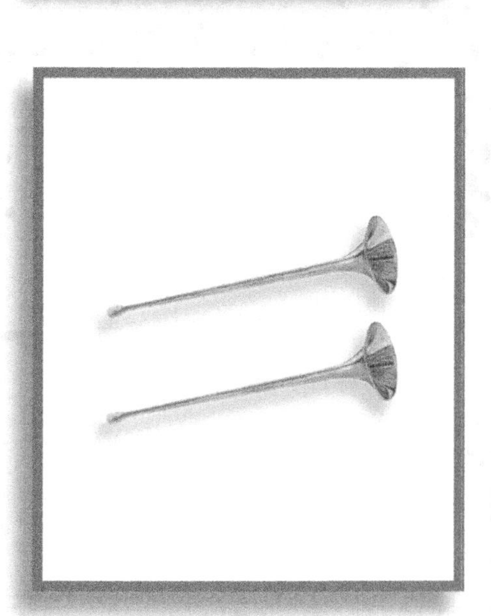

Part 1 – The Appointed Times

These are the appointed times of the LORD,
holy convocations which you shall proclaim at the times appointed for them.

Leviticus 23:4

You may have heard of the Jewish holy days such as the Sabbath Day, Passover, the Feast of Unleavened Bread, First Fruits, Pentecost, The Feast of Booths, The Day of Atonement, or The Day of Trumpets. If so, then you have encountered the Appointed Times. They include days of rest (Sabbaths), days of feasting (festivals), days of solemn ceremony, and various activities for the people and priests (Levites) throughout each year.

These special days were instituted by the Lord Himself. They are holy days and events that the Israelites were required to observe throughout each year at the specific times that the Lord prescribed.

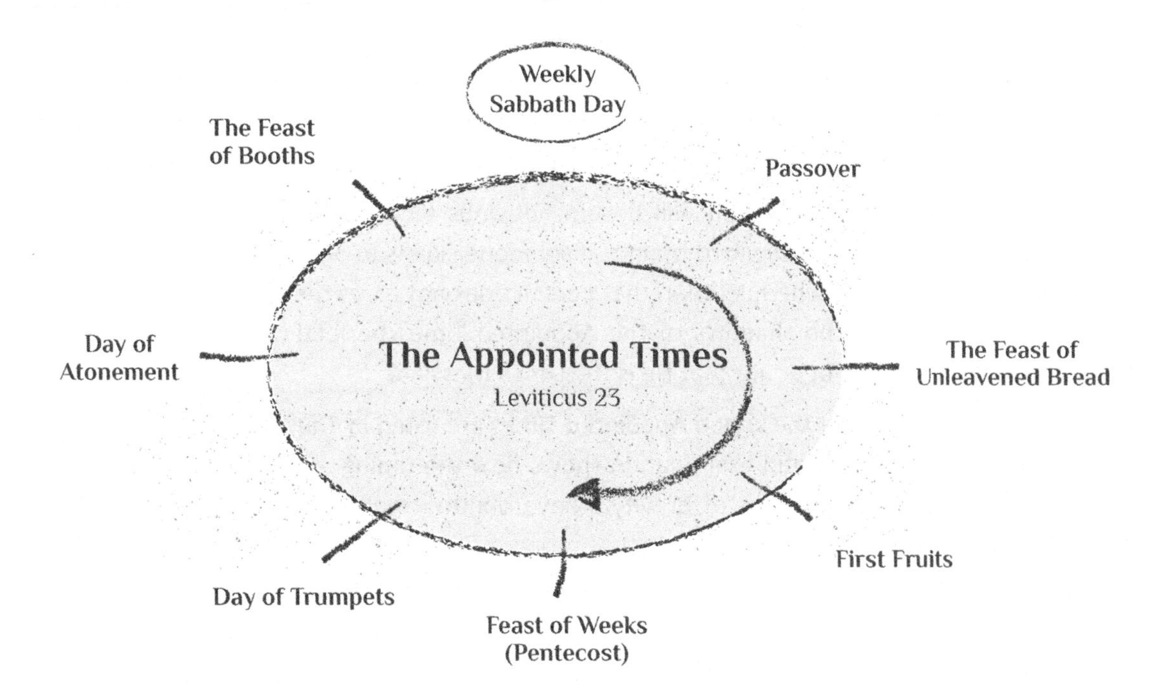

The Form of the Appointed Times

As we read about the Appointed Times in the 23rd chapter of Leviticus, we find that they are divided into two distinct seasons of the year—the spring and the fall. The spring Appointed Times speak of the first coming of the Messiah, highlighting key aspects of His ministry on earth 2,000 years ago. They speak of His purity and worthiness as a sacrifice, His death, His burial, His resurrection, and the giving of the Holy Spirit. The fall Appointed Times add further insights into His work, including His coronation, the resurrection and judgment of the dead, and the Messiah and His bride taking up residence in eternal homes.

The Spring Appointed Times
The Time Signature of the Messiah

What do we mean by the *time signature* of the Messiah? You may be thinking of a musical time signature, but this time signature refers to the well-defined schedule of *messianic* events that must be accomplished in perfect timing. As you would expect, the *spring* Appointed Times occur in the springtime of each year, beginning in the month of Abib[3], which is also called Nisan. When these events are studied together as a unit, it becomes clear that their timing forms a time signature that defines the timing of key events in the life of the Messiah.

The identity of the Messiah will become obvious when a person steps forward who fulfills these events in their prescribed timing. If someone claims to be the Messiah but does not accomplish these feats on schedule, then that person does not meet the criteria of the Messiah. Jesus, however, fulfilled the shadows of the Appointed Times perfectly, in their exact timing, proving beyond a shadow of doubt that He is the Lord's Messiah.

The components of the *spring* Appointed Times are listed in *The Spring Appointed Times* table on the next page. Careful examination shows how the timing and the events correspond to the life of Jesus. For the sake of brevity, I have omitted the details since it is provided in following chapters.

3 Abib is the first month of the Jewish year for religious observances. It is synonymous with Nisan, which was adopted during the Babylonian captivity. See Nehemiah 2:1 and Esther 3:7. We will use Abib throughout this book.

The Spring Appointed Times

Shadow	Appointed Time	Substance
	Abib 10 Inspect the Lamb for Purity In preparation for Passover, each household was to take an unblemished male lamb and observe it for its purity until the 14th. In a similar way, Jesus entered Jerusalem on the 10th day and was tested by the religious leaders regarding His purity in God's truth. He demonstrated such pure wisdom and truth that no one dared to continue questioning him.	
	Abib 14 (Passover) Kill the lamb and publicly display its blood The lamb was to be killed between 3:00pm and sundown, and its blood was to be applied to the doorposts and lintel of each house. In the same way, Jesus was crucified on Passover and died at 3:00pm—the same time that the Lord stipulated for the Passover lamb to be killed.	
	Abib 15–21 The Feast of Unleavened Bread When the sun set on Abib 14, the date changed to the 15th, which was the first day of the Feast of Unleavened Bread. On this evening, the people were to eat the lamb with bitter herbs and unleavened bread. Jesus was placed in the tomb on this same evening—the Lamb tasting the bitterness of death.	

The Sunday during the Feast of Unleavened Bread First-Fruits

First Fruits was to be observed on the day after the weekly Sabbath (i.e., on Sunday) during the seven-day Feast of Unleavened Bread. Thus, on the same day that the Israelites offered the sheaf of the First Fruits offering, Jesus rose from the dead as the first fruits of many brothers and sisters. The timing is stunning – the Israelites also arose alive from the sea at daybreak on First Fruits, and almost 1,500 years later Jesus arose alive from the tomb at daybreak on First Fruits.

50 Days after First Fruits
The Feast of Weeks
(i.e. Pentecost)

Fifty days after the Israelites arose alive from the sea on First Fruits, the Lord met them at Mount Sinai in a terrifying way and gave His Law to the people. Almost 1,500 years later, on the day of Pentecost, the Lord met with His disciples in the upper room in Jerusalem and lovingly indwelled them with His Holy Spirit.

As you can see, the spring Appointed Times provide a very clear time signature, which Jesus fulfilled with perfect precision.

Shadows

At this point we must ask, "Could it just be a coincidence that the timing and events of the Appointed Times just happened to match the timing and events of Jesus' life, or did the Lord intentionally place the Appointed Times in His Word to teach about the Messiah?" This is an excellent question, since we do not want to spend our time musing on mere coincidences that have little or no substance. Our focus must be on God's truth. Fortunately, the Scriptures provide a clear answer for us.

In Colossians 2:16–17, Paul tells us that no one should act as our judge in regard to "a festival, new moon, or Sabbath day—things which are a mere *shadow* of what is to come; but the substance belongs to Christ."[4] Did you know that the Jewish *festivals*, new moons, and *Sabbath days* were instituted by the Appointed Times? Although he did not use the term *Appointed Times*, Paul is referring to these holy days and telling us that they teach about the Messiah.

> ...a festival, new moon, or Sabbath day—things which are a mere **shadow** of what is to come; but the substance belongs to Christ.
>
> Colossians 2:16–17 (Emphasis added)

The book of Hebrews also teaches that the Law... has only a *shadow* of the good things to come and not the very form of things.[5] When we view these passages together, we learn that the Messiah is the substance or the true meaning of the Appointed Times, whereas the festivals, new moons, and Sabbath days simply cast shadows of His work.

What do we mean when we say that the Appointed Times are shadows of Christ? When we see a shadow on the ground or on a wall, we are able to discern details about the object that is casting it by simply observing its outline. Even though the shadow is all we can see, we can learn some key things about the object without being distracted by its many details.

In a similar way, the Appointed Times convey key truths about the work of the Messiah without overwhelming us with the splendor of His character and glory. From our human perspective, the Appointed Times help us understand the significance of events that we might otherwise miss amidst the complex and glorious details of the Messiah. For this reason God gave us shadows to help us see the forest despite the multitude of trees—forms and rites from the unfamiliar realm of heaven. It is up to us to meditate on these shadows so we can gain deeper and clearer understanding of the work of the Messiah.

Notice also that Paul said the Appointed Times are a shadow of what is to come. Some of the prophetic aspects have already occurred, but the fulfillment of others are still in the future, even from the time of Paul—even from our own time in the 21st century. We also find

4 Colossians 2:16 – "Therefore no one is to act as your judge in regard to food or drink or in respect to a festival or a new moon or a Sabbath day—things which are a mere shadow of what is to come; but the substance belongs to Christ" (Emphasis added).

5 Hebrews 10:1 (Emphasis added)

that the Lord has given special meaning to these dates in His plan for the ages. They include divinely significant events that have already occurred on these appointed dates in the past, but they also speak of divinely significant events that will occur on the same dates in the future.

Speaking of Jesus!

After His resurrection from the dead, Jesus had a very interesting conversation with two men on the road to Emmaus, making it very clear that the Hebrew Bible[6] speaks of Him. "Then beginning with Moses and with all the prophets, He explained to them the things concerning Himself in all the Scriptures."[7] Later in the same chapter, He told His disciples, "These are My words which I spoke to you while I was still with you, that all things which are written about Me in the *Law of Moses* and the *Prophets* and the *Psalms* must be fulfilled."[8] Did you get that? Jesus said that the Law of Moses contains prophesies about Himself, which brings us back to the Appointed Times. So we are on the right path when we look into the Hebrew Bible in our search for the Messiah.

It is essential for followers of Christ to study both the New Testament and the Hebrew Bible. Without the Hebrew Bible, the New Testament has very little context, relying on itself for credibility. But since the Scriptures of old give context and credibility to the New Testament, it is essential that we become intimately familiar with both bodies of Scripture. Many false Christs have come and gone throughout the centuries, but we determine whether a person meets the messianic criteria by examining his or her claims and works to see if they align with the entirety of God's Word.

The fall Appointed Times occur during the September–October timeframe of each year during the Hebrew month of Tishri. In general, the messianic events which they shadow have yet to be fulfilled, so it is more difficult to speak with certainty about how and when the events will unfold. Nonetheless, the New Testament provides insightful clues that align with the Appointed Times that the Lord originally conveyed to Moses. Please examine the *The Fall Appointed Times* table on the next page which contains a summary of these messianic events.

The latter chapters of this book will fill in the gaps and address objections, along with the apparent contradictions and concerns regarding Jesus' fulfillment. You will see that it becomes very clear that the Appointed Times clearly confirm that Jesus is the Messiah.

---

6 The Hebrew Bible, also called Hebrew Scriptures, is the same body of Scripture that is referred to as the Old Testament of the Bible.

7 Luke 24:27

8 Luke 24:44 (Emphasis added)

The Fall Appointed Times

Shadow	Appointed Time	Substance
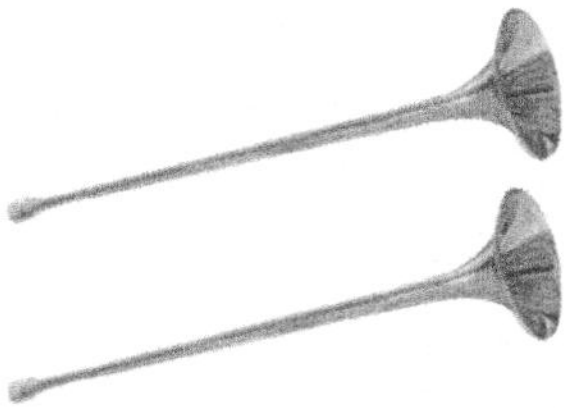	Tishri 1: The Day of Trumpets (Yom Teruah) The Return of the Messiah "Then the seventh angel sounded; and there were loud voices in heaven, saying, 'The kingdom of the world has become the kingdom of our Lord and of His Christ; and He will reign forever and ever.'"[9]	
	Tishri 10: The Day of Atonement (Yom Kippur) Full Atonement by the Messiah "...when Christ appeared as a high priest of the good things to come, He entered through the greater and more perfect tabernacle... through His own blood, He entered the holy place once for all, having obtained eternal redemption."[10]	
	Tishri 15–21: The Feast of Booths Taking Up Residence "And I saw the holy city, new Jerusalem, coming down out of heaven from God..."[11] "...and the throne of God and of the Lamb will be in it, and His bond-servants will serve Him; they will see His face, and His name will be on their foreheads."[12]	

9 *Revelation 11:15*

10 *Hebrews 9:11-12*

11 *Revelation 21:2*

12 *Revelation 22:3-4*

Leviticus 23 – The Chronology of the Appointed Times

Where do we find the Appointed Times in the Bible? They are listed in chronological order in the 23rd chapter of Leviticus. You will see, however, that this chapter does not provide all of the details regarding how the events are to be observed. Because of this, it is necessary to search the other books of Moses so we can see the bigger picture.

As we explore each Appointed Time, we will look to Leviticus 23 as our starting point for the chronology (i.e. the chronological order). We will then look into the related passages in the Pentateuch (the five books of Moses) to expand our understanding of each event. Thus, Leviticus 23 will be our starting point, which will lead us to related passages in the Pentateuch. The related passages for each Appointed Time are listed in the Quick Facts tables in Appendix E.

The entire chapter of Leviticus 23 has been printed in Appendix A. I strongly encourage you to become familiar with it, since it is central to our study of the Appointed Times. The introductory information for each Appointed Time from Leviticus 23 has been printed on the next page with my emphases added:

Part 1: The Appointed Times

Leviticus 23

1 The LORD spoke again to Moses, saying, 2 "Speak to the sons of Israel and say to them, 'The LORD'S appointed times which you shall proclaim as holy convocations—My appointed times are these:

The Weekly Sabbath Day – Lev 23:3

3 'For six days work may be done, but on the seventh day there is a sabbath of complete rest, a holy convocation. You shall not do any work; it is a sabbath to the LORD in all your dwellings.

<u>The Spring Appointed Times</u>

Passover – Lev 23:5

5 'In the first month, on the fourteenth day of the month at twilight is the LORD'S Passover.

The Feast of Unleavened Bread – Lev 23:6

6 'Then on the fifteenth day of the same month there is the Feast of Unleavened Bread to the LORD; for seven days you shall eat unleavened bread.

First Fruits – Lev 23:10–11

10 'When you enter the land which I am going to give to you and reap its harvest, then you shall bring in the sheaf of the first fruits of your harvest to the priest. 11 He shall wave the sheaf before the LORD for you to be accepted; on the day after the sabbath the priest shall wave it.

The Feast of Weeks – Lev 23:15–16

15 'You shall also count for yourselves from the day after the sabbath, from the day when you brought in the sheaf of the wave offering; there shall be seven complete sabbaths. 16 You shall count fifty days to the day after the seventh sabbath; then you shall present a new grain offering to the LORD.

<u>The Fall Appointed Times</u>

The Day of Trumpets – Lev 23:24

24 'In the seventh month on the first of the month you shall have a rest, a reminder by blowing of trumpets, a holy convocation.'

The Day of Atonement – Lev 23:27

27 "On exactly the tenth day of this seventh month is the day of atonement; it shall be a holy convocation for you, and you shall humble your souls and present an offering by fire to the LORD.

The Feast of Booths – Lev 23:34

34 'On the fifteenth of this seventh month is the Feast of Booths for seven days to the LORD.'"

Moed – Appointed Time

The Hebrew word that is translated as Appointed Time is *MOED*. This word has several meanings, and it occurs outside of the context of the Appointed Times; there is nothing mystical about the word itself. Moed has multiple meanings, including a place of meeting, a signal, an appointed sign or time, a place of solemn assembly, a congregation, a feast, or even a synagogue.

Terminology

There is one more item that I should mention about the Appointed Times. People frequently refer to them as the Jewish Festivals, which is not a completely accurate description. In order to clarify the terms for our study, you should know that only three of the Appointed Times are festivals: the Feast of Unleavened Bread, the Feast of Weeks (aka Pentecost), and the Feast of Booths (aka. the Feast of Tabernacles). The word feast in the name indicates that it is a festival.

The other Appointed Times are not actually feasts or festivals. For example, First Fruits is a "day," and the Day of Atonement is also a "day;" neither of these are feasts or festivals. Referring to the Day of Atonement as a feast would be a serious misrepresentation of the solemn nature of the ceremony. Sometimes, for the sake of convenience, we might refer to the Appointed Times as the Jewish feasts or festivals, but we should at least be aware that this is a misnomer—they are more accurately called the Appointed Times.

Chapter 1: The Messiah

We have found the Messiah...

What do we mean by "Messiah?" What does the word mean? *Messiah* is a Hebrew word that simply means *anointed one*, referring to someone who was anointed with oil by pouring it over the head[13] to signify that this person was appointed to a specific purpose or office. There were many messiahs in the Bible. In the history of Israel, priests and kings were anointed with oil to signify that they were in an official role for God—they were *messiahs* in a technical sense.

Just for the record, priests and kings were not the only objects of anointing. In the tabernacle, the altar, the tent of meeting, and the Ark of the Covenant were anointed, along with its various furnishings and utensils. [14]It is interesting that anointing in the religious realm was not normally done with simple olive oil.[15] The oil that was used for anointing priests and items of worship was a special formulation given to Moses from the Lord, a perfumed mixture of fine spices combined with olive oil. This anointing oil was sacred and, under the penalty of being *cut off*[16] from Israel, was never to be compounded or used for any other purpose than those which were designated by the Lord.[17]

---

13 *Leviticus 8:12, 1 Samuel 10:1, 2 Kings 9:3, Psalm 133:2*

14 *Exodus 29:36, 30:26, 40:9–11*

15 *Exodus 30:22–25*

16 *Cut Off (Hebrew: Kareth) "means not necessarily physical dissolution but extinction of the soul and its denial of a share in the world to come." – (Ehrman 1965) Volume 1*

17 *Exodus 30:33 – "Whoever shall mix [any] like it or whoever puts any of it on a layman shall be cut off from his people."*

On a lighter note, anointing also seemed to be a normal part of general hygiene and people's daily routine, as they probably anointed themselves with oil to groom their hair or to give a glow to their skin. Naomi advised Ruth to wash and anoint herself and put on her best clothes[18] so she could attend a harvest celebration and meet the man of her dreams.[19] Jesus told the people to anoint their heads and wash their faces so they would look acceptable and no one would suspect that they were fasting.[20]

In a sense, all of these people and items were *anointed ones*, but there is an exceedingly special individual whom we will refer to as ***the** Anointed One* or ***the** Messiah*. There is only one person who can claim this title. Even the greatest kings of Israel, although they were anointed ones, were not ***the** Anointed One*; they were not ***the** Messiah*.

The concept of the Messiah was introduced through a somewhat mysterious statement near the outset of the Scriptures. As part of the curse on the serpent in Genesis 3:15, the Lord said,

> *"I will put enmity between you and the woman,*
> *and between your offspring and her offspring;*
> *he shall bruise your head, and you shall bruise his heel." (ESV)*

The words of the curse are mysterious indeed, and their meaning runs much deeper than the idea of women disliking snakes. In the book of Revelation, the serpent is identified as the devil and Satan,[21] who deceives the whole world. As Eve listened to the voice of the serpent, she was actually deliberating with Satan himself. But as we explore these words of God, we must ask, "Who is the offspring of the woman who will strike the serpent—Satan—with a deathblow, despite the serpent striking him with a temporal wound?" As history unfolds throughout the Bible, it becomes evident that the offspring of the woman is the Messiah himself.

Progressive Revelation

God designed the Scriptures in a curious way. Key themes are sometimes introduced in brief and somewhat cryptic statements. But as the Spirit of God developed the themes through subsequent authors, He provided additional information and insights that increase

---

18 *Ruth 3:3*

19 *Okay—I took a little liberty with Naomi's description of Boaz—maybe she did not refer to him as the man of her dreams. Nonetheless, it was truly a match made in heaven!*

20 *Matthew 6:17*

21 *Revelation 12:9 - "And the great dragon was thrown down, the serpent of old who is called the devil and Satan, who deceives the whole world; he was thrown down to the earth, and his angels were thrown down with him."*

our understanding. This is the case with subjects like the Messiah, the Law of Moses, the Sabbath Day, and the Kingdom of God—we refer to this phenomenon of progressively revealing information as *progressive revelation*.

The term "Messiah," however, was used only one time in the Hebrew Bible to describe this special, promised individual. Daniel 9:25 makes this connection, saying,

"So you are to know and discern that
from the issuing of a decree to restore and rebuild Jerusalem
until **Messiah *the Prince*** *there will be seven weeks and sixty-two weeks..."*
(Emphasis added)

Nonetheless, it is clear from the progressively revealed Scripture passages that the Lord promised to send a Redeemer-King, a Savior, who would reign eternally over an everlasting kingdom, ruling with justice and righteousness. By the first century AD, this special individual had become commonly known as the Messiah or the Christ.

Speaking of the Christ, we have already mentioned that "messiah" is the Hebrew word that means *anointed one*. But as the apostles penned their writings in Greek, they usually used the Greek word for Messiah, which is Christos (Χριστός) or Christ. In other words, Messiah and Christ have the same meaning.

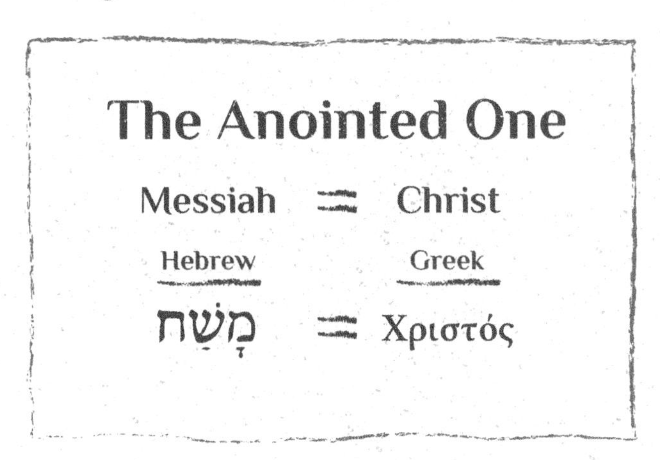

Think about it—when a person refers to Jesus Christ, they are actually saying, "Jesus Messiah" or that Jesus is the Messiah. In a similar way, when a person is called a Christian, they are essentially being called a follower of the Messiah or a person who believes in Christ and is Christ-like in their ways.

Watching for the Messiah

During the first century, the faithful were sometimes described as those watching for the appearing of the Messiah and His kingdom. There was certainly a lot of excitement and expectation about the appearing of the Messiah, as we will see in *Part 3 – The Messiah in the Spring Appointed Times*, but the people were somewhat uncertain about how they would recognize Him.

As we study the prophesies of the Hebrew Bible, we find many promises about the Messiah who will come as a mighty, conquering king to rescue Israel from the tyranny of her oppressors, heal infirmities, forgive sins, and restore the kingdom. We learn that this king will be a descendant of King David and will rule His people in righteousness and justice forever—there will be no end to His kingdom.[22] Without question, there is something supernatural and divine about this highly anticipated individual.

Surely the people of Israel must have envisioned that the Messiah would rise up as a mighty statesman and warrior with supernatural powers, overthrowing their Roman captors, purifying the hearts of the people, and restoring true worship. Even King Herod feared the Messiah. The thought of losing his throne to the Messiah haunted him to the extent that he ordered his soldiers to kill every male child of Bethlehem who was under the age of two years old, in order to eliminate all possible challenges to his own throne.

It's no wonder that the Jewish people during the time of Jesus were perplexed about whether He was the Messiah, since the prophecies taught that the Messiah was to reign for all eternity. But when the crowd heard Him say that He must be *lifted up*, which is a euphemism for crucifixion, they must have thought, *wait a minute—we do not understand!* They asked, "We have heard out of the Law that the Christ is to remain forever; and how can You say, 'The Son of Man must be lifted up'?"[23] And indeed, they asked an excellent question. But Jesus replied that He would be with them only for a little while longer, implying that His death was certain.

The Messiah's Death

Let's explore the excellent question that the Jewish people posed to Jesus. How could Jesus be the Messiah if He was going to die? Isn't the Messiah supposed to live and reign forever with divine power and authority?

---

22 *Examples: Psalm 110:4, Isaiah 9:6–7, Jeremiah 23:5–6, Daniel 2:44–45, Daniel 7:13–14*

23 *John 12:34*

This question also confounded the Jewish sages of old. There are two predominate types of prophesies regarding the Messiah in the Hebrew Bible. Many of the prophesies spoke of Him as a mighty conquering king, but others spoke of Him as a humble, servant-like individual who would suffer and die at the hands of men. Since the Scriptures teach that the Messiah will come as a conquering king, how should we interpret the prophecies about His suffering and death? The conquering-king prophecies outnumber the suffering-servant prophesies by a ratio of eight-to-one, but we must still explain how the suffering-servant prophesies fit into the mysterious divine plan. Were the ancient prophesies actually foretelling two distinct Messiahs—two different individuals?

Truly these differing types of prophesies presented a dilemma for students of God's word. But as God's revelation unfolded, it became obvious that the Scriptures were not prophesying about two different Messiahs. Instead, they were prophesying about two *visitations* of the same Messiah. We will see how the Appointed Times clearly teach that the Lamb—the Messiah—would die, but that there would also be a resurrection of the same Lamb, who will, one day, return as a mighty, conquering king.

Who would have ever imagined that the Messiah, the one who was sent by the Father to rule over the nations, would die by the hands of those He came to save? But He did. It is even more difficult to comprehend that this was the intention of the Father from the very beginning. The fourth chapter of Acts records a brief prayer of the apostles and saints that confirms this truth:

*"And when they heard this, they lifted their voices to God with one accord and said, '**O Lord**, it is You who made the heaven and the earth and the sea, and all that is in them... For truly in this city there were gathered together against Your holy servant Jesus, whom You anointed, both Herod and Pontius Pilate, along with the Gentiles and the peoples of Israel,* ***to do whatever Your hand and Your purpose predestined to occur.'"***

Acts 4:24, 27–28
(Emphasis added)

Jesus was not a martyr and He was not a casualty of the Romans or the Jews—His death on the cross was very deliberate, planned long before He came to earth. It is mind-boggling that the Father would send the Son into a fallen and hostile world, not with the possibility that He might suffer harm and death, but with the certainty that He would. Even more shocking is that the Father took pleasure in crushing the Son and causing Him grief if He would offer himself as a sacrifice.[24] Does this change your opinion about the love of God or about His justice? If this idea is new to you, I advise you not to pass judgment on Him too quickly. When the full story comes to light you will see that it reveals a magnificent, compassionate dimension to His love that soars far beyond even the greatest love of mankind.

24 *Isaiah 53:10 – "But the Lord was pleased to crush Him, putting Him to grief; If He would render Himself as a guilt offering"*

Chapter 2 – Why Did He Have to Die?

Then the eyes of both of them were opened…
Genesis 3:7

I imagine, at this point, you may be wondering about the reason behind this violence and bloodshed that was ordained from the throne of the Almighty. Why did the Messiah have to suffer and die? I am pleased to tell you that there is a very, very good reason for such a strange plan from heaven, and I am even more pleased to tell you that the plan was conceived in love for the great benefit of the people of this earth, including you and me.

In order to understand the necessity of the Messiah's death, we must return to the early pages of the Bible and go back to the Garden of Eden during the days of creation. Recall how the words of the Bible express God's pleasure at the end of each day after He looked upon the work of His creation and saw that it was good. At the end of the day on which He created man, male and female,[25] it was declared to be **very** good. Certainly, if it was very good in the eyes of God, then it was a world that was free of evil, sickness, mourning, crying, and pain.

Can we infer from the account in Genesis that the relationship between God and Adam and Eve was tender and warm? I imagine God enjoying tender fellowship with His creatures in the garden during the cool of the day, listening to their stories of what they had seen and learned and their fascination with their new world. Perhaps He winked at them as He dropped hints about the inner workings of His creation and ways to enjoy its riches. Like parents marveling as they watch their infant child discover their fingers and learn to control their hands,

25 *Genesis 1:27 – "God created man in His own image, in the image of God He created him; male and female He created them."*

so God must have felt great delight as He watched the amazement of Adam and Eve as they learned and increased in innocent understanding of His world.

But something terrible happened—an unimaginable catastrophe occurred that corrupted creation down to its very core. Sometime after God's creation was declared to be very good, the pride of Lucifer—the serpent and Satan—swelled within him and drove him to rebel against the Almighty. As a result, he was banished from the heavens and cast down to earth with his minions. It was Satan who used the serpent as his mouthpiece to deceive Eve so that she spurned the words of the Lord and ate from the tree of the Knowledge of Good and Evil. Because of the serpent's words, Adam also spurned the command of God and ate the fruit.

The Knowledge of Good and Evil

There were two trees of note in the center of the Garden of Eden.[26] One was the tree of life, which had the power to rejuvenate the human frame to the extent of eternal life. The other had a somewhat sinister sounding name: *the tree of the knowledge of good and evil*, for which God gave the direst warning against eating. If the consequences for partaking of this fruit were so severe, why did God allow it to flourish in plain sight, within reach of innocent hearts? Regardless of our speculations, there it stood.

The tree was delightful and its fruit was enticing—its beauty must have called to Adam and Eve and stirred their hearts with wonder and desire. The serpent's temptation did not take long to bear fruit in Eve. Perhaps she had already wondered about the fruit's effect on a heart—perhaps she wondered what it meant to be wise and what it meant to die—perhaps she wondered what it would be like to know both good and evil, rather than innocence. Whatever the knowledge of good and evil is, it resulted in a devastating toxic effect,[27] figurative or literal, that humans were not designed to possess.

The serpent's temptation hit its mark and resulted in the worst catastrophe that could ever have happened to humanity. You doubt? Imagine the story of creation if it had continued without the influence of that toxin. Our world would have never come to know jealousy, envy, hatred, murder, and war. God's design for humanity was to be pure, innocent, and wise; individuals, families, and cultures were to be characterized by love, compassion, and joy.

---

26 Genesis 2:9 – "The Lord God made all kinds of trees grow out of the ground—trees that were pleasing to the eye and good for food. In the middle of the garden were the tree of life and the tree of the knowledge of good and evil." (NIV)

27 I am using toxin figuratively to refer to the distortion of the nature of mankind as a result of disobeying God's commandment not to touch the tree or eat the fruit. Whether it was something innate within the fruit, or the rebellion in the act of disobedience, or a sin nature, or something else, for the sake of simplicity we will refer to it as a toxin.

Chapter 2: Why Did He Have to Die?

But with the knowledge of good and evil in our systems, our minds became hopelessly corrupt, treacherous, nefarious, and depraved. Our hearts and minds and reasoning were distorted to the extent that our thoughts became exceedingly wicked and our every intention was driven by evil.[28] A black river of sin was infused into the heart of man, ever groping for lower and more depraved ground, spreading its tentacles to the far reaches of the mind. The only possible hope being the intervention of the Creator Himself.

We are all beside ourselves because of the knowledge of good and evil within, each struggling to master the other. Mankind was not designed to coexist with the knowledge of good and evil, and the result was the universal imbalance of the heart and soul. Solomon tells us that the hearts of the sons of men are full of evil and insanity is in their hearts throughout their lives.[29] Jeremiah tells us that the heart of man is sick and desperately wicked.[30]

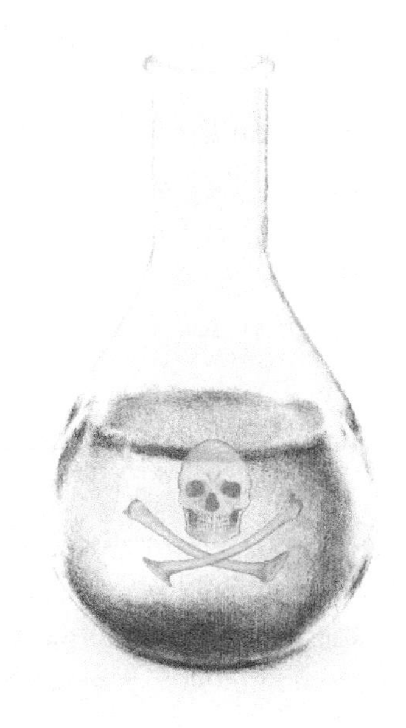

Does that explain some of the stories in the news headlines? Does the idea that mankind gravitates toward evil and is not basically good bother you? Can we really study history or read the news and honestly believe that man is basically good? Nonetheless, it is certainly correct that man was created to be good. But it is only because of God's love and His plan to restore us to pure goodness through His Messiah that mankind has hope—magnificent hope!

Certainly, we see much good in our world and in many people, but even the best will admit that they sometimes face this struggle within. Even if we veil our anger as righteous anger, we must concede that our desires fall short of the innocence of the newly created Adam and Eve. Even though the depths of depravity may not be evident in everyone, the cliff that borders the dark abyss is within walking distance for all of us.

---

28 *Genesis 6:5 – "Then the Lord saw that the wickedness of man was great on the earth, and that every intent of the thoughts of his heart was only evil continually."*

29 *Ecclesiastes 9:3 – "...the hearts of the sons of men are full of evil and insanity is in their hearts throughout their lives."*

30 *Jeremiah 17:9 – "The heart is more deceitful than all else And is desperately sick; Who can understand it?"*

The Curse

The fall of man incurred an additional toll as the Lord cursed creation with hardships that were not part of its original design. The curse brought thorns and thistles onto the earth, sentencing the farmer to a lifetime of toil. As the effects of the knowledge of good and evil multiplied, the earth became corrupt and filled with violence. Yet, even after God destroyed almost all of mankind with the great flood, the knowledge of good and evil still flowed through the veins of Noah and his family, extending its effects even to our day.

Didn't God anticipate this catastrophe? Was He unaware of the unimaginable distortion and horror that would result from placing an alluring temptation as the centerpiece of the garden? I believe that He knew—and if you allow me to speculate, I would suggest that in His mysterious way, it was to fulfill an even greater loving purpose for the human race—a relationship between God and man that will be perfect and eternally incorruptible.

There is no scheme or serum that can be concocted to restore the innocence of man. The hopes and worn out ideas for reversing the effects of sin—monastic separation, isolated communes, gene therapy, DNA manipulation, the chemistry of psychiatry, hypnosis, animal husbandry, and all others—are incapable of restoring innocence to the race of men. The corruption and depravity are so thorough and complete that the only possible remedy must come from the hand of the Creator Himself. Jesus referred to the healing remedy as the *regeneration*[31] and being *born again*,[32] and because of His divine work, He is the only one who is able to restore humanity in this way.

The Promise

And I will put enmity
Between you and the woman,
And between your seed and her seed;
He shall bruise you on the head,
And you shall bruise him on the heel.

Genesis 3:15 (Emphasis added)

31 *Mat 19:28 – "...in the regeneration when the Son of Man will sit on His glorious throne..." (Emphasis added) Also see Titus 3:5*

32 *John 3:3 – "Jesus answered and said to him, 'Truly, truly, I say to you, unless one is born again he cannot see the kingdom of God.'" (Emphasis added)*

Within the words of the curse, however, there is a glimmer of a promise stemming from God's immense love for mankind, the seed of a plan that will unfold throughout the ages, blossoming into a glorious resolution to the story of God and His creation. Indeed, the serpent, who is Satan, will be destroyed along with his minions, never to corrupt the earth again. The prospects that are offered by science and visionaries are miniscule when compared to the promises of God through His Messiah.

Holiness

There are so many delights that I could mention about God's re-creation of the world, but let's return to the question about why the Messiah had to die, since it is, indeed, a fundamental question. Recall how the concept of good or *goodness* appears so often throughout the story of God's creation. It is a goodness that is completely pure—it is the nature of God—completely other *than* evil. If we were to apply a word to this otherness, it would probably be *holiness*. You see, God is holy—completely pure, thoroughly good—to heights beyond our imaginations. But when Adam and Eve ingested the fruit of the knowledge of good and evil, their nature and minds were enjoined by evil and became reprehensible to God—He cannot and will not have fellowship with evil. As a result, His tender fellowship with the man and woman came to an abrupt end, even though His deep love for them continued.

And as offensive as it may seem to our civilized, twenty-first-century world, the only way to restore that fellowship and absolve the guilt of the race of men is by bringing about the death of the offenders. It was as God warned in the beginning—the day that you eat of the fruit, you shall surely die.[33] Fortunately for mankind, God's love for the world was so great that He sent His Messiah to take their place—to be their substitute in death so that they could be restored and live.

But what about the Messiah. Didn't He have to give the ultimate sacrifice so that others could live? Consider this: The Messiah did not have sin or the influence of sin in His system. He was without evil, so the penalty of death did not extend to Him. Because of this, God raised Him from the dead after He was put to death by sinful men. But God the Father did far more than simply raise Him from the dead. Because of the humble obedience of the Messiah in this role, God exalted Him by anointing Him and crowning Him the eternal king over the entire universe.

33 *Genesis 2:17 – "but from the tree of the knowledge of good and evil you shall not eat, for in the day that you eat from it you will surely die."*

Part 1: The Appointed Times

"But of the Son He says,
'Your throne, O God, is forever and ever,
And the righteous scepter is the scepter of His kingdom.
You have loved righteousness and hated lawlessness;
Therefore God, Your God, has anointed You
With the oil of gladness above Your companions.'"

Hebrews 1:8–9

Now the picture starts to come into focus—the Messiah died for the human race, but He endured death and was not bothered by the shame, since He had His sights set on the future joy[34] of reigning on the throne of God and the prospect of enjoying loving relationships with those He died to save. And with the hope of eternal life that God offers through His Messiah, even our own death is little more than a bump in the road as we journey toward the prize of immortality.

The idea of blood sacrifice is primitive, base, and reprehensible in the mind of our twenty-first-century world,[35] but that was part of God's reason for choosing it as the means of restoration. It is to hide it from those who are wise and enlightened in their own eyes while making it fully accessible to all who will humble themselves and believe. He offers this magnificent gift to everyone, but only the humble will enter the Kingdom of God.[36]

You might be wondering what the Messiah accomplished by His death. Was it simply a substitutionary one-for-many exchange, or did it involve something more? The words of Jesus and the apostles certainly provide the answer to that question, but we gain some additional, fascinating insights when we explore it from the foundation that was established in the Law of Moses through the Lord's Appointed Times.

---

34 Hebrews 12:2 – *"...fixing our eyes on Jesus, the author and perfecter of faith, who for the joy set before Him endured the cross, despising the shame, and has sat down at the right hand of the throne of God."*

35 1 Corinthians 1:27 – *"but God has chosen the foolish things of the world to shame the wise, and God has chosen the weak things of the world to shame the things which are strong."*

36 Matthew 18:3 – *"Truly I say to you, unless you are converted and become like children, you will not enter the kingdom of heaven."*

Chapter 3 – The Sabbath Days

For we who have believed enter that rest...

Hebrews 4:3

The Sabbath Day – The First Appointed Time

The concept of the Sabbath or resting is foundational to the Lord's plan through His Messiah. It is essential that we understand the Sabbath in order to understand the message of the Appointed Times. I would be remiss if I did not emphasize that the Sabbath day, the *weekly* Sabbath day, is the first Appointed Time that is mentioned in Leviticus 23.[37] The Sabbath day serves as a perpetual reminder of the eternal rest that the Lord is preparing for His own. So, let's explore the concept of the *weekly* Sabbath day so we can equip ourselves to understand the other Sabbath days that were given in this key chapter of the Bible.

The Sabbath

"Remember the sabbath day, to keep it holy.
Six days you shall labor and do all your work,
but the seventh day is a sabbath of the Lord your God;

...

37 *Some of the information about the Sabbath in this chapter was excerpted from the Tracking Time in Israel compendium.*

For in six days the Lord made the heavens and the earth,
the sea and all that is in them, and rested on the seventh day;
therefore the Lord blessed the sabbath day and made it holy."

Exodus 20:8–11

The Sabbath is observed on the seventh day of every week. Since Jewish days begin and end at sundown,[38] the Sabbath also begins at sundown on the sixth day of the week and ends at sundown on the seventh day. Or, stated differently, the Sabbath begins at sundown on Friday and ends at sundown on Saturday evening. Since the Sabbath occurs on the seventh day of *every* week, we sometimes refer to it as the weekly Sabbath in order to avoid confusion with *great* or *high* Sabbaths, which we will explore in a later section.

The Sabbath is the commemoration of the Lord's rest from His work after completing the six days of creation[39] and is intended to be a day of rest for everyone. The Hebrew word for Sabbath is shabbath, based on the Hebrew word that means "and He rested," referring to God resting after His work of creation.[40] Resting from our labors is the essence of the Sabbath. It was given as a loving gift from God so we can be refreshed as He was refreshed when He ceased from His labor.[41]

The Sabbath day is not just a commemoration, however. It is one of the hallmarks of God's covenant with Israel, to the extent that they would forever be known as God's people through keeping the Sabbath commandments.[42] Every Israelite was required to rest on the weekly Sabbath, including the head of the household, the entire family, the slaves/servants, guests, and even the animals that belonged to the household. The penalty for not keeping the Sabbath was extremely severe, so the entire nation honored it religiously.

If someone were to ask you, "Which day is the Sabbath?" how would you respond? The Israelites observe the Sabbath as the seventh day of the week, which is Saturday.

38 Refer to the Tracking Time in Israel compendium for additional information about Hebrew days.

39 Exodus 20:11 – "For in six days the Lord made the heavens and the earth, the sea and all that is in them, and rested on the seventh day; therefore the Lord blessed the sabbath day and made it holy."

40 Genesis 2:2 – "By the seventh day God completed His work which He had done, and He rested on the seventh day from all His work which He had done."

41 Exodus 31:17 – "It is a sign between Me and the sons of Israel forever; for in six days the Lord made heaven and earth, but on the seventh day He ceased from labor, and was refreshed."

42 Exodus 31:16–17a – "'So the sons of Israel shall observe the sabbath, to celebrate the sabbath throughout their generations as a perpetual covenant.' It is a sign between Me and the sons of Israel forever..."

Chapter 3: The Sabbath Days

"If because of the sabbath, you turn your foot
From doing your own pleasure on My holy day,
And call the sabbath a delight, the holy day of the Lord honorable,
And honor it, desisting from your own ways,
From seeking your own pleasure
And speaking your own word,
Then you will take delight in the Lord,
And I will make you ride on the heights of the earth;
And I will feed you with the heritage of Jacob your father,
For the mouth of the Lord has spoken."

Isaiah 58:13–14

The origin of the Sabbath rest is very interesting. The Scriptures taught it as the way of the Lord even before the Law of Moses was given (see Exodus 16:22–30). In the creation accounts in Genesis chapters 1 and 2, God rested on the seventh day, and the passage implies that mankind should follow His example by resting also. Indeed, the Lord designed humans to be refreshed and recharged with a day of rest as He did. What does your day of rest look like?

Great or High Sabbaths

In addition to the weekly Sabbaths, seven special Sabbaths were established by the Lord in His Appointed Times in Leviticus 23—we refer to these Sabbaths as great or high Sabbaths. For convenience, we will simply refer to them as high Sabbaths. Almost all of the high Sabbaths are defined as calendar days, rather than as specific days of the week.[43] For example, the Lord told Moses that the Feast of Unleavened Bread must be observed on the 15th day of the month, which is completely unrelated to a specific weekday.

The *high Sabbath* terminology is not common in the Scriptures, but it is certainly there. John 19:31, for example, refers to the first day of the Feast of Unleavened Bread as a *high* Sabbath, thus differentiating it from a weekly Sabbath. The underlying Greek word is *megas* (μέγας), from which we get the prefix meg or mega. Even in our modern world, when something is said to be *mega*, then you know it is big or special. The term carries multiple meanings, all of which suggest something of great magnitude or magnificence.

43 The timing of First Fruits and Pentecost were not defined by calendar days since they always occur on Sunday, the day after a weekly Sabbath.

Why would the Lord require a day of rest as part of His Appointed Times? Simply stated, I believe it is a way of telling us to honor the Lord by stopping, pausing, and considering what is being taught by this Appointed Time. We will explore the timing and substance of each high Sabbath in detail in the upcoming chapters.

The seven high Sabbaths of Leviticus 23 are listed in their annual order in the following table:

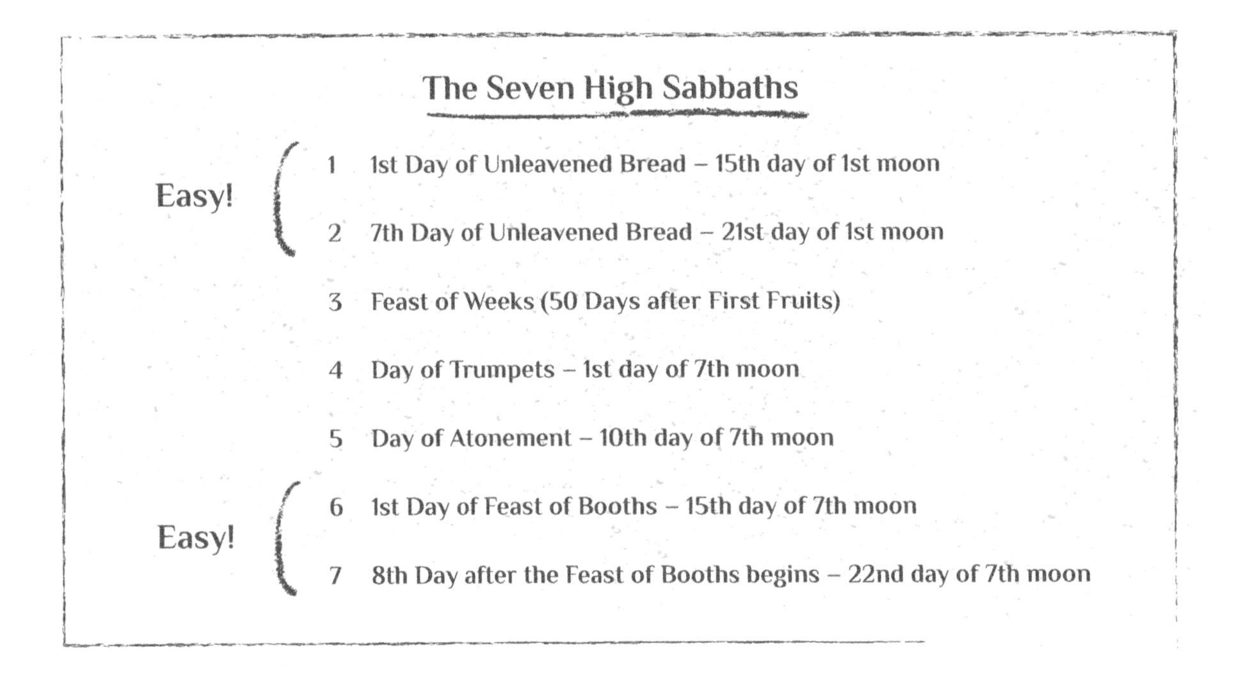

The Seven High Sabbaths

	#	High Sabbath
Easy!	1	1st Day of Unleavened Bread – 15th day of 1st moon
	2	7th Day of Unleavened Bread – 21st day of 1st moon
	3	Feast of Weeks (50 Days after First Fruits)
	4	Day of Trumpets – 1st day of 7th moon
	5	Day of Atonement – 10th day of 7th moon
Easy!	6	1st Day of Feast of Booths – 15th day of 7th moon
	7	8th Day after the Feast of Booths begins – 22nd day of 7th moon

Since the high Sabbaths are mentioned throughout the Scriptures, it would be worth your time to memorize them—it's really quite simple. Just remember that the Appointed Times in Leviticus 23 begin and end with week-long feasts. The first is the Feast of Unleavened Bread and the last is the Feast of Booths. You might picture them as bookends for the Appointed Times. Each feast begins and ends with a high Sabbath Day, which makes it easy to remember. That means that you already know four of the seven. The remaining three high Sabbaths occur in between these feasts.

Important Distinction

It is important to remember that weekly Sabbaths always fall on Saturday, the seventh day of the week. High Sabbaths, on the other hand, can fall on any day of the week since they are based on calendar dates. In a similar way, we also have special days (such as birthdays), which are tied to a specific calendar date but fall on a different day of the week each year.

The Sabbath Shadow

Since each Appointed Time is a shadow of a future event that is related to the Messiah, we must ask ourselves, "What does the Sabbath foreshadow?" The Scriptures give some hints, the clearest of which is found in the fourth chapter of Hebrews. There the writer refers to a *promise of entering His rest*,[44] which he connects to the Sabbath rest.[45] It is not just a one-day Sabbath; it is, rather, an eternal lifetime of rest.

Thus, it appears that the one-day weekly rest is a shadow of the eternal rest of God. Think about it—when God rested on the seventh day, there was no subsequent first day of the week on which He resumed His work.[46] His rest began on the seventh day, continues through today, and will continue through all eternity. The great hope of believers is to enter into His rest in His kingdom for all eternity. This is the hope that the Sabbath shadow represents.

Further Reading about the Sabbath Days

For more information about the Sabbath, please refer to the *Tracking Time in Israel Compendium* in the sections entitled *Week* and *The Sabbath Day*. Information about *great* or *high* Sabbaths can also be found in the compendium.

44 *Hebrews 4:1 – "Therefore, let us fear if, while a promise remains of entering His rest, any one of you may seem to have come short of it." (emphasis added)*

45 *The Sabbath is implied in Hebrews 4:4 by quoting Genesis 2:2 – "And God rested on the seventh day from all His works" and in Hebrews 4:9 – "So there remains a Sabbath rest for the people of God."*

46 *Hebrews 4:3–11*

Chapter 4 – The Historical Background of the Appointed Times

At what point in history did God unveil His Appointed Times? Once again, we must turn to the Law of Moses since it forms the foundation of the Bible. In this chapter, we will take a brief look at the events that led up to the Appointed Times so we can gain insight into the reasons God revealed them in His Word. In this journey, we will consider the life of Moses and explore how God groomed him to write His Word and to fashion the nation that would bring the Messiah into the world. We will start at the beginning, at the creation of the heavens and earth.

Three Events of Profound Significance

The first eleven chapters of Genesis tell of three events that are sometimes viewed as elementary Bible stories for children. But when the stories are properly understood, they create an illuminating backdrop to the global theater of the Scriptures. In this chapter, we revisit these stories with the intent of offering a fresh perspective of the truths they hold. The three events are The Fall of Man, The Great Flood, and The Tower of Babel.

The Fall of Man

When we open our Bibles to the very beginning of Genesis, we read about the account of creation. But immediately afterward, in the third chapter of Genesis, we read about the great catastrophe that the race of men brought upon themselves when they chose to have their eyes opened to know good and evil, hoping to become like God. We explored the significance of the fall of man in Chapter 2, so rather than reviewing it again, I refer you to that section for a refresher of the subject.

The term "Fall of Man" sounds simplistic and innocuous, but if we are going to use that metaphor, it might be more accurate if we picture it as a trapdoor that opened beneath Adam and Eve, causing them to plunge helplessly a thousand feet onto rugged rocks, in a hostile land with unforgiving terrain, climate, and predators. Their moral compass turned like a vane in a storm with no hope of finding their way back to their Father.

Following that horrific fall, the Bible records God's curse on the offenders and on creation. To the woman, He said:

"'I will greatly multiply
Your pain in childbirth,
In pain you will bring forth children;
Yet your desire will be for your husband,
And he will rule over you.'

Then to Adam He said,

'...Cursed is the ground because of you;
In toil you will eat of it
All the days of your life.
Both thorns and thistles it shall grow for you;
And you will eat the plants of the field;

By the sweat of your face
You will eat bread,
Till you return to the ground,
Because from it you were taken;
For you are dust,
And to dust you shall return.'"

Genesis 3:16–19

From that point, the narrative of Genesis takes us from innocence to iniquity, from the murder of a brother to global violence, to the point that God had to intervene to change the course of humanity.

The Great Flood

The race of men had become deranged because of the knowledge of good and evil to the extent that sin, corruption, and violence, ran rampant and unchecked throughout the world. The Lord saw the great wickedness on the earth and that every motive behind the thoughts of man was continually evil.[47] Humanity had degenerated to such low level of depravity that God chose to destroy the entire world by deluging it in a horrific, global flood. No one survived except a small family of eight people, who took refuge in the enormous ark that God directed Noah to build. Thus, they continued the human race and perpetuated many varieties of animals from the earth.

What was God's reason for doing this? I believe it was to convey to following generations how abhorrent and odious sin is to His holiness. It was not a simple matter of exacting some

47 Genesis 6:5 – "Then the Lord saw that the wickedness of man was great on the earth, and that every intent of the thoughts of his heart was only evil continually."

parental discipline upon the human race. More importantly, the flood reveals the potency of the toxin and the intense anger that was kindled within the Almighty because of the distortion it infused into the heart of man.

Sin is not a small thing that God will simply wink at and then move on. It is so abhorrent and reprehensible to Him that He actually regretted creating mankind.[48] The corruption in the heart of man could only be repaired by God Himself, by one day taking a strategic action that would have an impact that was far greater than the great flood—God becoming a man.

The Tower of Babel

After the great flood, human civilization revived and flourished to the degree that God, once again, had to take action to limit the growing power of mankind. So He brought confusion to their single, worldwide language at the Tower of Babel[49] by preventing the race of men from understanding each other through their common language. Thus, the civilization was divided, and humanity was scattered across the seas and across the face of the earth.[50]

At first glance, the story of Babel might sound like a simplistic explanation about how the diverse languages of the earth came into being and how the varied races of humanity came about. But please

48 Genesis 6:6 "And the Lord regretted that he had made man on the earth, and it grieved him to his heart." (ESV)

49 Genesis 11:1 – "Now the whole earth used the same language and the same words."

50 Genesis 11:9 – "Therefore its name was called Babel, because there the Lord confused the language of the whole earth; and from there the Lord scattered them abroad over the face of the whole earth."

allow me to speculate for a moment about a deeper reason for God's action at Babel:

The great flood destroyed the masses of humanity. Even so, God loved the world and desired that the human race continue and flourish. But by dividing humanity into diverse groups and races at Babel, He created a mechanism with which He could govern the development of civilizations and cultures, thus limiting the forward progress of man. The mechanism utilizes the glorious achievements that come from the spirit of man, as well as the dark perversions of hearts that are polluted by sin.

Slowing the progress of man became a simpler matter of pitting nations and civilizations against each other rather than destroying the entire earth. For example, the magnificent achievements of science and medicine move civilizations forward, while the twisted reasoning of despots and tyrants who invade, destroy and kill reverse the progress and synergy of mankind. You might ask, "Would God do that? Would He actually manipulate civilizations as He pleases?" The answer is yes, and we are going to explore just one of those instances in the following chapters, as He altered the destiny of the nation of Egypt.

The story of Babel is not suggesting that an ancient brick tower was such a marvelous feat that God had to intervene, fearing the intelligence and innovation of His own creation. Certainly, the technical prowess behind an ancient tower cannot compare to modern inventions such as automobiles, aircraft, modern medicine, artificial intelligence, or instant electronic communication. God endowed mankind with intellectual brilliance, but the corruption within would have brought civilization to a premature end before His divine plan for creation could be completed—before those whom He lovingly predestined to become His children could be born and adopted into His family. Thus He throttled the advancement of mankind by dividing them into competing nations, who would topple each other's accomplishments on His timetable so He would not have to again destroy the world.

When the Lord fragmented humanity at Babel, He created an arena of competing nations that He could use to enhance or stifle progress. He raises and razes civilizations so He can orchestrate the events of the world, building toward a crescendo when He will, one day, transfer the kingdom of the world to the kingdom of His Messiah.[51] A day will come when He will no longer limit the brilliance of humanity. In that day, the corrupt brilliance of man will accelerate to a white-hot arrogance, provoking God's wrath and bringing an abrupt end to the madness.

---

51 *Revelation 11:15 – "Then the seventh angel sounded; and there were loud voices in heaven, saying, 'The kingdom of the world has become the kingdom of our Lord and of His Christ; and He will reign forever and ever.'"*

Genesis 1-11

2,000 years from the Fall to God's Action at Babel

All three of these events, the Fall of Man, the Great Flood, and God's action at Babel, occurred within a 2,000-year timeframe. Yet it is interesting that they are condensed into only 11 chapters in Genesis, while the remaining 39 chapters span only a couple-hundred years. At this point, rather than reporting the global events that shaped the world, the scriptural narrative turns its focus to one man, Abram, who would become the forefather of the Messiah, the savior of the world.

Abraham

Soon after the account of the Tower of Babel, we are introduced to a man named Abram in the land of Ur, whom God told to leave his country and his family and go to a land that He would show him. Abram had an excellent reason for following the instructions, since God had chosen him to be the recipient of His great promise—to bless him, to make his name great, and to make him into great nation. In a somewhat mysterious way, God added, "And in you all the families of the earth shall be blessed,"[52] most certainly referring to Abram's role in God's salvation through His Messiah.

You may know the story—God changed Abram's name to Abraham, which means "the father of many nations." And in a miraculous way, He blessed him with the promised son when he was at the ripe old age of 100 years. Indeed, Abraham became the father of many nations. Ishmael, his eldest son, was the father of twelve princes,[53] from whom the North Arabian tribes

52 Genesis 12:3 – "And I will bless those who bless you, And the one who curses you I will curse. And in you all the families of the earth will be blessed."

53 Per Genesis 17:20, Ishmael would become the father of twelve princes, the descendants of whom are with us today in the Arab nations. Two prominent North Arabian tribes, the Qedarites and the Nabateans, are named after two of Ishmael's sons, Kedar and Nebaioth in Genesis 25:13.

descended. But the Lord promised to fulfill His everlasting covenant[54] through Isaac, the son of Abraham's wife Sarah.

The Lord followed through on His promise to Abraham. One of Isaac's sons, Jacob, was given the name Israel, meaning "one who strives with God," after a physical encounter with an angel. It was from this man that the nation of Israel received its name, and it was through this nation that God sent His Messiah into the world. Thus, all the families of the earth are blessed in Abraham.

But it was Israel's next generation that set the stage for the Appointed Times. Israel fathered twelve sons, who became known as the twelve tribes of Israel and eventually became the nation of Israel. The names of his sons are:

Reuben, Simeon, Levi, Judah, Zebulun, Issachar
Dan, Gad, Asher, Naphtali, Joseph, Benjamin

As you can imagine, the antics of twelve brothers can get pretty wild, and some of their antics were truly shameful. Even so, God used one of their more deviant acts to bring about His good will and His most loving act. In His sovereign way, He elevated one of the sons, Joseph, to become the second in command of the entire nation of Egypt. And, through a series of miraculously ironic events, He moved the entire family, including Israel himself, into the land of Egypt to escape the great famine that had reached their homeland in Canaan.

Now, you should be aware that Israel and his family were not squatters in the land. On the contrary, they came to Egypt at the invitation of Pharaoh himself, as his honored guests, since he highly esteemed Joseph. Pharaoh insisted that they settle in Goshen, which was the best of the land of Rameses. Israel, his twelve sons, and their entire families were together in the land of Egypt under the protection of Pharaoh. They were living good lives in a good land, enjoying ample food, provisions, and security provided by the sovereign of Egypt.

54 *Genesis 17:19 – "But God said, 'No, but Sarah your wife will bear you a son, and you shall call his name Isaac; and I will establish My covenant with him for an everlasting covenant for his descendants after him.'"*

Even though Joseph seemed to be in the most enviable position that anyone could imagine, he still did not consider Egypt to be his home. When he was on his deathbed, he charged his brothers, saying, "I am about to die, but God will surely take care of you and bring you up from this land to the land which He promised to Abraham, Isaac, and Jacob," and he made them swear that they would carry his bones up from Egypt to the promised land.[55]

---

55 Genesis 50:24–25 – "Then Joseph made the sons of Israel swear, saying, 'God will surely take care of you, and you shall carry my bones up from here.'"

Painting by Sir Edward Poynter - *Israel in Egypt* - 1867
Used with permission: Guildhall Art Gallery, City of London

Predestined Change

The good life for the Israelites was not intended to last forever. Three generations before they entered Egypt, God had already informed Abram of things to come, telling him, "Know for certain that your descendants will be strangers in a land that is not theirs, where they will be enslaved and oppressed four hundred years."[56] God had determined to forge Israel into a nation in a unique way that would gain the attention of the entire world.

So let's jump forward from the last chapter of Genesis to the first chapter of the book of Exodus. Here we find the entire nation of Israel in a very different situation in Egypt. Many years had passed since Israel and his family were the honored guests of Pharaoh. But in time, Israel and his sons died, and a new king had come to power. As Israel's family grew, the Egyptians became concerned about the strength of the foreign nation that was living within their borders. They were worried that Israel might side with their enemies if they were attacked by another nation. Thus, the new king's shrewd solution was to enslave the entire nation of Israel, forcing them into hard labor to build storage cities in the land of Rameses.[57]

Despite the severity of their slavery, the population of Israel continued to increase, and it seemed that increasing the affliction only increased their numbers. In response, the Egyptians tried to subdue them further by demanding greater production from them, making their lives bitter through making bricks and laboring in the fields. Even so, their population continued to grow.

In an attempt to stem the Israeli tide, Pharaoh commanded the Egyptian midwives to slay all male babies that were born to the Hebrew women but allow the females to live. Fortunately, the midwives feared God and did not obey the command. In desperation, Pharaoh commanded *all* of his people to throw newborn Hebrew boys into the Nile River. Can you imagine that? If an Egyptian were walking through a neighborhood and saw a newborn Hebrew boy, they were to grab the baby and toss it into the croc-infested Nile River! Yet, the Israelites lived under these horrific conditions for many years. They groaned in the misery of Egypt's iron furnace, until the Lord raised up Moses as their deliverer from the tyranny of Egypt.

---

56 *Genesis 15:13*

57 *Exodus 1:11 – "So they appointed taskmasters over them to afflict them with hard labor. And they built for Pharaoh storage cities, Pithom and Raamses."*

The Birth of a Prince

In order to gain greater appreciation for the nation of Israel, for the Bible, and for the Appointed Times, it is important that we provide some background information about Moses, the leader and humble servant of God. The liberation of the Israeli slaves was not masterminded or instigated from within by a vigilante slave who led an uprising against the king of Egypt. Instead, it was initiated by God Himself. He heard the groaning of the people, and He answered by sending a specially groomed deliverer from the royal house of Egypt—an Israelite by the name of Moses.

With this as our backdrop, let's turn our attention to a husband and wife from the family of Levi[58] who were living under the harsh conditions in Egypt—their names were Amram and Jochebed. Jochebed gave birth to a son and successfully hid him from the tormentors for three months. But as the child grew, she resorted to a desperate measure to preserve his life, by waterproofing a wicker basket with tar and pitch, and setting it afloat on the Nile River with her son as its only passenger.

The timing and location of the voyage were, no doubt, strategically planned by his mother and controlled by the hand of God, since it was the time of day when Pharaoh's daughter and her maidens came to the river to bathe. Seeing the basket lodged in the reeds, Pharaoh's daughter sent one of her attendants to retrieve it. When the basket was opened, the boy was crying, and she felt compassion for him, realizing that he was a Hebrew boy who was under the condemnation of her father.

No doubt with some fear and apprehension, the boy's sister, Miriam, stepped forward and asked the princess if she should find a nurse for the child from the Hebrew women. She agreed and even paid wages to the nurse, which turned out to be Jochebed, the mother of the boy—smart sister! When the boy grew, Jochebed brought him to the princess to be her son, and she named him Moses, which means, *drawn from the water*.

58 Levi was the third son of Israel and his wife, Leah.

The Deliverer – Groomed by God

Moses was raised as a prince in the palace of Pharaoh, the son of a princess, with everything that a person could ever desire. Dressed in splendor, servants, guards, and nobles bowed as he strode through the palaces of Egypt. Wealth was his and all things were accessible to him, the highest education, tutoring in nobility, warfare, horses, chariots, ships, royal celebrations, beautiful women, sages, magicians, philosophers, museums, monuments, archives, and libraries. He was in the inner circle of royalty—among nobles, princes, princesses, and queens; even the doors to the court of Pharaoh would open for him. Moses was a prince in perhaps the mightiest, most refined, and most affluent nation on earth—the kingdom of Egypt. He was a royal prince and a general in the Egyptian army[59]—the grandson of the sovereign of Egypt.[60]

Perhaps he heard it through whispers in the palace. Perhaps his Egyptian cousins sneered that he was not one of them, or perhaps he was haunted by the prophecy of the Egyptian sacred scribe that he would, one day, bring down the dominion of Egypt.[61] Whatever it may have been, something tormented the man deep inside, and he refused to be called the son of Pharaoh's daughter, choosing instead to identify with the people of God.[62] Something caused him to exchange riches, affluence, and pleasures for a life of nomadic hardship. He gave up the ease of his princely position and stepped into the iron furnace of Egypt so he could alleviate the affliction of his enslaved brethren. Certainly, only a man of great character and conviction would make such a sacrifice; he persevered as if he could actually see the unseen God[63] of his forefathers. Moses had his eyes on something far greater than earthly position and power.

59 *(Josephus 1994) Antiquities of the Jews, 2:10:1(241)*

60 *Acts 7:21–22 – "Pharaoh's daughter took him away and nurtured him as her own son. Moses was educated in all the learning of the Egyptians, and he was a man of power in words and deeds."*

61 *(Josephus 1994) Antiquities of the Jews, 2:9:7(234)*

62 *Hebrews 11:24 – "By faith Moses, when he had grown up, refused to be called the son of Pharaoh's daughter..."*

63 *"...for he endured, as seeing Him who is unseen."*

My suspicion is that Moses, after learning that he was the son of Hebrew slaves, spent much of his time in the libraries of the kingdom, searching through the archives and poring over the annals of his ancestors who sojourned in Egypt generations before. From those annals he no doubt read that his forefathers, Abraham, Isaac, and Jacob, had encounters with God and were the beneficiaries of sworn covenants of enormous blessing from the only true Sovereign.[64]

At one point, when he was almost forty years old,[65] Moses' burden for his countrymen eventually resulted in committing a crime that drew a death sentence from Pharaoh. In desperation, he fled to the land of Midian and assumed a new life as a shepherd, finding friendship with a man named Reuel, the priest of Midian. Moses had endeared himself to Reuel by rescuing his seven shepherdess daughters from some local, menacing shepherds, and he went above and beyond the call by also watering their flocks.[66] To Moses' delight, Reuel invited him to live with them and gave his eldest daughter, Zipporah, to be his wife.

Moses' station in life had quickly changed from royal prince to humble shepherd, but he was about to experience an even more radical change of life through an encounter with the angel of the Lord on the mountain of God. As he was shepherding his father-in-law's flock in the wilderness, Moses came to Mount Horeb[67] and saw a very strange sight—a bush engulfed by a blazing fire, yet the bush itself was not burning.

His curiosity drew him closer, and the angel of the Lord appeared to him in the flame and called him by name, "Moses, Moses! ... Do not come near here; remove your sandals from your feet, for the place on which you are standing is holy ground."[68] The voice identified Himself as "the God of your fathers, the God of Abraham, the God of Isaac, and the God of Jacob," and upon hearing this, Moses shook with fear and hid his face, not daring to look at God.[69]

64 *Genesis 15:18–21, Genesis 26:1–5, Genesis 28:10–17*

65 *Acts 7:23*

66 *Exodus 2:19*

67 *Mount Horeb is referred to as the mountain of God in Exodus 3:1. It is used synonymously with Mount Sinai.*

68 *Exodus 3:4–5*

69 *Exodus 3:6*

During this encounter, God told Moses that He had seen the affliction and suffering of His people and had come down to deliver them from the Egyptians. He promised to bring them to a good and spacious land, and He then told Moses, "I am sending you to tell Pharaoh to let my people go." Thus, after some discussion with God, Moses became the designated deliverer of Israel.

God heard the groaning of the Israelites as they writhed in the agony of their slavery. He turned His attention to them and orchestrated their deliverance through Moses, a deliverance that would be miraculous, magnificent, and terrifying. The mighty arm of God was outstretched with muscles flexed against the mightiest nation on earth, and He would soon devastate the land, crops, cattle, people, and Pharaoh with plagues so severe that the Egyptians would beg the Israelites to leave lest they all die.[70]

The Judgment of God

As Pharaoh refused to comply with Moses' requests to allow the people to leave, God responded by assailing the land of Egypt with plagues of apocalyptic severity. Imagine horrific plagues being inflicted at a national level, pandemic in proportion, instilling dread and fear in the hearts of the Egyptians. Nonetheless, Pharaoh was unbending.

70 Exodus 12:33

Chapter 4: The Historical Background of the Appointed Times

The first eight plagues inflicted physical misery on the people, their livestock, and their crops, but the ninth plague penetrated the hearts and minds of the people with oppressive gloom, dread, and even madness. The Lord said to Moses, "Stretch out your hand toward the sky, that there may be darkness over the land of Egypt, a darkness that can be felt." Moses did so, and thick darkness descended on the land of Egypt, a darkness so thick and pervasive that the people could not see each other or even leave their homes. The darkness loomed over the land of Egypt for three days. Even so, the Israelites had light in their homes.

It was on the heels of the plague of darkness that Pharaoh became enraged with Moses, shouting, "Get away from me! Beware, do not see my face again, for in the day you see my face you shall die!" And Moses countered, "You are right; I shall never see your face again!"[71]

And he went on to tell Pharaoh that the Lord will soon go into the heart of Egypt around midnight, and all the firstborn in the land of Egypt shall die, from your firstborn, even to the firstborn of the slave girl who grinds with the millstone; even all the firstborn of the cattle will die. There will be a great cry in the land of Egypt, such as has never been heard before and such as shall never be again. But not even a dog will bark against the Israelites—neither against man or beast. And all of your servants will come to me and bow down, and plead with us to leave the land. Then Moses left the presence of Pharaoh in hot anger.[72]

71 *Exodus 10:28-29*

72 *Exodus 11:4–8*

It is in this prophetic threat from Moses that we encounter the Appointed Times. How would the Lord judge Pharaoh and his people while protecting the Israelites from the same destruction? Enter the Appointed Time that is known as Passover, an event that enabled Israel to step out of the iron furnace of Egypt and begin the journey to becoming their own sovereign nation.

Part 2 – The Spring Appointed Times

Our Direction

The spring Appointed Times commemorate key events of Israel's exodus from Egypt, but, of far greater importance, they cast shadows of the key events of the Lord's Messiah. Annually the Israelites observe and annually they proclaim the mysteries of Christ.

In this section, we will look into each of the spring Appointed Times to confirm their place in the messianic timeline and explain how they are shadows of things to come, but are ultimately about the Messiah. Remember that Paul referred to these festivals, new moons, and Sabbath Days as shadows of what is to come, but their substance, or true meaning, belongs to Christ.

The spring Appointed Times are most clearly understood when they are viewed together as connected events. We will explore them in the order they are listed in Leviticus 23, beginning with Passover, which shadows the purity of the lamb and its death—a death that was in lieu of the death of others. Our next area of investigation will be the Feast of Unleavened Bread and how its timing and symbolism are revealed in the Passover meal, consisting of the sacrificed lamb, unleavened bread, and bitter herbs. These symbols foreshadow the bitterness of the death of Jesus, as He was placed in the tomb on the same evening.

We will then look into the First Fruits offering, which coincides with the Israelites rising alive from the sea, foreshadowing Jesus rising alive from the grave. Both events took place around dawn on the first day of the week, which is the day of First Fruits.

The last spring Appointed Time is the Feast of Weeks, which is also known as Pentecost. This feast is to be observed exactly fifty days after First Fruits, which is the reason it is called Pentecost—the Greek word for fiftieth. It can be demonstrated from the Scriptures that the Lord met with Moses and gave His Law to Israel on this day. In a similar way, on the day of Pentecost almost 1,500 years later, the Lord met with mankind again, giving His Holy Spirit to all who would believe.

It is of the greatest importance that we become familiar with the details of these holy days since they confirm that the Appointed Times are truly shadows of the Messiah and that Jesus fulfilled them with perfect precision. It may sound like a lot of information and somewhat overwhelming, but we will take it slowly and provide enough background information so you can clearly understand their importance.

Why is this so important? It is because the Appointed Times give clear evidence that Jesus is truly the Messiah. His sacrifice provided the means for God to save us. But the story of the Messiah does not end with our salvation. As we look into the fall Appointed Times, we see shadows of magnificent events, both terrifying and eternally delightful, that are yet to come. It is clearly worth our time to learn and seek to understand these mysteries that the Lord has hidden in His word.

Chapter 5 – Passover

In the first month, on the fourteenth day of the month at twilight
is the Lord's Passover.

Leviticus 23:5

The Events of Passover

In Chapter 4, we briefly reviewed the historical background of the Appointed Times. Recall that Moses delivered an impassioned ultimatum to Pharaoh, warning him that all the firstborn in Egypt were going to die because of his stubborn refusal to release the Israelites. He warned that the impending plague would take the life of every firstborn in Egypt—from Pharaoh's firstborn to the firstborn of the slave girl. It would even take the life of the firstborn in the homes of Israelites if they did not follow God's instructions for survival. Those who followed the instructions, however, would be completely unharmed by the calamity since their obedience would provide a sign for the destroyer[73] to pass over the household. It is in these instructions about Passover that we begin to see shadows of God's Messiah.[74]

After storming out of Pharaoh's palace, Moses gathered the elders of Israel and conveyed the words of the Lord regarding the final plague on Egypt.[75] The news involved much more than a warning of imminent danger for the firstborn, as he explained that the Lord would also render severe judgment on Pharaoh, his armies, and even on the gods of Egypt. It would be

73 *Exodus 12:23 – "...the Lord will pass over the door and will not allow the destroyer to come in to your houses to smite you."*

74 *The Passover Quick Facts table can be found in Appendix E*

75 *Exodus 12:21*

a swift and decisive judgment, resulting in the complete annihilation of Pharaoh and his armies and the complete emancipation of Israel from the tyranny of the Egyptians. The Lord told Moses,

> *"I will go through the land of Egypt on that night,*
> *and will strike down all the firstborn in the land of Egypt,*
> *both man and beast; and against all the gods of Egypt*
> *I will execute judgments—*
> *I am the Lord."*
>
> *Exodus 12:12*

In addition to the plague, the Lord also granted favor to the Israelites in the sight of the Egyptians. He told the people to ask their Egyptian neighbors for articles of gold, silver, and clothing. It seems like they would have needed wagons and carts to carry all their newly acquired wealth, but it is certain they had pack animals from their herds to carry the goods. It is interesting that the Lord told Abraham about this providential favor, hundreds of years before.[76]

76 Genesis 15:13–14

The Timing of Passover

As always, we will begin our exploration in Leviticus 23 since it provides a chronological listing of all the Appointed Times. From there, we will examine related passages in the Pentateuch to see what we can glean from them. Let's begin with Leviticus 23:5.

*"In the **first month**, on the **fourteenth day** of the month at twilight*
is the Lord's Passover."

Leviticus 23:5 (Emphasis added)

Notice that the Leviticus 23 verse contains very little information about Passover. From it, we learn the date and the timing, but it says nothing about instructions for its observance or the significance of the event. It tells us that Passover must be observed in the first month of the year, which is Abib,[77] occurring in the March-April timeframe.[78] Thus, Passover is one of the *spring* Appointed Times.

☆ ***Important fact to remember: Passover is always on Abib 14*** ☆

Let's continue our investigation of Passover by exploring related passages in the Pentateuch. A listing of related passages along with other valuable information can be found in the Passover Quick Facts table in Appendix E. We encourage you to familiarize yourself with the Quick Facts tables for each Appointed Time.

Instructions for Passover

Let's begin learning about the Passover in the 12th chapter of Exodus. The Lord instructed Moses to

"Speak to all the congregation of Israel, saying,
*'On the **tenth of this month** they are each one to take a lamb for themselves, according to their fathers' households, a lamb for each household.*

Now if the household is too small for a lamb, then he and his neighbor nearest to his house are to take one according to the number of persons in them; according to what each man should eat, you are to divide the lamb...

77 *The month is identified as Abib in Exodus 13:4, 23:15, 34:18, and Deuteronomy 16:1*

78 *Refer to the Month section of the Tracking Time in Israel compendium to see a chart that compares the relative timing of the Gregorian months and the Hebrew months.*

You shall keep it ***until the fourteenth day of the same month,*** *then the whole assembly of the congregation of Israel is to kill it at twilight."*

Exodus 12:3–4, 6 (Emphasis added)

The Two Events of Passover

Notice from the above passage that Passover is comprised of **two specific events, occuring on:**

Abib 10 and **Abib 14.**

Let's look into these events.

Abib

Corral the Lamb

10

Abib 10 – Corral the Lamb

In Exodus 12:3–4, Moses told the people to take a lamb for themselves ***on the tenth of this month***; one lamb for each household. They had to make sure the lamb was large enough to feed all the residents of the household. If a household was too small for a lamb, then the people of that household were to go to their nearest neighbor's house to share a lamb, dividing it according to the number of people and what each man could eat.

Notice that smaller households were to go to their nearest neighbor, rather than traveling a distance to be with family or friends. This is because Passover was not intended to be a festive celebration wherein people visit family and friends and gather to enjoy a meal together. Instead, the mood is dark and ominous. Something terrible is about to happen. Imminent danger is looming, and the people must seek protection in their own homes or with their nearest neighbor in order to survive. It has an eerie sound—like the angst that we feel from the warning sirens for tornados or tsunamis or even the bombs of war. The calamity that is coming is not a festive occasion. It is, instead, a solemn, grievous event that will result in death and mourning for Egyptian friends and neighbors, launching the nation of Israel into a terrifying yet fascinating journey with God.

The requirements for the lamb were very specific. It was to be an unblemished male a year old, and it could be either a sheep or a goat.[79] The lamb was to be kept until the 14th day of the month, set apart for five days so it could be observed to make sure that it was truly unblemished—without defect. The purity of the lamb speaks of the sinless purity of the Messiah, which we will see in Chapter 9.

An Unblemished, Spotless Lamb

What is meant by unblemished in the context of a sacrifice? In the book of Leviticus, Moses identified several types of defects or imperfections that would render an animal imperfect and thus unacceptable as a sacrifice. It is likely that these are the same criteria that would be considered blemishes on a potential Passover lamb, disqualifying it as an acceptable sacrifice. The imperfections that are mentioned in Leviticus 22:22–24 include:

- Blindness
- Bone Fractures
- Maimed
- Running sores
- Eczema
- Scabs
- Injured Tesicles

It is sometimes said that the Passover lamb must be a pure white lamb, but this idea is not found in the Scriptures. Notice that there is no mention about the color or spots of color on the lamb's coat; coloration or spots are not indications of blemishes or of impurity.

79 *Exodus 12:5*

Abib 14 – Kill It at Twilight

On the 14th of the month, all the Israelites were to kill the Passover lamb at twilight.[80] From the *Tracking Time in Israel* compendium we learn that twilight literally meant *between the evenings*,[81] which is between 3:00pm and sundown, so they had a couple hours to complete this task.

"You shall keep it until the ***fourteenth day of the same month****, then the whole assembly of the congregation of Israel is to kill it at twilight.*

Moreover, they shall take ***some of the blood*** *and* ***put it on the two doorposts and on the lintel of the houses*** *in which they eat it.*

They shall ***eat the flesh that same night****, roasted with fire, and they shall* ***eat it with unleavened bread and bitter herbs****."*

Exodus 12:6–8 (Emphasis added)

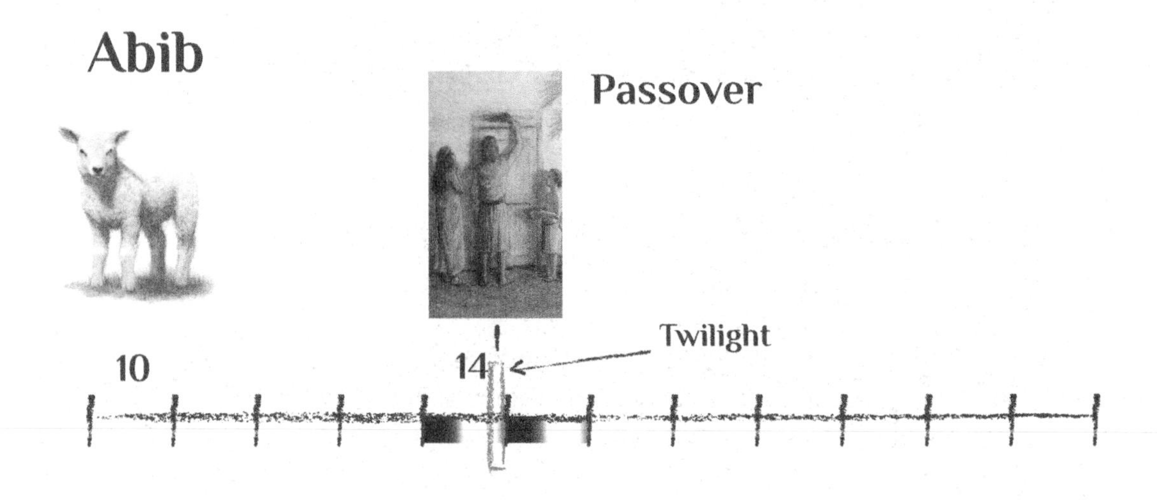

Figure 1

80 *Exodus 12:6*

81 *Refer to the Tracking Time in Israel compendium to learn more about twilight.*

After they killed the lamb, they were to take a bunch of hyssop[82] and dip it into the blood that was in the basin and apply it to the lintel and the two doorposts of the house.[83] The blood would provide a sign for them on the houses where they lived, and when the Lord would see the blood on the lintel and two doorposts, He would pass over the house and not allow the destroyer to enter to kill their firstborn.[84] Thus, the plague would not affect those who obeyed these instructions as it would the others in the land of Egypt.

It may be helpful to remember that the Hebrew people were shepherds and herdsmen. Even though they were slaves, they owned large flocks and herds,[85] which were a primary source of their diet. The act of killing a lamb was probably a routine task in meal

82 *Hyssop is a wild herbaceous shrub that is common in the Mediterranean region; it produces small, blue flowers in the summertime.*

83 *Exodus 12:22*

84 *Exodus 12:23*

85 *Exodus 12:38 – "A mixed multitude also went up with them, along with flocks and herds, a very large number of livestock."*

preparation—blood and the sight of death were common among the people in this context. Even though the Passover lamb had a special significance, the Hebrew people probably did not have an emotional attachment to the animal that a person would have toward a pet. I imagine, however, that they must have wondered what was special about the lamb, that it had to die and its blood be publicly displayed around the door, thus sparing them from death.

Preparing the Lamb

The Lord gave Moses some detailed guidelines for preparing the lamb for the Passover meal. From Exodus 12:8–10 we learn:

- It must be roasted with fire—the Talmud adds that is should be roasted on a pomegranate spit.[86]
- Do not eat any of it raw or boiled with water.
- Prepare it with its head and its legs, along with its entrails.
- None of it should be left until morning—anything that is left over must be burned with fire.
- You are not to break any bone of the lamb (Exodus 12:46).

Do you remember the words from the gospel of John? The Roman soldiers had been sent to break the legs of those who were crucified, "but coming to Jesus, when they saw that He was already dead, they did not break His legs... For these things came to pass to fulfill the Scripture, **'Not a bone of Him shall be broken.'**"[87] John is clearly equating the Passover lamb with the Messiah—it is a shadow of the Messiah. The apostle Paul explicitly refers to "Christ our Passover" in 1 Corinthians 5:7, which further makes the connection between the Passover lamb and the Messiah.

The Passover Meal

The Passover lamb must be eaten with unleavened bread and bitter herbs. Unleavened bread is simply bread that is made without a leavening agent such as yeast. Therefore it does not rise and is sometimes referred to as flatbread. The sound of bitter herbs may not immediately

86 (Rodkinson, The Babylonian Talmud 1916) – Volume 3, TRACT PESACHIM (PASSOVER), CHAPTER VII, p. 143 – The Talmud stipulates that the lamb was to be roasted on a pomegranate stick (i.e., a roasting spit)
87 John 19:33, 36

appeal to you, but the traditional bitter herbs of Passover are actually quite tasty and common, even in our day. The traditional bitter herbs of Passover, according to Jewish tradition, are listed in Figure 2.

The Talmud contains the following quote about the bitter herbs that are acceptable for the Passover meal:[88]

> "MISHNA: the duty of eating bitter herbs on the Passover may be acquitted with the following herbs:
>
> with **lettuce, wild endive** and **garden endive**, with **Harhabinah**, with **bitter coriander, and bitter herbs (horseradish)**"

Figure 2

Notice, however, that Moses did not stipulate which bitter herbs should be used in the Passover meal; he simply used the Hebrew word mĕror or maror, which means bitter herb. So any available bitter herb would have probably sufficed. The important characteristic was that it must be bitter in order to symbolize the bitterness of the Israelites' upcoming journey, which has important implications regarding the Messiah.

In reality, the traditional bitter herbs of Passover are probably different from those that were readily available in Egypt. For example, horseradish does not grow naturally in the Middle East. Even though it has a long tradition in the Passover meal, it was probably not used in the first Passover meal during the year of the Exodus. Does it matter? Of course it is important to follow the instructions as carefully as possible, but in this case there is some latitude since bitterness and herbs are the only stipulations for the meal.

Figure 3

88 *(Rodkinson, The Babylonian Talmud, 1916) Volume 2, Tractate Pesachim (Passover), Chapter II, p. 59*

The Talmud states that Hillel, a renowned Jewish scholar, held that one would make a sandwich from the ingredients and eat them together,[89] while other Jewish scholars insisted that the ingredients must be eaten separately. Thus, for the sake of simplicity, we will depict the Passover meal as a sandwich, which might be similar to that in Figure 3.

Ready to Go...

The sun was setting on the 14th day of Abib, and the preparatory work had been completed – the lamb had been killed, its blood had been applied to the doorposts and lintel, and it was roasting over an open fire. The unleavened bread had been baked and bitter herbs were prepared for the meal. The next step was in the hands of God.

The year was 1446 BC. As the sun set on the land of Egypt that night, the sons of Israel retreated to their homes to consume the special meal they had prepared and await the journey of a lifetime. They were not to get too comfortable since the command to leave their homes and depart from Egypt could come at any moment in the night.

The Lord had instructed the Israelites to eat the lamb that same night, while they were fully dressed,[90] with their sandals on their feet and staff in hand. They were to eat it quickly and be ready to go. This event, the Lord's Passover, would be executed swiftly and become a hallmark of this newly forged nation and a stunning wakeup call to the entire world.

The Judgment

That night, the entire nation of Israel sheltered in their homes, dreading the imminent words of Moses. The Egyptians huddled to protect their beloved firstborn while Israel wondered where this fearful event would lead and if they would survive the wrath of Pharaoh that would surely come. How would the God of Moses, the God of their forefathers, deliver them? How far could they travel with their young, old, and possessions in a desert wilderness? Where would they find water and provisions for hundreds of thousands of people and herds and flocks? Their questions were valid, but the God of Abraham was their hope.

89 *(Rodkinson, The Babylonian Talmud 1916) – Volume 3, TRACT PESACHIM (PASSOVER), CHAPTER X, p.238*

90 *Exodus 12:11 – "[With] your loins girded" is an idiom for being fully dressed.*

Chapter 5: Passover

It happened at midnight that the Lord fulfilled His promise. He took the lives of all the firstborn in the land of Egypt in every household that was not protected by the blood of the lamb. The life of the firstborn in every household in Egypt was taken, from the lowly to the greatest—the child of the slave girl, the child of the prisoners in the dungeons, the firstborn of the cattle—even the firstborn of Pharaoh, the heir to the throne of Egypt. Every home in Egypt suffered the pain of death and the entire nation cried out in anguish.[91] Yet, the destroyer passed over the homes that displayed the lamb's blood on the doorposts and lintel.

In fear and anger, Pharaoh arose in the night with all of his servants and advisors and called for Moses and Aaron. "Get up and get out!" he shouted. "Get away from my people and go and worship the Lord as you said. Take your flocks and your herds and go... and bless me also."[92] Pharaoh had become a believer, but his faith would be short-lived. His pride had been broken, but his hardened heart would soon cause him to break his word to Moses and the Israelites, setting the stage for one of the most stunning defeats in all human history.

The Israelites' anticipated journey was about to begin. They took their possessions and took their dough before it was leavened, with their kneading bowls bound up in the clothes on their shoulders.[93] And they baked the dough into cakes of unleavened bread since it had not become leavened, as they were in a great hurry to leave Egypt.

Unleavened bread... does that sound familiar? Let's briefly step away from our story of the Israelites' exodus on the evening of Passover, since it has brought us to our next Appointed Time, which is the **Feast of Unleavened Bread**. But don't worry—we will return to the story of the exodus right where we left off.

Passover, with its two key dates of Abib 10 and the 14th at twilight, form the initial entries of the time signature of the Messiah.

91 *Exodus 12:30 – "...for there was no home where there was not someone dead."*

92 *Exodus 12:29–32 (Author's paraphrase)*

93 *Exodus 12:34*

Chapter 6 – The Feast of Unleavened Bread

Then on the fifteenth day of the same month there is
the Feast of Unleavened Bread *to the Lord;*
for seven days you shall eat unleavened bread.

Leviticus 23:6 (Emphasis added)

The Feast of Unleavened Bread begins when the sun sets on Abib 14—it always begins on the evening of the day on which the Passover lamb was sacrificed. It is very important to understand that the day and the date change when the sun sets. Thus, when the sun sets on Abib 14, the date changes to Abib 15.[94] From our modern perspective, sunset simply announces the evening of the same day, but not so with the Hebrew calendar. Simply stated, the Feast of Unleavened Bread begins on the same day as Passover, but at sundown.[95]

The purpose of the Feast of Unleavened Bread is to be a perpetual reminder of the Lord bringing the Israelites out of the land of Egypt; it is to be observed throughout all their generations.[96]

94 *Refer to the Tracking Time in Israel compendium to learn how the Israelites reckon days.*
95 *The Feast of Unleavened Bread Quick Facts table can be found in Appendix E.*
96 *Exodus 12:17*

Part 2: The Spring Appointed Times

As always, we will begin our exploration of this Appointed Time in the 23rd chapter of Leviticus:

"Then on the ***fifteenth day of the same month*** *there is*
the ***Feast of Unleavened Bread*** *to the Lord;*
for seven days you shall eat unleavened bread.
On the first day *you shall have a holy convocation;* ***you shall not do any laborious work.***
But for seven days you shall present an offering by fire to the Lord.
On the seventh day *is a holy convocation;* ***you shall not do any laborious work."***

Leviticus 23:6–8 (Emphasis added)

Notice from the above passage that the first and seventh days are high Sabbaths, meaning that two high Sabbaths are embodied within this feast. Carefully read the instructions in Leviticus 23:6–8 (above) and refer to the calendar image in *Figure 4 - The Timing of The Feast of Unleavened Bread:*

1. Notice that the feast begins on the 15th of the month (i.e., when the sun sets on the 14th).
2. The feast lasts for seven days, from the evening of the 15th until sunset on the 21st.
3. The first day of the feast, which is Abib 15,
    a. is to be a day of rest from ordinary work. In other words, it is a Sabbath.
    b. It is the **first** great or high Sabbath for this feast.
    c. The people attend a holy gathering (convocation) on this day.
4. The seventh day of the feast, Abib 21,
    a. is also a day of rest from ordinary work. It is a Sabbath.
    b. It is the **second** great or high Sabbath of the feast.[97]
    c. The people attend a holy gathering (convocation) on this day.

97 Refer to the Tracking Time in Israel compendium to learn more about great Sabbaths, which are also referred to as high Sabbaths.

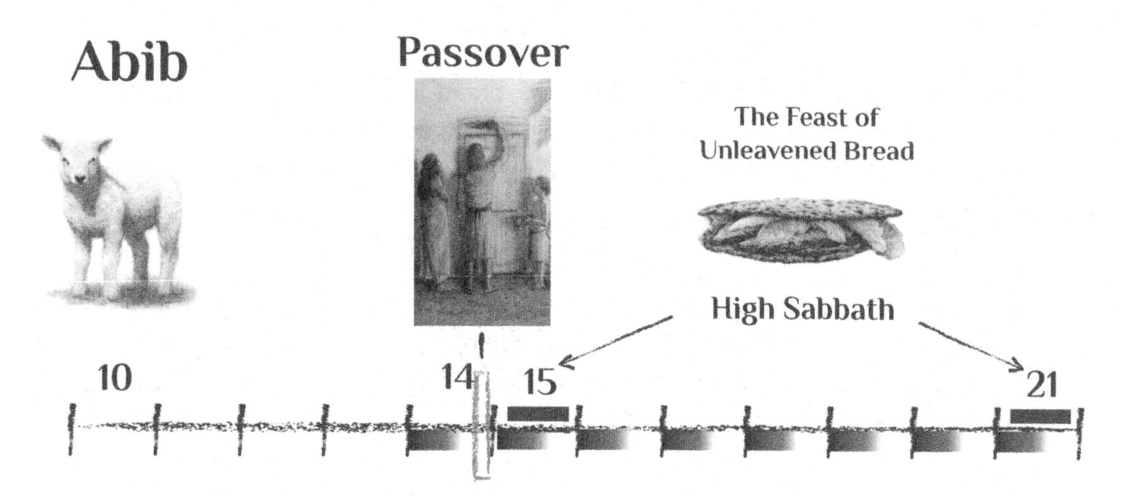

Figure 4 - The Timing of The Feast of Unleavened Bread

Even though this feast is the second spring Appointed Time in Leviticus 23, it is also the first high Sabbath of the year—recall that Passover, Abib 14, is **not** a **high Sabbath** day.[98]

A Holy Convocation

You may be wondering what is involved in a convocation or a holy gathering. Simply stated, it is a gathering of the people for a holy purpose—it could be called a sacred meeting or a worship service. Convocations involved teaching, reading the Law, prayer, worship, and giving praise to God.

Unleavened Bread

As the name implies, unleavened bread is the only kind of bread that the Israelites were allowed to eat during this week. But the command of the Lord actually goes further than a simple prohibition against leavened bread; it goes on to say that no leaven may be found in the Israelites' houses during this week.[99]

---

98 Refer to the Tracking Time in Israel compendium to learn more about Passover as a day of preparation rather than a high Sabbath.

99 Exodus 12:19–20

This means that anything containing leaven is strictly forbidden during this seven-day feast; the people were not allowed to have any leaven or leavened items in their houses or in their entire territory.[100] For modern Jewish people, this would include bread, pretzels, pizza, cakes, muffins, donuts, stuffing, croutons, bread pudding, beer, and many other alcoholic beverages. If it sounds like a difficult week to endure, then you are on the right track. Subsequent generations were required to observe this one-week feast in remembrance of the affliction that their forefathers experienced while on their journey out of Egypt, denying themselves some of the pleasures of life as a mild form of self-affliction.

Just so you know, it is fully permissible for Jewish people to eat and enjoy leavened bread and other leavened delights outside of the week of the Feast of Unleavened Bread. This feast is not a sweeping prohibition against leavened foods throughout the year. The restrictions against leaven are only in force during this springtime feast.

The Significance of Unleavened Bread

You may have heard that leaven always represents sin or evil when used as a metaphor in the Bible. But we must be careful when making such sweeping statements. Moses told the people that unleavened bread is the *bread of affliction*,[101] so it has nothing to do with sin in this case. It is used as a metaphor to represent the affliction that the Israelites endured during their exodus from Egypt. Since they were in such a hurry to escape from their tormentors, their dough did not have time to become leavened, so they baked it into unleavened cakes.

"You shall not eat leavened bread with it;
seven days you shall eat with it
unleavened bread, the bread of affliction
(for you came out of the land of Egypt in haste),
so that you may remember all the days of your life
the day when you came out of the land of Egypt."

Deuteronomy 16:3 (Emphasis added)

100 *Deuteronomy 16:4*

101 *Deuteronomy 16:3*

Another indication that leaven does not always represent sin or evil is that leavened cakes are to be presented to the Lord for peace offerings.[102] Furthermore, two loaves of leavened bread were to be presented as a new grain offering at the Feast of Weeks (i.e., Pentecost).[103] Jesus taught that the kingdom of God is like leaven, which a woman took and hid in some flour until it was entirely leavened[104]—He is certainly not teaching that the kingdom of God is evil or sinful.

Somber Reflection

For subsequent generations, the ritual of eating unleavened bread during this feast was not to be a casual, lighthearted meal. The meal is intended to be a thoughtful time of deep reflection about the anguish of their forefathers. Each person was to envision him or herself enduring the journey out of Rameses, walking alongside their forefathers through the sea and into the wilderness. From its inception, the nation of Israel has endured monumental afflictions that have continued throughout the centuries, but she endures.

Once again, the nation of Israel is the theater of God. He established the nation to declare and demonstrate His truth to the world, as the conduit through which He would send His Messiah. Israel will continue to exist even though the affliction continues, even to our day, but their tribulations should come as no surprise. It is the fury of the serpent raging against the Messiah, the promised son of this nation, who will, one day, inflict a death blow upon him.[105] John the apostle saw a great vision that explains the reason behind the persecution of Israel and of those who believe in the Messiah.

102 *Leviticus 7:13*

103 *Leviticus 23:16–17*

104 *Luke 13:20–21*

105 *Genesis 3:15 – The meaning of this somewhat cryptic passage is revealed through progressive revelation.*

"And when the dragon saw that he was thrown down to the earth,
he persecuted the woman who gave birth to the male child...
So the dragon was enraged with the woman,
and went off to make war with the rest of her children,
who keep the commandments of God and hold to the testimony of Jesus."

Revelation 12:13 & 17

The Amazing Journey

Let's return to the city of Rameses to see how the journey of affliction unfolds. The Lord brought the multitudes of Israel out of the land of Egypt sometime after sunset on the day they ate the Passover lamb with the bitter herbs and unleavened bread.[106] The day of the week is not mentioned in the Bible, but a passage in the Talmud says,

"on the fourteenth day of the month of Nissan [i.e., Abib],
during which (month) the Israelites went out of Egypt,
they killed the Passover sacrifice;
on the fifteenth they went out, and that day was Friday."

Talmud (Emphasis added).[107]

From this, we can deduce that **the Passover lamb was sacrificed on a Thursday during the year of the exodus**, since it was to be killed before sunset on that day.[108]

The Scriptures do not tell us when Moses gave the command to begin the exodus, but we know that the destroyer did his work at midnight and that Pharaoh called for Moses *sometime in the night.*[109] We also know that the departure began in the nighttime since Deuteronomy 16:1 says, "the Lord your God brought you out of Egypt *by night*." (Emphasis added). So, we really only know that the Israelites departed sometime in the night of Abib 15, but the exact time is uncertain.

106 Exodus 12:51

107 (Rodkinson, The Babylonian Talmud 1903), Volume 1, TRACT SABBATH, CHAPTER IX, p.161

108 Recall that the date changed from the 14th to the 15th when the sun set, but it was essentially the same day. Refer to the Day section of the Tracking Time in Israel compendium for more information about how a new day always begins at sundown.

109 Exodus 12:30

The Israelites had followed the instructions of Moses and requested articles of silver and gold and clothing from their Egyptian neighbors. The Lord truly gave them favor with their neighbors, who generously gave them everything they requested. But on the night of the Passover, the Egyptians begged them to get out of their land quickly, "otherwise we will all be dead!"[110]

With the full moon illuminating their way, the people of Israel emerged from their homes in the middle of the night, uncertain of what they would encounter outside in the wake of the destroyer's work. Perhaps they beheld the ominous flaming pillar of fire[111] towering in the distance, waiting to lead them to their new home. The wails and cries of the Egyptians were the only human sounds that were heard as Israel boldly assembled themselves together in martial array[112] and readied their families, flocks, and newly acquired possessions for the odyssey that lay ahead.

The Israelites' journey was about to begin. As they advanced toward the pillar of flame, their ranks expanded as they walked. But as they moved together, the entire multitude, even their children and livestock, seemed to instinctively follow the pillar.

They journeyed from Rameses to Succoth on foot, about six hundred thousand men, in addition to their children and flocks and herds, and they walked in the sight of the Egyptians who were burying their firstborn.[113]

A Plan with a Ploy

As you would expect, the Lord did not allow the Israelites to simply walk out of Rameses without a plan; their route was well planned, and it included a ploy to draw Pharaoh and his armies into a deadly trap. Their destination was Mount Horeb (i.e., Mount Sinai), the mountain of God. Recall that Moses received instructions from God at the burning bush to bring the people back to this mountain to worship Him after he led them out of Egypt.[114]

The first item of business, however, was to keep their forefathers' promise to Joseph, to carry his bones out of Egypt when they left.[115] So they managed to retrieve his bones from what

110 Exodus 12:33

111 Exodus 13:21 – *"The Lord was going before them in a pillar of cloud by day to lead them on the way, and in a pillar of fire by night to give them light, that they might travel by day and by night."*

112 Exodus 13:18 – *"and the sons of Israel went up in martial array from the land of Egypt."*

113 Numbers 33:3–4

114 Exodus 3:12 – *"...when you have brought the people out of Egypt, you shall worship God at this mountain."*

115 Genesis 50:25

was probably a prominent Egyptian tomb and take them on their journey to the Promised Land. It is unlikely that the entire multitude of Israel made the journey to retrieve his bones—Moses probably sent a small band of able raiders to do the job. Joseph's body had been embalmed many years prior, so he was ready to go.

Three Encampments

Israel is on the run—Numbers 33 tells us that they stopped to camp three times. How far did they travel on the first leg of their journey? How long can such a mixed multitude travel after being awake the entire night? How long did they remain at each camp site? Did they camp during the daylight hours or did they walk until dark? Since their journey began in the night of Abib 15, they might have been ready for a rest sometime during the daytime of that same day. The information is not explicitly provided in the Bible, but it is interesting and possibly of messianic significance that they stopped to camp three times, perhaps indicating a three-day journey. We will explain the implications further in *Chapter 11 – Unleavened Bread and the Bitterness of Death.*

Moses recorded the names of the encampment sites in Numbers 33:5–8 as follows.

1. "Then the sons of Israel journeyed from **Rameses and camped in Succoth.**"
    - Note: Succoth is believed to be about 15 miles (24 kilometers) southeast of their starting point.[116]
2. "They journeyed **from Succoth and camped in Etham**, which is on the edge of the wilderness."
3. "They journeyed **from Etham** and turned back to Pi-hahiroth, which faces Baal-zephon, and they **camped before Migdol.**"[117]

116 (Byers 2008) - Archeologists have attempted to identify the locations of the exodus encampments based on excavations in the eastern Nile Delta region. This article by Gary Byers provides some excellent information.

117 Numbers 33:5–8 (Emphasis added)

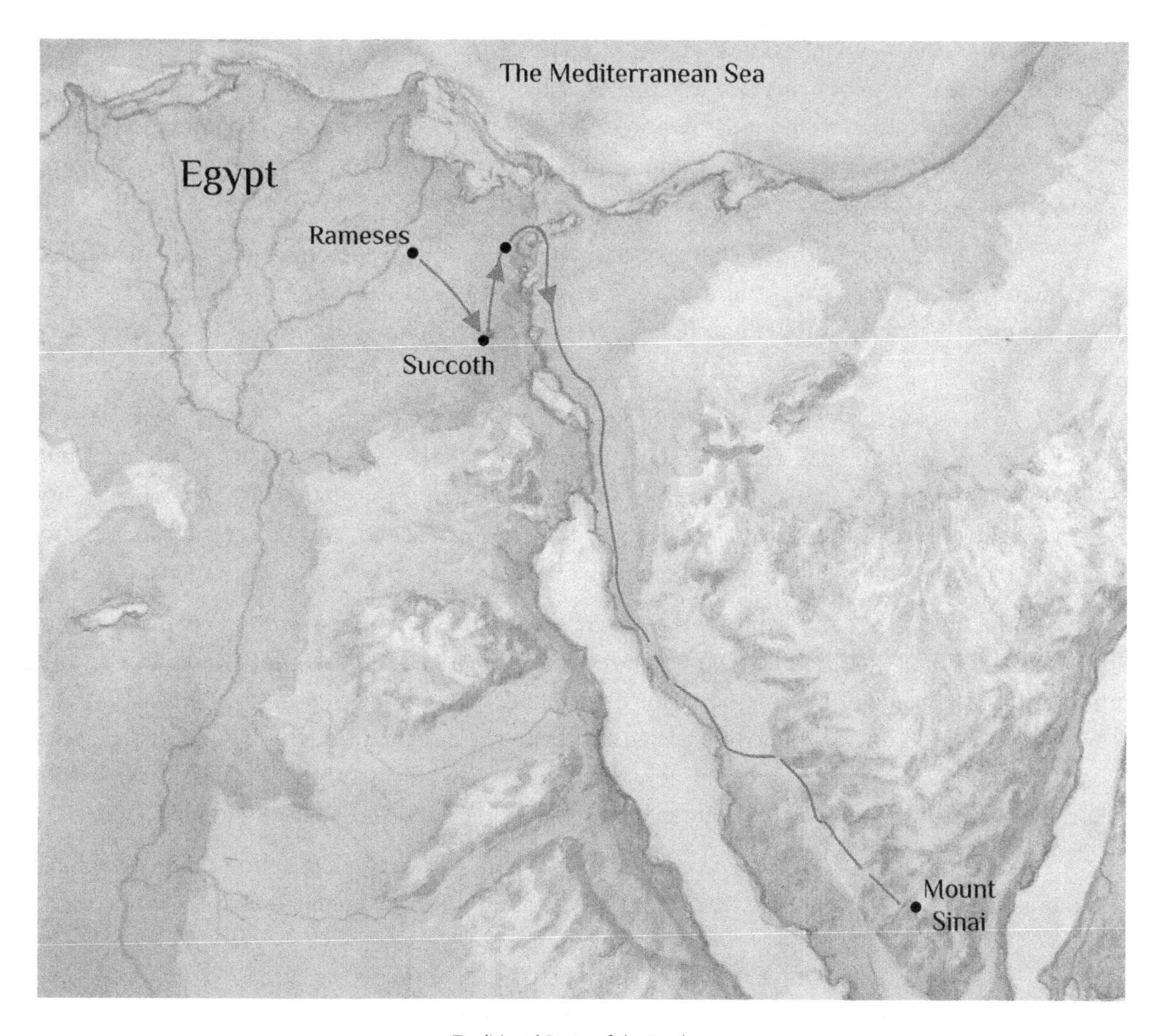

Traditional Route of the Exodus

The Ploy – What have we done???

It may have been during the Israelites' encampment at Etham that the Lord instructed Moses to have the people turn back in a way that would cause Pharaoh to believe they were wandering in confusion and helplessly shut in by the wilderness. It was through this ploy, however, that God once again hardened Pharaoh's heart so that he would chase after Israel.[118]

118 *Exodus 14:1–4*

When the news of Israel's apparent confusion was reported to Pharaoh, he and his servants had a change of heart and asked, "What have we done by releasing them from serving us?" So they mounted an all-out assault on Israel. Pharaoh readied his own chariot and ordered six hundred select chariots to follow him, leading all of the other chariots of Egypt, enjoined by their officers, and joined by horsemen and foot soldiers.[119]

It was probably during the daylight hours that Pharaoh's fearsome war machine reached the unarmed Israelites. We surmise this since the pillar that was leading them was in the form of a cloud at that time, rather than fire.[120] When the armies caught up with them, they were camped beside Pi-hahiroth, with their backs against the sea, with no way to escape.

To give you an idea of how thoroughly God hardened Pharaoh's heart, here we see the man pursuing a people whose God had selectively wiped out every first-heir of Egypt and was now leading His people by a giant pillar of fire. Like a dog chasing a truck, Pharaoh did not even consider what might happen if he caught it; he never stopped to consider the supernatural danger that was signaled by this phenomenon.

The affliction that is represented by the unleavened bread does not completely capture the fear and terror that the people must have felt as they beheld the fury of Pharaoh's chariots, horsemen, and soldiers bearing down on their children, parents, and entire families. It was a harrowing three days. They were exhausted from their flight through day and night[121] with minimal sleep and nourishment, and now they found themselves trapped against the sea with nothing between themselves and immanent annihilation by a furious king and his angry army.

"Were there not enough graves in Egypt that you had to bring us here to die? Why have you done this to us?" the people demanded of Moses. But Moses boldly replied,

"Do not fear! Stand by and see the salvation of the Lord
which He will accomplish for you today;
for the Egyptians whom you have seen today,
you will never see them again forever.
The Lord will fight for you while you keep silent."

Exodus 14:13–15

---

119 *Exodus 14:18 includes horsemen, and Exodus 14:10 implies foot soldiers by the phrase "marching after them" (Emphasis added).*

120 *Exodus 14:19 – "The angel of God, who had been going before the camp of Israel, moved and went behind them; and the pillar of cloud moved from before them and stood behind them."*

121 *Exodus 13:21 – "The Lord was going before them in a pillar of cloud by day to lead them on the way, and in a pillar of fire by night to give them light, that they might travel by day and by night."*

Then the Lord said to Moses, "Tell the people to go forward." "For what reason?" Moses must have wondered. But as the people began walking toward the edge of the sea, the Lord told Moses to "lift up your staff and stretch out your hand over the sea and divide it, and Israel shall go through its midst on dry land."[122]

As Moses raised his staff and his hand toward the sea, the Lord swept back the waters and drew them away from the center, exposing a path of dry land for the nation's escape. Then the angel of God, who had been leading the people, moved and took his stand in the pillar of cloud, in front of Pharaoh's army, shielding the people of Israel from the oncoming torrent. All night long, the wind dried a path in the sea for Israel while the pillar of cloud and fire halted the onslaught of Pharaoh. **Sometime in the night, by the light of the angel's fire, the people began to cross through the sea and ascended alive on the other side**.

At the Morning Watch

"At the morning watch,
the Lord looked down on the army of the Egyptians
through the pillar of fire and cloud and brought the army of the Egyptians into confusion. He caused their chariot wheels to swerve, and He made them drive with difficulty..."

Exodus 14:24–25 (Emphasis added)

As the last of Israel's hosts passed through the corridor of the sea in the night, Pharaoh gave the command to pursue them through the divide. Chariots and horsemen thundered down the embankment of the sea, certain to seize the trailing ranks of Israel. But ***at the morning watch,***[123] the Lord looked down on the army through the pillar of fire and cloud, and once again He influenced the minds of the Egyptians.

The Lord brought the army into confusion, causing the wheels of their chariots to swerve and confounding their ability to drive. "Retreat! Back to shore! The Lord is fighting for Israel against us!" the soldiers shouted, but they were ensnared in the trap, unable to free themselves.

"Then the Lord said to Moses, 'Stretch out your hand over the sea so that the waters may come back over the Egyptians,'"[124] and Moses did so. The walls of the sea roared back to

122 *Exodus 14:16 (Author's paraphrase)*

123 *Refer to the section in the Tracking Time in Israel compendium to learn more about the nighttime and the morning watch.*

124 *Exodus 14:26a*

their normal state, over the chariots and horsemen and all the Egyptians who went in after Israel. The sea returned to its normal state at daybreak, consuming Pharaoh's entire army so that not one of them survived. After the torrent had settled, Israel stood on the opposite side of the sea and beheld the bodies of their tormentors, spread along the seashore. As for Israel, the Lord saved them from the Egyptians, restraining the waters like walls as they passed through the midst of the sea. And when Israel beheld the great power of the Lord, they feared and believed in Him and also in Moses.[125]

Did You Catch That?

Yes, the Israelites arose from the sea before dawn, and judgement came upon their foe during the morning watch. But let's back up a few days in their story to highlight some details that will bring the time signature of the Messiah into focus:

1. The Passover lamb was corralled or isolated from the other sheep on **Abib 10**, for the purpose of inspecting its purity—Jesus submitted himself to be tested by Israel when He entered Jerusalem on **Abib 10**.
2. The Passover lamb was slain at twilight on **Abib 14**—Jesus died at the ninth hour (3:00pm), the beginning of the twilight hours, on the afternoon of Passover, **Abib 14**.
3. When the sun set on that same day, the date changed to **Abib 15**.
4. Shortly after sundown, the Passover lamb was eaten with bitter herbs and the bread of affliction. In a similar way, Jesus, the Lamb of God, tasted the bitterness of death as His body was placed in the tomb on the evening of **Abib 15**.
5. Sometime during the nighttime hours of Friday, **Abib 15**, the people began their journey of affliction.
6. The Israelites traveled on foot and camped three times.
7. **At the morning watch on the third day**, the Israelites arose alive from the sea.
8. **Jesus arose alive from the grave before dawn (i.e., during the morning watch) on the third day.**

125 *Exodus 14:31 (Author's paraphrase)*

Chapter 6: The Feast of Unleavened Bread

As we carefully observe the timing of the spring Appointed Times, it becomes clear that they reveal the time signature of the Messiah. But there is more to come, since all of the spring Appointed Times comprise this unique time signature. Indeed, the Lord choreographed these events for the purpose of placing the spotlight on His Messiah so everyone would recognize Jesus as the main performer in Theater Israel—the entire production is about Him.

Does the New Testament truly bear witness to these corresponding dates and events? Does the timeline in Jesus' life match the timing of the spring Appointed Times? Indeed, it does! Stay tuned—we will see how all four of the gospels are in perfect harmony with the timing of the Appointed Times.

Chapter 7 – First Fruits

*...you shall bring in the sheaf of the **first fruits** of your harvest to the priest.*
He shall wave the sheaf before the Lord for you to be accepted;
on the day after the sabbath the priest shall wave it.

Leviticus 23:10–11 (Emphasis added)

The Day of First Fruits is the third *spring* Appointed Time mentioned in Leviticus 23. The timing of First Fruits has been highly controversial for thousands of years, but as we will demonstrate, the answer is right before our eyes in the Law of Moses. Understanding the timing is of great importance since it casts a shadow of the resurrection of the Messiah—a feat that could only be accomplished by the *true* Messiah.[126]

Think about It... What Is Meant by First Fruits?

Before we look into the timing of First Fruits on the Hebrew calendar, let's consider the meaning of the term itself. If someone were to ask you, "What is meant by first fruits?" what would you say? The name in itself offers some valuable clues. Obviously, *first* is a common word that implies a sequence or series of events. If someone were to give you some money and tell you that this is the first payment, you would probably assume that more payments will follow; there will likely be a second, possibly a third, and so on. The word fruits is referring to the fruit of the harvest, which in this case is the barley harvest.

126 The First Fruits Quick Facts table can be found in Appendix E.

The First Fruits offering is not, however, suggesting that this is the first of many offerings to the Lord. Instead, this sheaf is the first of many sheaves that will come *from* the Lord back *to* the giver, and the offering expresses an expectation that the Lord will provide more fruit in the coming harvest. The First Fruits offering is a way of honoring the Lord by acknowledging that the produce came from Him with the hope and expectation that He will bless with more fruit.

☆ ***First Fruits is giving thanks for the first of God's many gifts to us.*** ☆

Even though the sheaf of grain is presented to the Lord through a priest, it really should not be viewed as a sacrifice. A sacrifice is something of significant value that a person gives for the purpose of gaining something of more value (e.g., forgiveness) or to prevent some sort of evil (e.g., King David's burnt offerings to prevent the angel from striking down the people—see 2 Samuel 24:15–25). In the case of First Fruits, the sheaf that is offered has relatively little value when compared to the amount of grain in the field. Thus, the First Fruits sheaf should be understood as a token or acknowledgement that the giver is thankful and fully aware that the produce came from the Lord.

When the Israelites eventually moved into the Promised Land and were able to grow their own crops, they were required to bring a sheaf from their barley crop to the priest as a First Fruits offering during the Feast of Unleavened Bread. The priest would take the sheaf and wave it or raise it before the Lord so the giver would be accepted. Incidentally, this is referred to as a wave offering or an elevation offering (the priest would simply raise it up toward the Lord). Notice also that the people were forbidden from eating bread, roasted grain, or the new growth of their crops until they offered their first fruits offering on this day.[127]

Which Sabbath? – Good Question!

"When you enter the land which I am going to give to you and reap its harvest,
then you shall bring in the sheaf of the first fruits of your harvest to the priest.
He shall wave the sheaf before the Lord for you to be accepted;
on the day after the sabbath *the priest shall wave it."*

Leviticus 23:10–11 (Emphasis added)

127 *Leviticus 23:14*

Chapter 7: First Fruits

Now that we have a better feel for the meaning of first fruits, let's explore the timing of the event. Immediately after saying, *he shall wave the sheaf before the Lord,* for you to be accepted, the Lord stipulates that the priest should wave the sheaf on the *day after the Sabbath*. The big question is which Sabbath is He referencing? Is it the first **high Sabbath** that occurs on Abib 15, which is the first Day of the Feast of Unleavened Bread, or is it the **weekly Sabbath** that occurs during the Feast of Unleavened Bread? That's a good question—a pivotal question.

Is the Exact Date Really Important?

Determining the exact date is very important, obviously because we are dealing with God's Word and we want to be in the truth, but there are other reasons that we must correctly identify it. The first is that the date has messianic significance, and we must identify the correct Sabbath in order to correctly see the shadow of the Messiah. The second is that the timing of the next Appointed Time, the Feast of Weeks, is based on the date of First Fruits. If we do not correctly identify the day on which First Fruits is to be observed, then we will misjudge the timing for the Feast of Weeks. Thus, two very important shadows of the Messiah's work would be distorted.

The "*Which Sabbath?*" question reflected the deep divide between the leading Jewish religious sects, the Pharisees and the Sadducees, during the time of Jesus. The dispute began sometime during the latter half of the Second Temple Period (516 BC – AD 70). In this chapter, we present a high level overview of the differences between the two sects regarding the timing of First Fruits, but I encourage you to read the more detailed information that has been provided in *Appendix B - The Timing of First Fruits.*

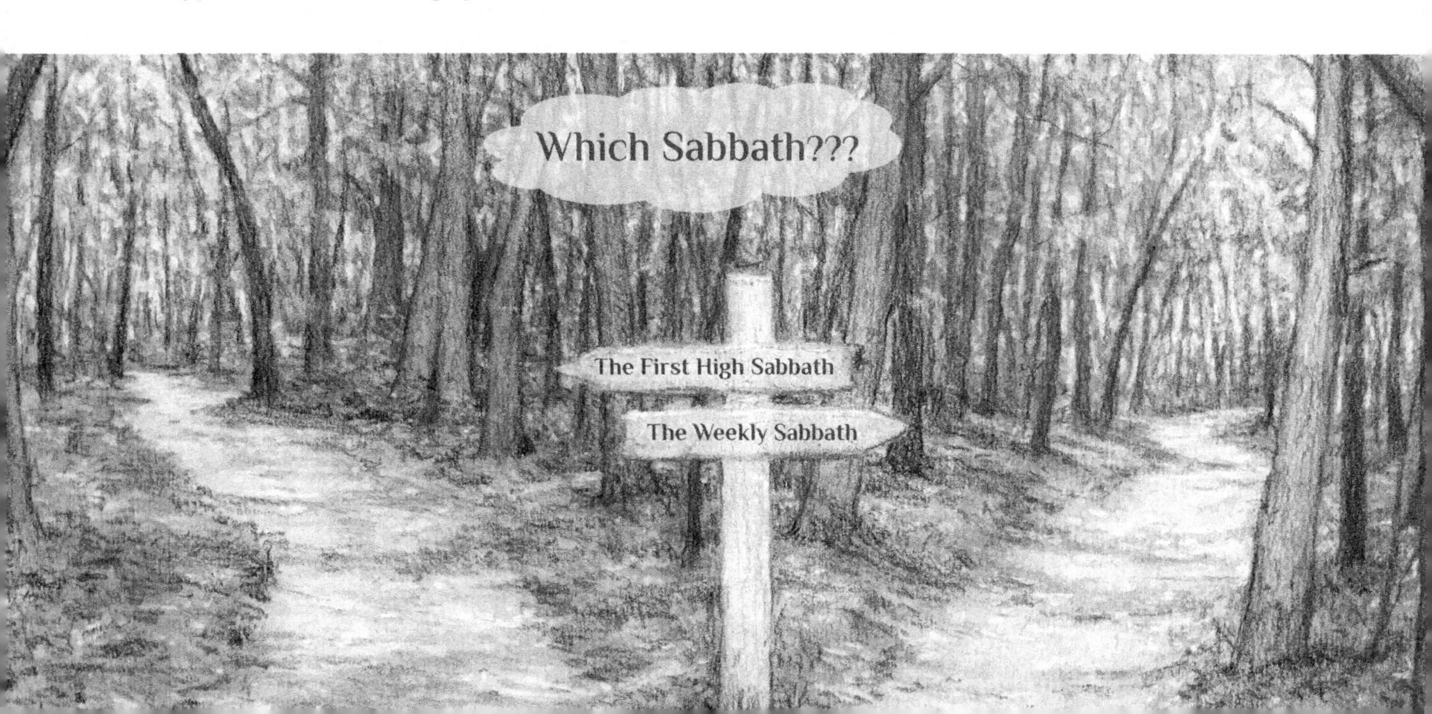

***...on the day after the sabbath** the priest shall wave it.*

Leviticus 23:11 (Emphasis added)

Let's explore the viewpoints of these two groups:

***According to the Pharisees...* the First Fruits offering is to be presented on Abib 16, the day after the first *high* Sabbath day of the Feast of Unleavened Bread.**

The Pharisees believed that Moses was referring to the first high Sabbath of the Feast of Unleavened Bread, which is Abib 15. Thus, according to their belief, First Fruits should always be observed on Abib 16, the day after that Sabbath. And so it is, even in our modern day, that the great majority of the Jewish community—those who adhere to the Oral Law, the Talmud—observe First Fruits on Abib 16. By this interpretation, First Fruits is always observed on Abib 16, and therefore, can fall on any day of the week (i.e. Monday, Tuesday, Wednesday, etc.). Refer to the image in Figure 5 to help visualize the Pharisee's understanding of the timing of First Fruits.

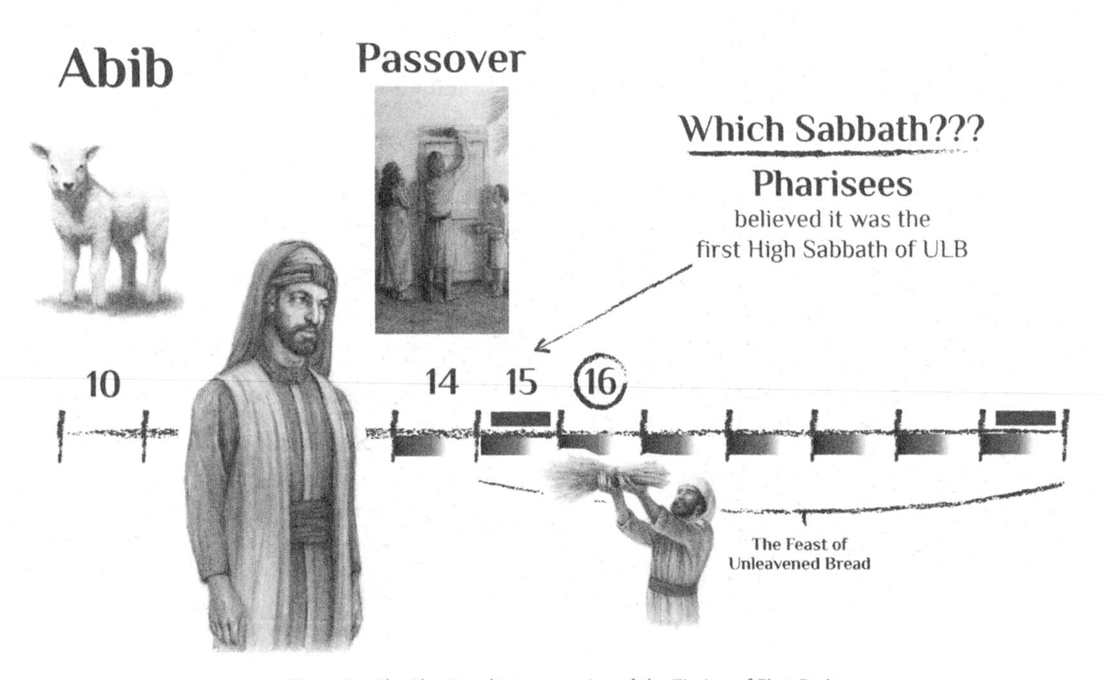

Figure 5 – The Pharisees' Interpretation of the Timing of First Fruits

***According to the Sadducees...* the First Fruits offering is to be presented on the Sunday that occurs during the Feast of Unleavened Bread.**

The Sadducees, on the other hand, believed that Moses was referring to the *weekly* Sabbath (i.e., the Saturday) that occurs during the week-long Feast of Unleavened Bread. Of course, that means that First Fruits would be observed on the Sunday during Unleavened Bread. It also means that the date of First Fruits would vary—it could fall anywhere between Abib 15–21, rather than only on the 16th. Stated simply, the Sadducees believed that First Fruits would be observed on the Sunday that occurs during the Feast of Unleavened Bread. Refer to Figure 6 to help visualize the Sadducee's understanding of the timig of First Fruits.

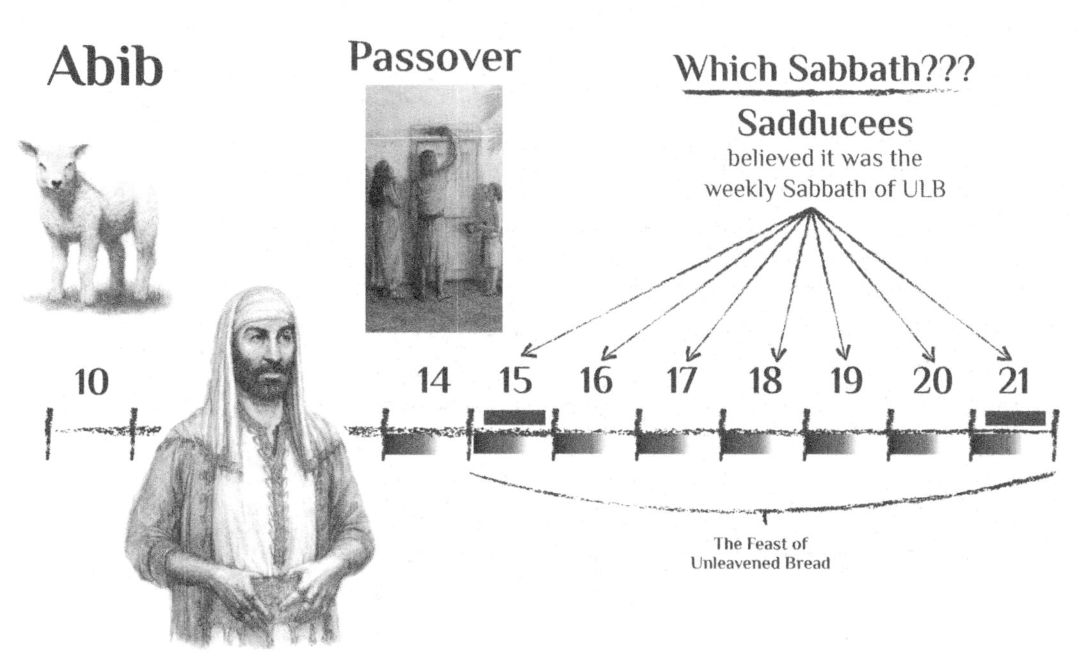

Figure 6 – The Sadducees' Interpretation of the Timing of First Fruits

How Can We Know?

If the Pharisees and Sadducees had not resolved the dispute more than 1,000 years after Moses prescribed it, then how are we to answer the question? Fortunately, the answer is not complex—it is a simple matter of observing the details of God's Word. You see, the issue is not that the Scriptures are not clear; instead, their dispute can be traced back to different approaches to interpreting them. The Sadducees held to a literal interpretation of the Scriptures to determine the dates, whereas the Pharisees chose to determine the dates by their calendar, even when it differed from the Scriptures. When we allow the Scriptures to speak for themselves, we will find the clue that makes the timing of First Fruits very clear, removing the need for guesswork. *Let's take a look...*

The timing of First Fruits can be determined from Moses' instructions about the next Appointed Time, which is the Feast of Weeks. Leviticus 23:15–16 gives the following instruction:

"You shall also count for yourselves from the day after the sabbath,
from the day when you brought in the sheaf of the wave offering..."

Note: Since you are now an expert in this subject, you recognize that Moses is referring to the day of First Fruits in "brought in the sheaf of the wave offering," which he uses to determine the date of the Feast of Weeks (Leviticus 23:15).

He continues:

"...there shall be seven complete sabbaths.
You shall count fifty days ***to the day after the seventh sabbath****;*
then you shall present a new grain offering to the Lord."

Leviticus 23:15–16 (Emphasis added)

With this information, we simply draw on our knowledge that a sabbath can also refer to a seven-day period, which is one week.[128] Thus, seven complete sabbaths (i.e., seven weeks) is forty-nine days, and the fiftieth day is the day after the seventh sabbath. We also know that the day after a weekly Sabbath is always Sunday, the first day of the week.

128 *Refer to the section in the Tracking Time in Israel compendium to learn more about Weeks..*

The Key

Therefore, the only way the Feast of Weeks can consistently fall on a Sunday is if the day of First Fruits, which is 50 days prior, also falls on Sunday. Thus, Moses must have been referring to the weekly Sabbath in Leviticus 23:11 when he stipulated,

"...on the day after the sabbath the priest shall wave it."

On the other hand, if he was referring to the day after Abib 15 (the first high Sabbath of the Feast of Unleavened Bread), as the Pharisees believed, then there could be no assurance that the Feast of Weeks would fall on the first day of the week, which the Lord stipulated in Leviticus 23:16.

It looks like the Sadducees had it right!

I should mention, however, that just because the Sadducees arrived at the right conclusion in this case does not mean that their interpretation approach is always correct, since their excessively literal methodology became the source of many errors. For example, in

his English translation of the Babylonian Talmud, Levi Rodkinson explains how the Sadducees, in their "attempt to get at the profound meaning of the Scriptures,"[129] resorted to theological philosophizing in order to explain common figures of speech, such as God's hand, eye, or finger—expressions that should simply be viewed as literary personifications of God.

The Pharisees, on the other hand, who compiled the Talmud, are on the other end of the interpretation spectrum, preferring a figurative interpretation even when it may not be appropriate. As we interpret the Scriptures, we should always have the goal of understanding the intended meaning of the original writer or speaker. If a figure of speech was used then we should interpret it as such; if something was intended literally, then we should interpret it literally. Serious error can arise from interpreting the literal in a figurative sense, just as much as interpreting the figurative in a literal sense.

The Shadow of First Fruits

Now that we know that First Fruits is to be observed on the Sunday that occurs during the Feast of Unleavened Bread, let's return to the story of the exodus to explore the shadow that is cast by the day of First Fruits. Consider the following timing for the first few days of the Israelites' journey of affliction, as follows.

Recall that:

- The Passover lamb was slain on Abib 14, which was a **Thursday afternoon,**[130] at twilight (i.e., between 3:00pm and sunset).
- When the sun set, the date changed to Abib 15 (recall that it was a Friday that year), and the Israelites ate the Passover meal and later that night, began their journey from Rameses.
- We saw that they **camped in three different locations**:
    1. They journeyed **from Rameses** and **camped in Succoth**
    2. They journeyed **from Succoth** and **camped in Etham**
    3. They journeyed **from Etham** and camped **before Migdol.**[131]

---

129 (Rodkinson, The Babylonian Talmud 1903) – Volume 10, HISTORY, CHAPTER VII, p. 28. Note: this quote is in Rodkinson's History of the Talmud; it is not in the Talmud per se.

130 As mentioned earlier, we deduced that the Passover lamb was sacrificed on Thursday from the Talmud, which states that the Israelites went out on a Friday. Refer to "The Amazing Journey" section in "Chapter 6 – The Feast of Unleavened Bread."

131 Numbers 33:5–8

It is difficult to know when the Israelites camped, since their journey began in the nighttime. Perhaps they camped during the daytime and nighttime in order to get some rest and have something to eat. But for the sake of simplicity, let's divide their journey into even parts to see what it might look like:

Abib 15 Nighttime: Journey

Abib 15 Daytime: Camped in Succoth

Abib 16 Nighttime: Journey

Perhaps they camped sometime in the night in Etham

Abib 16 Daytime: Journey

Perhaps they camped late in the day before Migdol

Then, late in the daylight hours of Abib 16, Pharaoh and his army caught up with the Israelites. In order to protect them, the angel in the pillar of cloud took his stand between the army of Egypt and the camp of Israel. Pharaoh and his army threatened through dusk and into the night of Abib 17, but **sometime during the nighttime of Abib 17, the Israelites began crossing through the corridor of the sea.** As the trailing ranks of Israel were moving toward the other side, Pharaoh gave the order to attack, and his forces entered the pathway in the sea and pursued the people with the intent of utterly destroying them.

It was at the **morning watch** of Abib 17—which was the first day of the week, a **Sunday**, the day after the weekly Sabbath, **the day of First Fruits**—that God looked down on the Egyptian army through the pillar of fire and completely destroyed them by collapsing the walls of the sea as they reeled in their confusion. But immediately afterward, at sunrise on that same day, we find the Israelites alive and safe on the opposite shore of the sea.

Would it be accurate to say that **the newly forged nation of Israel was a sort of First Fruits**? I believe it would. They were fulfilling the First Fruits shadow of this Appointed Time. As the priest would wave the barley sheaf before the Lord, giving thanks for the things that He had given, and even more for the things yet to come, so this fledgling nation was the first fruit of a holy nation from whom Christ was born, who is over all, God blessed forever.[132]

Indeed, the ultimate fulfillment, the substance of First Fruits is something much greater than the nation that God created. First Fruits is casting a shadow of the Messiah rising from the dead on the third day, after He conquered a much greater foe than Pharaoh.

---

132 *Romans 9:5*

Chapter 7: First Fruits

Is the Messiah truly greater than the entire nation of Israel? Yes, indeed, in the same way that the builder of a house is greater and worthy of greater honor than the house.[133] The Messiah is the builder and Creator, not just of Israel, but of all creation.[134] Stay tuned—we will explore this thought in greater detail in "Chapter 12 – The First Fruit of Many Brethren."

A Further Thought

Before we end this chapter, you should know that the First Fruits offering was not presented by the Israelites during the year of the exodus. Obviously, since they were oppressed slaves, they did not have crops from which they could present a sheaf of new grain to the Lord. Furthermore, the Lord stipulated that this command would become effective *"when you enter the land which I am going to give to you and reap its harvest."*[135] It was not in effect during the exodus, although the Passover and the Feast of Unleavened Bread certainly applied to their situation at that time.

The timing of First Fruits was designed to coincide with the Israelites' rising alive from the sea and the Messiah rising alive from the grave. Both events occurred at the morning watch on the day of First Fruits, which is an essential ingredient of the time signature of the Messiah.

133 Hebrews 3:3 – *"For He has been counted worthy of more glory than Moses, by just so much as the builder of the house has more honor than the house.*

134 Colossians 1:16 – *"For by Him all things were created, both in the heavens and on earth, visible and invisible, whether thrones or dominions or rulers or authorities—all things have been created through Him and for Him."*

135 Leviticus 23:10

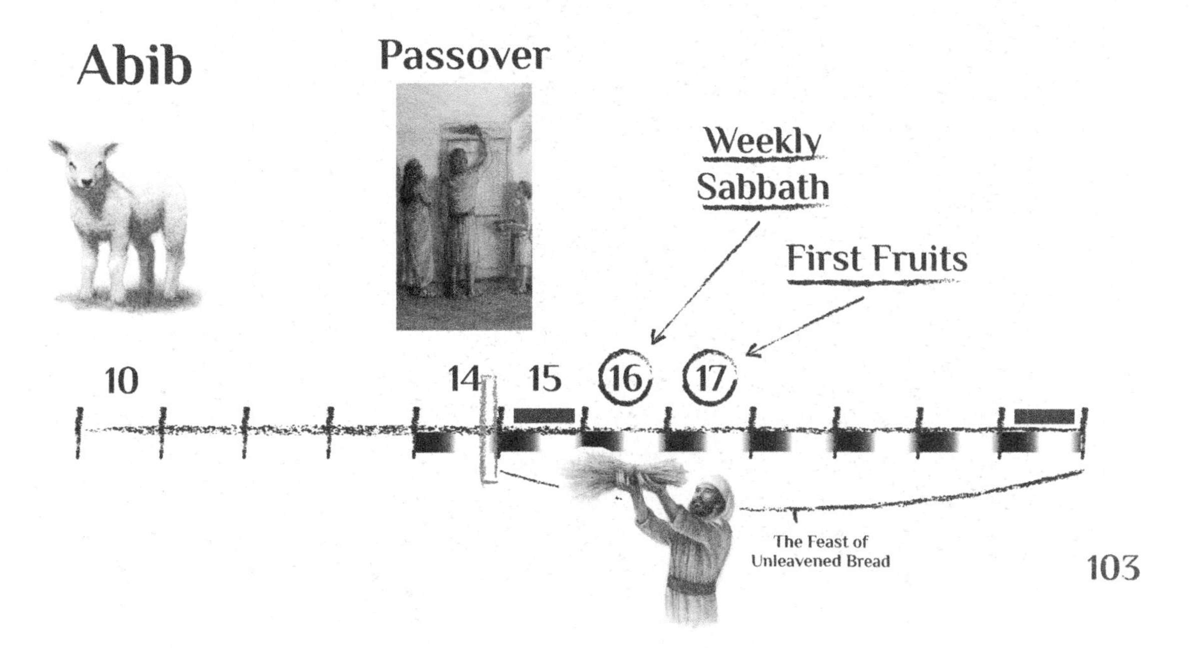

Chapter 8 – The Feast of Weeks

You shall also count for yourselves from the day after the sabbath,
from the day when you brought in the sheaf of the wave offering;
there shall be seven complete sabbaths.
You shall count fifty days to the day after the seventh sabbath;
then you shall present a new grain offering to the Lord.

Leviticus 23:15–16

The Feast of Weeks is the fourth spring Appointed Time in Leviticus 23. **It is observed exactly fifty days after the day of First Fruits.** The timing of the Feast of Weeks[136] is based on the timing of the day of First Fruits, which we discussed in the previous chapter. Notice in the passage above that the Israelites were required to count seven complete sabbaths,[137] which is seven full weeks from the day of First Fruits, and then present a new grain offering *on the next day*, which would be the fiftieth day. Since the feast is observed on the fiftieth day, it is commonly referred to as Pentecost, which is the Greek word for "fiftieth."

The Feast of Weeks is observed
exactly fifty days after the Day of First Fruits.

★ Pentecost is the Greek word that means "fiftieth" ★

136 *The Feast of Weeks Quick Facts table can be found in Appendix E.*

137 *Refer to the Tracking Time in Israel compendium to learn more about Sabbaths and weeks.*

The duration of the Feast of Weeks is only one day, unlike the Feast of Unleavened Bread and the Feast of Booths, which are both seven days in duration. The name *Feast of Weeks* might lead someone to incorrectly believe that the feast lasts for multiple weeks, but it gets its name from the weeks that are counted from the day of the First Fruits offering.

The emphasis of the Feast of Weeks is a first fruits offering, carrying the same idea as the first fruits offering during the week of Unleavened Bread. This first fruits offering, however, comes from the *wheat* harvest, whereas the first fruits offering during the Feast of Unleavened Bread comes from the *barley* harvest.[138] Another important detail is that this first fruits offering was not in the form of a sheaf, but in the form of *two loaves of bread* that were *baked with leaven* and were given to the priest.[139]

"You shall bring in from your dwelling places ***two loaves of bread for a wave offering,*** *made of two-tenths of an ephah; they shall be of a fine flour,*
baked with leaven as first fruits to the Lord.*"*

Leviticus 23:17 (Emphasis added)

Did you catch that? **The loaves were baked with leaven**—they were not unleavened bread, which is the bread of affliction. Since they contain leaven, they have the opposite connotation from affliction. Can we infer that the leavening in this offering represents life and vitality? It certainly fits the mood of this feast since it is festive and full of rejoicing—a celebration of the harvest. Regarding the Feast of Weeks, Moses told the people,

"**...you shall rejoice before the Lord your God**, *you and your son and your daughter*
and your male and female servants and the Levite who is in your town,
and the stranger and the orphan and the widow who are in your midst,
in the place where the Lord your God chooses to establish His name."

Deuteronomy 16:11 (Emphasis added)

138 Barley ripens earlier than wheat, which is the reason the first fruits of the barley harvest is offered during the Feast of Unleavened Bread in the month of Abib. Exodus 9:31–32 gives a practical insight about the development of barley, flax, and wheat. After the plague of hail, Moses recounted, "Now the flax and the barley were ruined, for the barley was in the ear and the flax was in bud. But the wheat and the spelt were not ruined, for they ripen late."

139 Leviticus 23:20 – "...they are to be holy to the Lord for the priest."

So, once again, the people were honoring the Lord by bringing the first fruits of their harvest, acknowledging that the produce came from Him and expecting that He will bless them with additional fruit from their harvest. As the name of this feast indicates, the focus is on counting the weeks just as much as on the feast day itself. As the Israelites counted the days and sabbaths until the Feast of Weeks, there was an exciting anticipation that something special and joyous was approaching.

The Shadow of the Feast of Weeks – Pentecost

Do you remember the meaning of the term *first fruits* from the previous chapter? Recall that it does not suggest that this offering is the first of many offerings from the worshipper. Instead, it is an acknowledgment that these fruits came from the Lord and are the first of many more that He will give back to the worshipper. It is a way of thanking the Lord for what He has given and will continue to give. The *first fruits* offering of the Feast of Weeks is an expression of thanks to the Lord for the produce from the wheat harvest, in the form of baked loaves of bread. In this offering, the worshipper expresses faith that the Lord will continue to bless the harvest.

This is the shadow of the Feast of Weeks, and we must now consider what it teaches about *things to come* and how the substance is the Messiah. Recall that Paul taught that the Appointed Times are shadows of things to come,[140] so we must keep the first fruits concept in mind as we consider possible fulfillments or commemorations of the shadows. But, of greater importance, we must consider the substance of this Appointed Time. What can we learn about the Messiah from this shadow through the concept of first fruits? Stay tuned—some fascinating and gratifying fruit await us.

The Timing of the Feast of Weeks

Recall that the Lord conveyed the Appointed Times to Moses after He gave His Law at Mount Sinai. The book of Leviticus, including the Appointed Times, were most likely written in the year that followed the giving of the law. In that light, it seems reasonable that the Feast of Weeks reflects back in time to commemorate the giving of the Law. Even though the Feast of Weeks was instituted as an Appointed Time after the Law was given, it can still be considered a shadow or commemoration of the giving of the law, since their timings correspond.

140 Colossians 2:16-17

So, let's take a look at the Hebrew calendar and count the weeks to see what we can learn. We know that the Israelites left the city of Rameses during the nighttime of Abib 15, which the Talmud says was a Friday. Furthermore, when we track the encampments of the Israelites and their passage through the sea, we can deduce that Abib 17 was a Sunday, the first day of the week. Let's refer to the calendar in *Figure 7 - Counting the Weeks* to see what we can learn.

First Fruits → Abib 17

	Sunday						Weekly Sabbath (Saturday)	
Abib	17	18	19	20	21	22	23	1
	24	25	26	27	28	29	30	2
Iyar	1	2	3	4	5	6	7	3
	8	9	10	11	12	13	14	4
	15	16	17	18	19	20	21	5
	22	23	24	25	26	27	28	6
	29	30						
Sivan			1	2	3	4	5	7
	(6)							

Figure 7 – Counting the Weeks

When we count seven *complete Sabbaths* from the day of First Fruits on Abib 17, we see

two full weeks in the month of Abib,

four full weeks in the month of Iyar, and

the seventh full week beginning on Iyar 29, ending on the fifth day of the month of Sivan.

The fiftieth day is the day after the seventh sabbath, which is **Sivan 6**.

Sivan – The Third Month – The Giving of the Law

Sivan 6 is a very interesting date since, according to the Jewish Oral Law, the Ten Commandments were given to Moses on that date.[141] The giving of the Law would indeed be a hallmark event that would, no doubt, be commemorated as an Appointed Time. But do the Scriptures support Sivan 6, the 50th day after First Fruits, as the day the Lord gave His Law to Moses?

Let's take a look by resuming with the journey from Egypt:

> *"In the **third month** after the sons of Israel had gone out of the land of Egypt, **on that very day** they came into the wilderness of Sinai... and there Israel camped in front of the mountain."*
>
> *Exodus 19:1–2 (Emphasis added)*

The first two verses of Exodus 19 tell us that the Israelites came into the Sinai wilderness in the third month, which is called Sivan. From this we see that they set up camp in front of the mountain on Sivan 1. Does anyone know the exact location of Mount Sinai and the wilderness around it? The location is the subject of great debate in our age. I certainly do not know the answer, but fortunately, it is not necessary to know the exact location in order to understand the significance of the events that occurred there.

141 *(Rodkinson, The Babylonian Talmud 1903) – Volume 1, TRACTATE SABBATH, CHAPTER IX, p. 158 – "The rabbis taught: The Decalogue was given to Israel on the sixth day of the (third) month"*

Sivan 1 – The First Day of the Third Month

Based on the passage above, let's assume that the Israelites set up their camp during the afternoon and evening of Sivan 1. Moses was, no doubt, anxious to ascend the mountain so he could meet with God in the rendezvous they had planned years before.[142] But as you can imagine from the picture above (one of the possible locations of Mount Sinai), climbing the mountain would be a significant feat for an afternoon walk. A modern travel brochure tells hikers to plan on 2 – 3 ½ hours for the trek. Most likely, Moses ascended the mountain in the morning of Sivan 2 rather than beginning the journey just before dark on Sivan 1.

Sivan 2

So Moses went up to God, and the Lord gave him some words to convey to the Israelites:

"You yourselves have seen what I did to the Egyptians,
and how I bore you on eagles' wings, and brought you to Myself.
Now then, if you will indeed obey My voice and keep My covenant,
then you shall be My own possession among all the peoples,
for all the earth is Mine; and you shall be to Me a kingdom of priests and a holy nation."

Exodus 19:4–6

142 *Exodus 3:12 – "And He said… 'when you have brought the people out of Egypt, you shall worship God at this mountain.'"*

After receiving these words, Moses returned to the camp, assembled the elders, and conveyed the Lord's words to the people. They enthusiastically replied, "All that the Lord has spoken we will do!" Can we infer that Moses came down from the mountain on the same day that he went up? I believe it's a reasonable assumption, even if he was more than 80 years old![143]

Sivan 3

Moses returned to the Lord on Mount Sinai and conveyed the people's acceptance of His words.[144] As Moses listened to the Lord with reverence and awe, the Lord explained how He would esteem him in the sight of all the people so they would believe in Moses forever—He would come to Moses in a thick cloud and speak with him so the people would hear God's voice. No one would be able to say that Moses was fabricating this deity with smoke, clouds, and pyrotechnics as a ruse to make the people follow him. No, the Lord was going to confirm him as His servant and friend[145] in the sight and hearing of the multitudes of Israel.

God told Moses to "go to the people and consecrate them **today** and **tomorrow**, and let them wash their garments; and let them be ready for the third day, for on the **third day** the Lord will come down on Mount Sinai in the sight of all the people."[146] Furthermore, they were to set bounds around the mountain to keep the people from trespassing on the holy site, for whoever went up the mountain or touched even its border would be put to death. When the ram's horn sounded a long blast, the people were to come to the edge of the mountain to meet their God.

Let's pause for a moment to check the dates. We speculated that Moses conveyed these instructions to the people on the same day that he came down from the mountain, but it is certainly possible that he met with the people on the day after he descended the mount and conveyed the words of the Lord in the morning. In other words, after returning to camp in the evening of his Sivan 2 meeting, he may have met with the people on Sivan 3 and delivered the news to them before he made the journey up the mountain to be with the Lord.

---

143 *Exodus 7:7*

144 *Exodus 19:8b*

145 *Exodus 33:11 "Thus the Lord used to speak to Moses face to face, just as a man speaks to his friend."*

146 *Exodus 19:11 – Emphasis added*

Sivan 4, 5, and 6

Thus, when Moses returned to the camp late in the day of Sivan 3, he may have waited until the next day, Sivan 4, to tell the people to consecrate themselves, "today and tomorrow... and let them be ready for the third day." These dates would be:

Sivan 4 (today),

Sivan 5 (tomorrow), and

the Lord would come down on Mount Sinai in the sight of all the people on

Sivan 6 (the third day).

Indeed, if the Lord descended on Mount Sinai and gave His Law on Sivan 6, then the date corresponds perfectly with the day of Pentecost, exactly fifty days after First Fruits. Am I trying to force an interpretation where it's not appropriate? I don't think so; it is a perfectly legitimate means of reckoning the dates. The Jewish rabbis who authored the Talmud reckon the timing in a similar way and arrive at Sivan 6 as the date of the giving of the Ten Commandments—the decalogue. The Talmud states, "The rabbis taught: The decalogue was given to Israel on the sixth day of the (third) month..."[147] So, there is widespread agreement that the day of Pentecost commemorates the Lord meeting the nation of Israel, giving His law, and making them His people.[148]

We can be reasonably confident that there were exactly fifty days from the day that Israel arose from the sea until the Law was given at Mount Sinai. Thus, the timing of the Feast of Weeks was probably established by the Lord to coincide with the giving of the law—an epic event that is certainly worthy of being marked by an Appointed Time.

The Feast of Weeks, which is also known as Pentecost, commemorates the date on which the Lord gave His law to Moses.

Once again, the timing of the Appointed Times synchronizes perfectly with a key historical event of the Bible. These are the events and dates that God declared to be significant when He declared that these are "My appointed times."[149] They are not the invention of Moses

147 *(Rodkinson, The Babylonian Talmud 1903) – Volume 1, TRACTATE SABBATH, CHAPTER IX, p. 159*

148 *Exodus 19:5–6 – "...you shall be My own possession among all the peoples... and you shall be to Me a kingdom of priests and a holy nation."*

149 *Leviticus 23:2*

or any man, sect, or religion—they are the Lord's shadows of things that are to come, and their substance belongs to the Messiah.

Is Pentecost Always on Sivan 6?

The Jewish Oral Law states that the Torah—the Law—was given on Sivan 6. But the Jewish sages who compiled the Talmud concede that Pentecost could fall on other dates as well if either the months of Abib or Iyar had only 29 days[150] during a particular year. That means that Pentecost, which is 50 days after the day of First Fruits, could be on Sivan 6, 7, or 8 on any given year, depending on the lengths of the preceding months.

But recall that the Pharisees incorrectly chose to determine the date for First Fruits as the day after the first high Sabbath of Unleavened Bread, which, by their reckoning, is always on Abib 16. The Sadducees, on the other hand, correctly calculated First Fruits as the day after the weekly Sabbath that occurs during Unleavened Bread. Thus, by the Sadducees' reckoning, it is possible that the Feast of Weeks could occur anywhere between Sivan 4 and 11. Furthermore, if we include two additional days in case Abib and Iyar were 29-day months, then the Feast of Weeks could occur anywhere between Sivan 4 and 13. But we must keep in mind that it **is not the *calendar date* that is important**. Instead, the Feast of Weeks, per the Law of Moses, is determined by counting fifty days from the day of First Fruits.

In the Shadow of the Feast of Weeks

At this point, it should be clear that the timing of the giving of the Law falls directly within the shadow of the Feast of Weeks. Indeed, this Appointed Time commemorates the monumental event when the Lord met Israel at Mount Sinai and gave His law, which included the Ten Commandments. The following excerpts from Exodus help us visualize the emotion and energy of the event.

"So it came about on the third day, when it was morning, that there were thunder and lightning flashes and a thick cloud upon the mountain and a very loud trumpet sound, so that all the people who were in the camp trembled. And Moses brought the people out of the camp to meet God, and they stood at the foot of the mountain. Now Mount Sinai was all in smoke because the Lord descended upon it in fire; and its smoke ascended like the smoke of a furnace, and the whole

150 Refer to the Tracking Time in Israel compendium for more information about months.

mountain quaked violently. When the sound of the trumpet grew louder and louder, Moses spoke and God answered him with thunder. The Lord came down on Mount Sinai, to the top of the mountain; and the Lord called Moses to the top of the mountain, and Moses went up."

Exodus 19:16–20

"All the people perceived the thunder and the lightning flashes and the sound of the trumpet and the mountain smoking; and when the people saw it, they trembled and stood at a distance. Then they said to Moses, 'Speak to us yourself and we will listen; but let not God speak to us, or we will die.' Moses said to the people, 'Do not be afraid; for God has come in order to test you, and in order that the fear of Him may remain with you, so that you may not sin.'

So the people stood at a distance, while Moses approached the thick cloud where God was. Then the Lord said to Moses, 'Thus you shall say to the sons of Israel,
"You yourselves have seen that I have spoken to you from heaven."'"

Exodus 20:18–22 (Emphasis added)

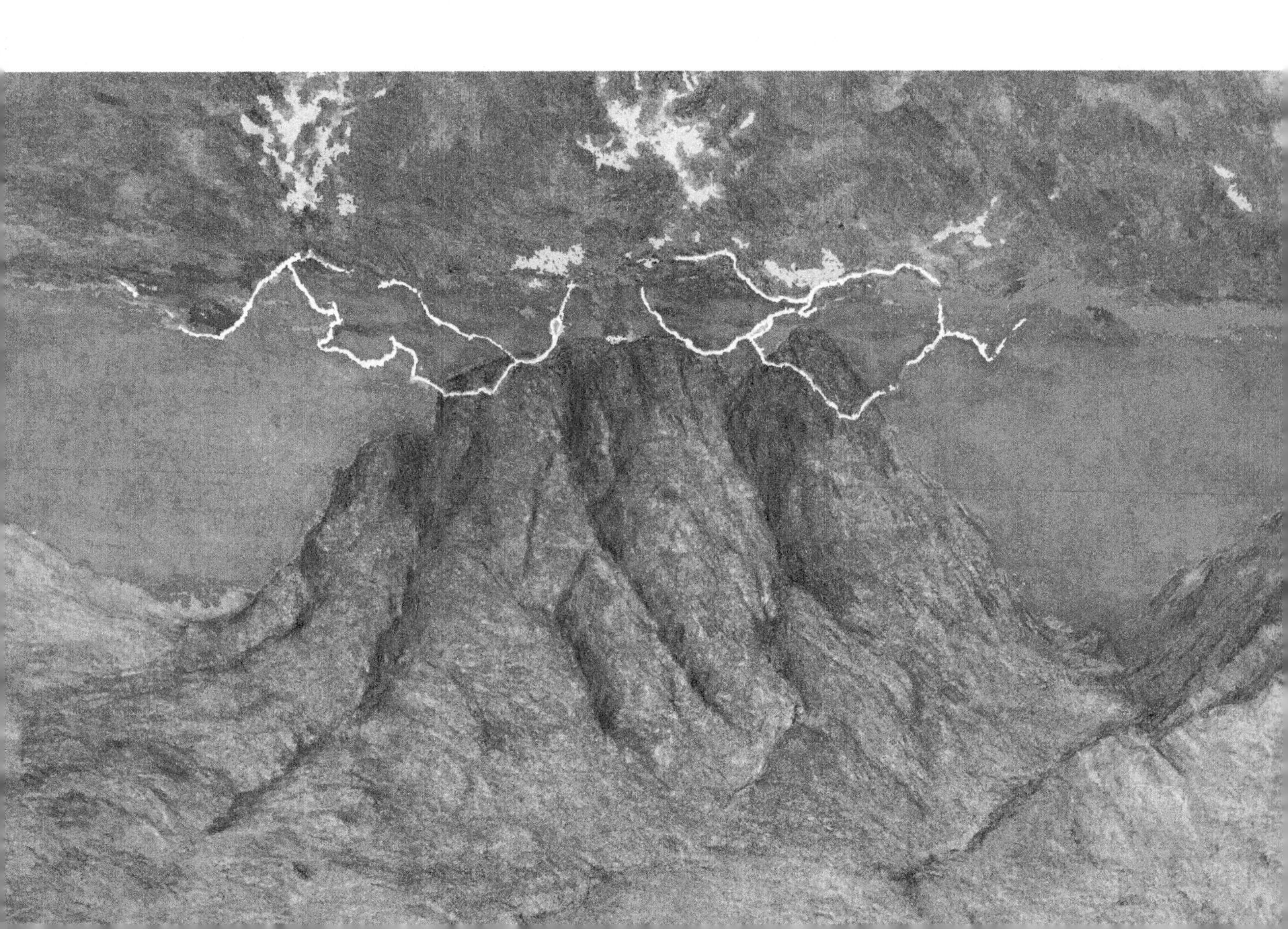

What Actually Happened at Mount Sinai?

At Mount Sinai, the Lord spoke to the Israelites from heaven—an event that is unparalleled in the history of the world. He reached down to man and made it abundantly clear that an enormous chasm exists between Himself and humankind. A great divide separated wretched, sinful man from the fearsome, holy God. It was a chasm that could not be crossed or bridged by man. The very idea of meeting the Lord was terrifying to humanity and absolutely forbidden by God.[151] How could such a divide ever be bridged?

Hundreds of years later, the Spirit spoke through Jeremiah the prophet, alluding to the peril of approaching the Lord. But within the same passage, God declared that a leader would come from Israel, and He would bring this man near to approach Him. The result would be a mending of the relationship between man and his God.

"Their leader shall be one of them,
And their ruler shall come forth from their midst;
And I will bring him near and he shall approach Me;
For who would dare to risk his life to approach Me?' declares the Lord.
You shall be My people, And I will be your God."

Jeremiah 30:21–22 (Emphasis added)

There is only one person who would dare to approach the Lord—only one person who could survive approaching Him. That is the pure and spotless Lamb of God—the Messiah of God. Indeed, the revelation at Mount Sinai presented a fearful dilemma, since the commandments of God raised the bar far above man's ability to comply. The problem was made known beyond a shadow of doubt, but the Lord had a plan for a remedy that was mysteriously intimated through the shadows of the Appointed Times—shadows of His Messiah.

The Time Signature of the Messiah

Now that we have the full time signature of the spring Appointed Times, we have updated our timeline in Figure 8 to include the Feast of Weeks. Part 3 of this book demonstrates how the key events of Jesus' ministry were perfectly synchronized with this timing. This is the time signature of the true Messiah—the signature of Jesus.

151 *Exodus 19:12 – You shall set bounds for the people all around, saying, 'Beware that you do not go up on the mountain or touch the border of it; whoever touches the mountain shall surely be put to death.'*

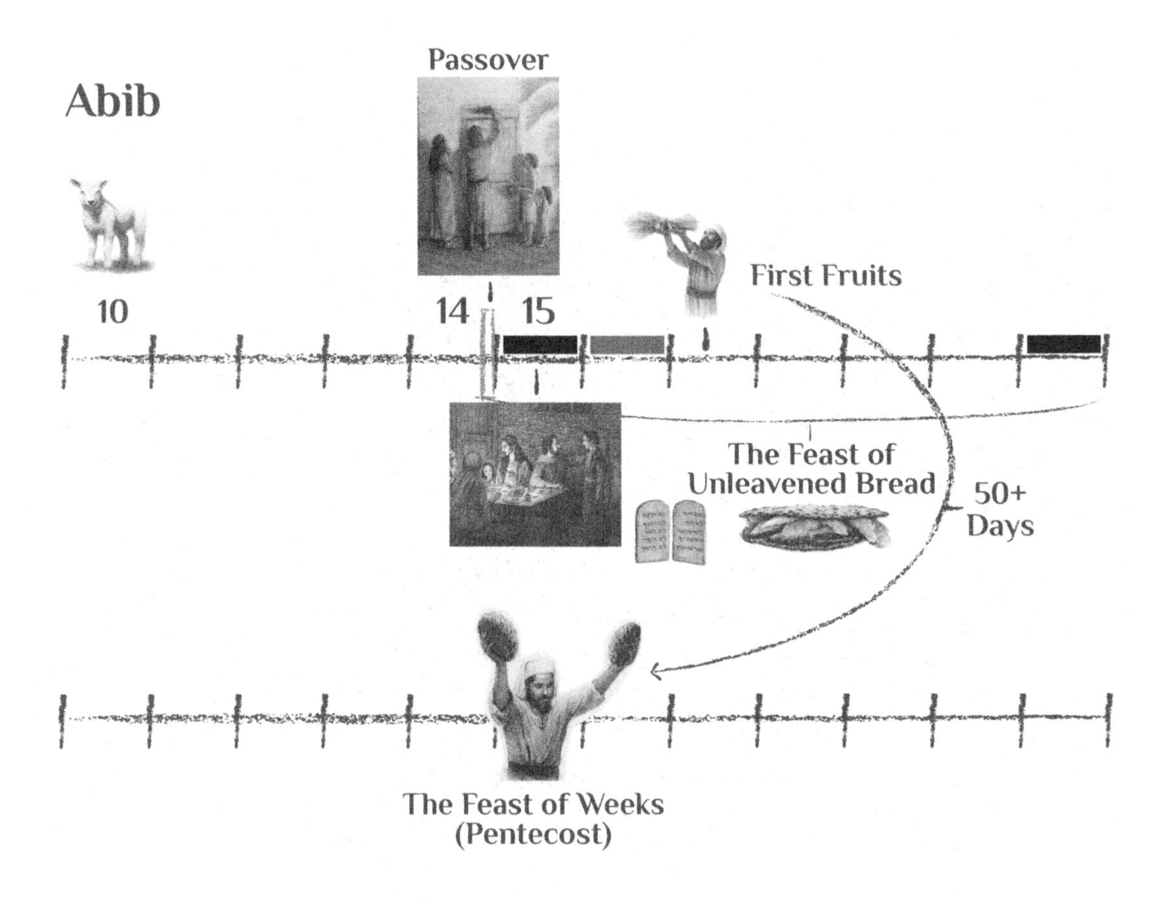

Figure 8 – The Time Signature of the Messiah

Please take some time to familiarize yourself with the diagram in Figure 8. I believe you will become convinced that the timing of the Appointed Times forms a time signature of the Messiah—the signature that Jesus precisely fulfilled almost 1,500 years later.

I look forward to introducing you to the Messiah's fulfillment in the following chapters.

Part 3 – The Messiah in the Spring Appointed Times

During the first century AD, there was a fervor among the people of Israel as they were watching for the appearing of the Messiah and the Kingdom of God. For example:

» Andrew told his brother Peter, "We have found the Messiah."[152]

» Philip found Nathanael and said to him, "We have found Him of whom Moses in the Law and also the Prophets wrote."[153]

» Nicodemus came to Jesus at night and told Him, "Rabbi, we know that You have come from God..."[154]

» The Samaritan woman who Jesus met at the well, told her friends to "come, see a man who told me all the things that I have done; this is not the Christ, is it?"[155]

» Joseph of Arimathea became a secret follower of Jesus, as he was waiting for the Kingdom of God.[156]

These are just a few of many who came to understand that Jesus was truly the Christ, which prompts us to ask, "How did they recognize that He was the Messiah?" The most obvious indications were, no doubt, His many healing miracles—undeniable confirmations to those who were healed and to those around them. Entire cities and regions beheld the blind seeing, the lame walking, lepers cleansed, the deaf hearing, the dead raised, and the poor having the gospel preached to them[157]—messianic fulfillments of prophecy that were awe inspiring and undeniable.

But in a more subtle way, events would unfold in Jesus' ministry that had not only been prophesied but were perfectly synchronized with the Appointed Times—events that were choreographed in ages past, revealing the time signature of the Messiah.

---

152 John 1:41

153 John 1:45

154 John 3:2

155 John 4:29

156 Mark 15:43, John 19:38

157 Luke 7:22 – "And He answered and said to them, "Go and report to John what you have seen and heard: the blind receive sight, the lame walk, the lepers are cleansed, and the deaf hear, the dead are raised up, the poor have the gospel preached to them.

Do you remember the words of Jesus, near the close of Luke's gospel?

> *"These are My words which I spoke to you while I was still with you,*
> *that all things which are written about Me in*
> *the* ***Law of Moses and the Prophets and the Psalms*** *must be fulfilled."*
>
> *Luke 24:44 (Emphasis added)*

Do you think Jesus explained the Appointed Times as He talked with the disciples? I have no doubt about it, especially since Paul told us that their substance is the Messiah.[158] So, let's explore the gospels to see how the events of Jesus' life were perfectly synchronized with the timing of the Appointed Times.

158 *Colossians 2:16–17*

Chapter 9: Abib 10 – Corral the Lamb

In what way was Abib 10 a *shadow* of the Messiah? The gospels tell us that Jesus entered Jerusalem several days before His crucifixion in an event known as the Triumphal Entry, on a day which became known as Palm Sunday. We will demonstrate from the Scriptures that this date was Abib 10 when Jesus submitted Himself to be tested for His worthiness as the Lamb of God. It was the same day that the Passover lamb was corralled for inspection.[159]

Recall that the purpose of this five-day isolation was to inspect the lamb for its purity, to make sure it was an acceptable sacrifice for Passover. In the case of the Messiah, Jesus presented himself to the people of Israel and to the Jewish leadership to be tested regarding His righteousness and His perfect adherence to God's Word. In a very real sense, He was demonstrating His own purity as the of the Lamb of God, without spot or blemish.

The Triumphal Entry is a key messianic event that is recorded in all four gospels.[160] Some have suggested that Jesus was presenting Himself to the nation as their king and He would have immediately set up His kingdom if the people and the religious leaders had accepted Him. Indeed, He was the king of the Jews, but in the Triumphal Entry, He was not offering Himself as their king, but as their Passover Lamb, for the purpose of laying down His life so they could have eternal life.

---

159 Exodus 12:3 – "...On the tenth of this month they are each one to take a lamb for themselves, according to their fathers' households, a lamb for each household."

160 The Triumphal Entry is recorded in Matthew 21, Mark 11, Luke 19, and John 12

The Two Events of Passover

Recall from Chapter 5 that Passover has two key events associated with it. The first is on Abib 10, when the Passover lamb was selected and isolated until the second event, which is the 14th day of the same month. Even though Abib 10 is not mentioned in Leviticus 23, Moses' instructions in Exodus 12:3 make it an inseparable component of Passover when he said,

> *"...**On the tenth of this month** they are each one to take a lamb for themselves, according to their fathers' households, a lamb for each household. ... You shall **keep it until the fourteenth day of the same month,** then the whole assembly of the congregation of Israel is to kill it at twilight."*
>
> *Exodus 12:3 & 6 (Emphasis added)*

We will, therefore, place the image of the Triumphal Entry on our timeline, in place of the image of the corralled lamb in Figure 9.

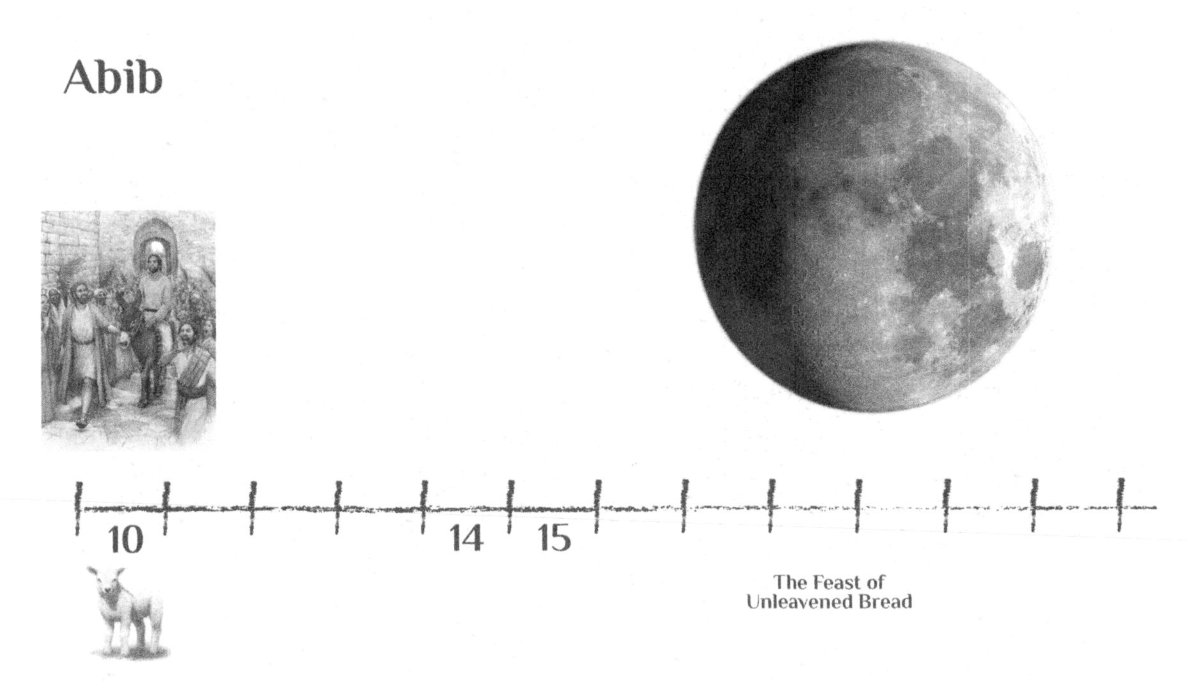

Figure 9

The Triumphal Entry – Abib 10

Is there evidence in the gospels that the Triumphal Entry occurred on Abib 10? John the apostle provided some valuable information about Jesus' journey to Jerusalem from which we can determine the date. In John 11:55, we are told that the Passover of the Jews was near, and many went up to Jerusalem." A few verses later, he says:

*"Jesus, therefore, **six days before the Passover,***
***came to Bethany** where Lazarus was, whom Jesus had raised from the dead.*
So they made Him a supper there, and Martha was serving..."

John 12:1–2 (Emphasis added)

Since you are now familiar with the spring Appointed Times, you are probably thinking that ***six days before the Passover*** would be Abib 8, since the date of the Lord's Passover is always Abib 14, and I would congratulate you for your grasp of the subject! Remember the Lord's words in Leviticus 23:

"In the first month,
*on **the fourteenth day of the month at twilight is the Lord's Passover."***

Leviticus 23:5 (Emphasis added)

The synoptic gospels (i.e., Matthew, Mark, and Luke) indicate that Jesus was traveling to Jerusalem from Jericho, but John adds the additional detail that they came through Bethany to be with Martha, Mary, and Lazarus. Bethany was Jesus' final stop before entering Jerusalem in His Triumphal Entry.

On which day of the week did Passover fall? Recall from Chapter 6 in the section entitled The Amazing Journey, the Israelites departed from the city of Rameses on a Friday night, Abib 15, which means that **Passover would have been on the preceding Thursday** afternoon during the year of the exodus. So, for our purpose of comparison, **we will also place Passover, Abib 14, on the Thursday during the week of Jesus' crucifixion**.

To help visualize the timing, we have placed the dates on a calendar in Figure 10. When we count six days prior to the 14th, we find that **Jesus came to Bethany on Friday, Abib 8**.

							Weekly Sabbath
Abib	3	4	5	6	7	(8)	9
	(10)	11	12	13	(14)	15	16
	17	18	19	20	21	22	23
	24	25	26	27	28	29	30
Iyar	1	2	3	4	5	6	7
	8	9	10	11	12	13	14
	15	16	17	18	19	20	21
	22	23	24	25	26	27	28
	29	30					
Sivan			1	2	3	4	5
	6						

Figure 10

It is important to be aware that the terms Passover and the Feast of Unleavened Bread are sometimes used interchangeably in the Bible, which can sometimes cause confusion. It is possible that John 12:1 is referring to the first day of the Feast of Unleavened Bread, which is Abib 15. But if that were the case, then six days prior to the 15th would have fallen on Abib 9, which was a Sabbath Day (refer to Figure 10), meaning that Jesus' journey would have been on a Sabbath day and would have exceeded the distance of a Sabbath Day's journey on His trek to

Bethany.[161] I therefore believe the best interpretation is that John was referring to Abib 14 as the Passover and **Jesus' journey to Bethany took place on Friday, Abib 8.**

If indeed Jesus arrived in Bethany on a Friday, then the next day would have been a Sabbath day, and we can conclude that

» He would not have journeyed to Jerusalem on the next day, Abib 9—the Sabbath Day—since the distance from Bethany to Jerusalem is about two miles[162] (3.2km), which is farther than a Sabbath day's journey;[163]

» He would not have ridden on an animal (i.e., a colt or donkey) on a Sabbath day,[164] since it was also forbidden on the Sabbath by the Law of Moses.

For the above reasons, the Triumphal Entry would certainly not have occurred on Abib 9, since it was a Sabbath day. Furthermore, the people would not have cut palm branches, since it was considered to be work, and all work was forbidden on the Sabbath day.

John 12:12, however, places the Triumphal Entry on the next day, which is most likely referring to the next weekday or the next non-Sabbath day, from a colloquial perspective. This means that **the Triumphal Entry would have occurred on Abib 10, a Sunday,** the first day of the week. In Christian circles, the day is commonly known as Palm Sunday because the crowds welcomed Jesus by waving palm branches and making a pathway for Him by laying their coats on the ground.

On Abib 10,
Jesus, the Lamb of God, was publicly set apart
for everyone to test and observe His purity,
the same day that the Passover lamb was set apart
to be observed for its purity.

---

161 Refer to the Tracking Time in Israel compendium to learn more about a Sabbath day's journey.

162 John 11:18 – "Now Bethany was near Jerusalem, about two miles off."

163 A Sabbath Day's journey is about .6 miles or .9km. Refer to the Tracking Time in Israel compendium to learn more about a Sabbath day's journey.

164 Deuteronomy 5:12–14

As Jesus approached Jerusalem on Abib 10, the size of the crowds swelled as they welcomed Him, hailing Him as their king and shouting messianic psalms, as "the one who comes in the name of the Lord."[165] He rode on a young donkey, traveling down the descent of the Mount of Olives. People removed their coats and spread them on the road in front of Him,[166] waving palm branches and shouting,

"Blessed is the King who comes in the name of the Lord;
Peace in heaven and glory in the highest!"

Luke 19:38

Their praises of joy came directly from Psalm 118, a psalm about the Messiah. It is interesting that the next verse of the psalm says,

"The Lord is God, and He has given us light;
Bind the festival sacrifice with cords to the horns of the altar."

Psalm 118:27 (Emphasis added)

165 *Psalm 118:26*
166 *Luke 19:36*

Indeed, the festival sacrifice was being brought to the people because of the Lord's everlasting lovingkindness. The disciples did not understand that prophesies were being fulfilled in these acts,[167] but Jesus' entry into Jerusalem fulfilled prophesies from the Psalms and Zechariah, and, in a more subtle way, it was the substance of the Appointed Times.

Inspecting the Lamb

Recall that the purpose of corralling the Passover lamb was to observe it to make sure that it was truly unblemished per the requirements of the Law of Moses. How would the idea of being blemished apply to the Messiah, the Lamb of God? The gospels demonstrate that the Lamb of God zealously loved and honored the Lord, His God, and that He was pure and uncompromising in teaching the truths of God. Furthermore, they clearly show that Jesus was completely pure and sinless, uncontaminated by the sinful nature of man. Let's see what we can learn from the events that confirm Jesus' purity in His final week in Jerusalem.

Zeal for Your House Will Consume Me

After entering the city of Jerusalem, the city of God, the home of the temple of God, the zeal of the Lord of Hosts consumed Jesus. He entered the temple and surveyed the worldly corruption that had infested the house of prayer. In jealous rage and love for His Father, He overturned the tables of the money changers and the sellers, driving them out with a scourge; His zeal and purpose were pure as He purged the temple of this calloused sacrilege.

The chief priests and elders demanded to know the source of Jesus' authority for His actions, miracles, teaching, and acceptance of messianic praise.[168] But He instead exposed their hypocrisy since they rejected the truth of John's teaching, asking if it was from heaven or from men.[169]

167 *John 12:16 – "These things His disciples did not understand at the first..."*

168 *Luke 19:39–40 – "Some of the Pharisees in the crowd said to Him, 'Teacher, rebuke Your disciples.' But Jesus answered, 'I tell you, if these become silent, the stones will cry out!'"*

169 *Matthew 21:23–27, Mark 11:27–33, Luke 20:1–8*

Test #1 – The Pharisees and Herodians Test the Lamb

The religious leaders continued their offensive against Jesus, trying to trap Him in a statement that would make Him guilty before Pilate under Roman Law.[170] The Pharisees plotted together with the Herodians[171] and sent their disciples to Jesus, pretending to be sincere inquirers. Take a look at their interaction below:

"Teacher, we know that You are truthful and teach the way of God in truth, and defer to no one; for You are not partial to any. Tell us then, what do You think? Is it lawful to give a poll-tax to Caesar, or not?"

But Jesus perceived their malice, and said, "Why are you testing Me, you hypocrites? Show Me the coin used for the poll-tax."

And they brought Him a denarius. And He said to them,
"Whose likeness and inscription is this?"

They said to Him, "Caesar's." Then He said to them, "Then render to Caesar the things that are Caesar's; and to God the things that are God's."

And hearing this, they were amazed, and leaving Him, they went away.

Matthew 22:16–22 (Emphasis added)

Test #2 – The Sadducees Test the Lamb

Perhaps the Sadducees would be able to find some blemishes or inconsistencies in the teachings of this Lamb. On that same day, the Sadducees, who say there is no resurrection,[172] asked Jesus to settle a little dispute for them. It was their classic One Bride for Seven Brothers

170 *Luke 20:20 – "So they watched Him, and sent spies who pretended to be righteous, in order that they might catch Him in some statement, so that they could deliver Him to the rule and the authority of the governor."*

171 *The Herodians were a small party of Hellenistic Jews who also hoped for the restoration of Israel but sought it through political means through King Herod.*

172 *Matthew 22:23–33, Mark 12:18–27, Luke 20:27–38*

story, and through it they hoped to demonstrate that the teachings of the resurrection were illogical and even absurd.

The Sadducees began by explaining that the Law taught that if a man died, having no children, then his closest of kin—i.e., his brother—would take the man's widow as his own wife so she could bear children in her deceased husband's name.[173] So, they related the story of a woman and seven brothers who were affected by this law. The first brother took a wife, but he died childless. The second brother took her for his wife with the hope of having a child by his sister-in-law, who would carry on the eldest brother's name, but the second brother died childless, as well. The Sadducees went on to say that the same happened with the third brother, all the way through the youngest, leaving no children, and finally the woman died. Probably with a smirk on their faces and checkmate on their minds, they asked,

"whose wife will she be in the resurrection since she was the wife of all of them?"

Their smirks and smiles quickly turned into frustration and frowns, as Jesus confidently responded,

"Is this not the reason you are mistaken,
that you do not understand the Scriptures or the power of God?
For when they rise from the dead,
they neither marry nor are given in marriage,
but are like angels in heaven."

Mark 12:24–25

He continued.

"But regarding the fact that the dead rise again,
have you not read in the book of Moses,
in the passage about the burning bush,
how God spoke to him, saying,
'I am the God of Abraham,
and the God of Isaac,
and the God of Jacob'?"

Mark 12:26

173 *Deuteronomy 25:5–10*

Truly, Moses did speak of the resurrection of the dead. When the voice in the burning bush said, "I am the God of your father, the God of Abraham, the God of Isaac, and the God of Jacob,"[174] the implication was that **Abraham, Isaac, and Jacob *are alive* and I AM their God**.

When the crowds heard this, they were astonished at His teaching.[175] Some of the scribes conceded that He was right and said, "Teacher, You have spoken well." For they did not have courage to question Him any longer about anything.[176]

Test #3 – The Pharisees Try Again...

But when the Pharisees heard that Jesus had silenced the Sadducees, they huddled themselves together again. A lawyer among the Pharisees tested Jesus with a question:

"Teacher, which is the great commandment in the Law?"

Jesus passionately quoted from the Law of Moses,

"'You shall love the Lord your God
with all your heart, and with all your soul, and with all your mind.'
This is the great and foremost commandment."

But He did not stop with the greatest commandment,

"The second is like it, 'You shall love your neighbor as yourself.'
On these two commandments depend the whole Law and the Prophets."

Matthew 22:36–40

Mark tells us that the scribe who posed the question thoughtfully replied, "Right, Teacher; You have truly stated that He is One, and there is no one else besides Him; and to love Him with all the heart and with all the understanding and with all the strength, and to love one's neighbor as himself, is much more than all burnt offerings and sacrifices."[177]

---

174 *Exodus 3:6*
175 *Matthew 22:33*
176 *Luke 20:39–40*
177 *Mark 12:28–33*

Seeing that the scribe had responded intelligently, Jesus responded with grace and compassion. Rather than posturing Himself as the victor in what seemed to be a small intellectual contest, He responded with beautiful candor, telling the scribe, "You are not far from the kingdom of God."[178]

You see, these interrogations were not mere academic contests—they were much more than that. They were decisive tests, the final examinations of the purity of the Lamb, and battles for the hearts, minds, and souls of those He came to save.

Testing the Pharisees

Jesus easily passed all of the examinations and, as His interrogators were gathered together, He posed a question to them:

"What do you think about the Christ, whose son is He?"
They replied, "The son of David."
Jesus responded, "Then how does David in the Spirit call Him 'Lord,' saying,
'The Lord said to my Lord,
"Sit at My right hand,
Until I put Your enemies beneath Your feet"'?

If David then calls Him 'Lord,' how is He his son?"

Matthew 22:41–45[179]
(Emphasis added)

What was the point of this little inquiry? Once again, it was not simple academic bantering in order to gain converts from the crowd. No, this question had profound implications about the authority and pedigree of the Messiah.

178 *Mark 12:34*

179 *A similar dialogue is recorded in Mark 12:35 and Luke 20:41*

"If David calls Him 'Lord,' how is He his son?"

Jesus was quoting Psalm 110, verse 1. I recommend that you read the entire Psalm since it is about the Messiah. When David said, "The Lord says to my Lord," he was actually saying, "When God said to my Lord." "My Lord," in this passage, is a reference to the Messiah. Thus, when David referred to this special person as "my Lord," he was revealing that the Messiah, his son, was far greater than himself—a son who is greater than his father. Honoring father and mother was a fundamental precept within Judaism, so it was incomprehensible for the experts in the Law to accept that a father would venerate his son by calling him "Lord."

What was Jesus' point when He posed this question to the Pharisees? He was making it very clear that King David honored the Messiah as one greater than himself and that the one who was now addressing the Pharisees is the same Lord and Messiah that David revered in Psalm 110. He is fully worthy of their honor, as well—the Son of Man, the Son of God, the Christ—the Messiah.

The Result of Testing Jesus

What was the result of these inspections of the Lamb?

"No one was able to answer Him a word,
nor did anyone dare from that day on to ask Him another question."

Matthew 22:46
(Emphasis added)

At this point, the Passover Lamb had been tried and tested and found to be pure. We would be missing the point, however, if we believed the inspection was merely a test of Jesus' doctrinal views. Instead, His responses attest to His being in the truth, and, even more so, they substantiate that He is the truth.[180] Truth is paramount with Jesus. He later told Pilate, "For this I have been born, and for this I have come into the world, to testify to the truth."[181] Jesus made no compromises. Truth is absolute, since it emanates from God the Father, and Jesus was found to be spotless and without blemish in the truth.

Unblemished and Spotless

I must mention another fundamental aspect of our Passover Lamb: Jesus was completely pure and perfectly sinless.

"...you were not redeemed with perishable things like silver or gold...
but with precious blood,
as of a lamb unblemished and spotless, the blood of Christ."

1 Peter 1:18–19

About six months before the Triumphal Entry, the crowds whom Jesus was teaching became highly antagonistic. At one point, during a heated exchange with those who did not believe, He boldly faced them and asked, "Which one of you convicts Me of sin?"[182] But no one stepped forward with an accusation. That is truly amazing—do you know anyone who could

180 John 14:6 – "I am the way, and the truth, and the life; no one comes to the Father but through Me."
181 John 18:37
182 John 8:46

stand in front of a crowd of antagonists and not be charged with an accusation? It might be easy for a beloved preacher or leader to stand before their own people and ask such a question, but who would dare ask enemies if they convict him of sin? *Unless, of course, the person was truly sinless and above reproach.*

When Jesus stood before the high priest and the Council in His first trial, "the chief priests and the whole Council kept trying to obtain false testimony against Him, so they would have grounds to put Him to death, They did not find any, even though many false witnesses came forward."[183] Clearly, the hearts of His enemies were intent on bringing about His death regardless of His innocence, even if they had to resort to fabricating a charge.

This Lamb, Jesus the Messiah, was tested by the experts, and no fault was found in Him regarding sin or untruths. His righteousness soared far above theirs, and His understanding sounded the depths of their wisest teachers and sages.

Without a doubt, the source of purity of the Messiah came from the lineage of His Father, who is none other than God the Father. From earthly appearances, Jesus was the son of Joseph the carpenter. But the Scriptures emphasize that Jesus' origin was supernatural. The angel Gabriel informed a virgin named Mary that she had been chosen to bear the Son of God by the power of the Holy Spirit. The angel "said to her, 'The Holy Spirit will come upon you, and the power of the Most High will overshadow you; and for that reason the holy Child shall be called the Son of God.'"[184]

The virgin birth is of the greatest importance as we consider the Messiah. Certainly, the fact that Jesus is the Son of God is a magnificent truth that answers and creates a myriad of questions. And as we consider the purity of this Lamb, it becomes clear that the sinful nature of man was not passed to Him since He did not have a human father. It was because He was completely pure, spotless, and innocent that He was able to stand before God the Father and make eternal redemption with His own blood.[185]

On Abib 10, Jesus, the Passover Lamb, entered Jerusalem for public inspection. During that week, He was found to be completely pure in truth and righteousness, fully worthy to be the Lamb of God, the ultimate sacrifice to God.

---

183 *Matthew 26:59–60*

184 *Luke 1:35*

185 *Hebrews 9:12*

Chapter 10: Abib 14 – The Lord's Passover

Caution – Interpretation Challenges Ahead

Dear reader, as we begin this section about the Lord's Passover, I want to make you aware that the gospel accounts about the crucifixion appear to be somewhat different when viewed at a surface level. Specifically, the synoptic gospels,[186] Matthew, Mark, and Luke, seem to present a different chronological message than that of the gospel of John. One of my goals for this book, however, is to highlight the points that lead to confusion and explain how all four gospel accounts are in full harmony with each other and demonstrate that the differences are merely superficial.

It is important that you are aware that apparent differences do exist that can easily lead to confusion. I have seen that teaching only one perspective, without acknowledging possible contradictions, can cause students to lose heart for a subject or to reject it altogether. There would be nothing to gain if I were to present a one-sided message and you later encountered the apparent differences in Matthew, Mark, and Luke but did not understand how they can be reconciled with John's gospel. My intention is to inform you of the different perspectives and help you understand them fully. In doing so, I believe you will sense the harmony between all four gospels and gain a great appreciation for Jesus' fulfillment of the Appointed Times.

186 Synoptic gospels refer to the three gospels, Matthew, Mark, and Luke, which look alike or are similar in their message, while the gospel of John conveys the good news (i.e., gospel) of Christ from a different perspective. The gospels tend to be grouped as the synoptic gospels versus John's gospel. Despite their different perspectives, a careful study of all four gospels will show that they complement and harmonize with each other, rather than contradict.

We will begin by exploring the account of the crucifixion from John's gospel since it presents the clearest harmony between the Appointed Times and the work of the Christ. After we have presented John's perspective, we will look into the seemingly contradictory passages in the synoptic gospels with the hope of harmonizing them beyond a reasonable doubt.

Abib 14 – Passover

Did Jesus die on the cross in the afternoon of Abib 14 or did He eat the Passover meal with His disciples in the upper room later that evening?

What happened on Abib 14? Did Jesus die on the cross on that afternoon, or did He eat the Passover meal with His disciples later that evening? This is the crux of one of the most interesting controversies related to the crucifixion of Jesus. Since Jesus is our Passover,[187] we would expect His crucifixion to have taken place in the afternoon of Abib 14, at the time the Passover lamb was killed. Indeed, all gospel accounts of the crucifixion confirm this is the case, so let's look into John's gospel to see what he recorded about the timing of the crucifixion.

*"Now **before** the Feast of the Passover,*
Jesus knowing that His hour had come
that He would depart out of this world to the Father,
having loved His own who were in the world, He loved them to the end. During supper, the devil
having already put into the heart of Judas Iscariot,
the son of Simon, to betray Him..."

John 13:1–2 (Emphasis added)

187 1 Corinthians 5:7

Figure 11

In the passage above, John sets the stage for the impassioned conversation between Jesus, His disciples, and the Father, which continues for five chapters. Notice that the timing of the last supper is before the Feast of the Passover (i.e., the Feast of Unleavened Bread). From Mark and Luke, we learn that Jesus and His disciples were together in a large, furnished upper room that had been prepared for the Passover.[188]

Why would they have supper together in a room that was prepared for the Passover if they were not eating the Passover meal? Consider this: the Law of Moses requires all the men of Israel to come to Jerusalem[189] three times per year to participate in the feasts of the Appointed Times.[190] In the days leading up to each feast, huge crowds flocked to the city in order to purify themselves and to secure lodging in or near Jerusalem. Inns and other lodging places were completely filled because of the flood of worshippers that descended on Jerusalem, a city that is relatively small by today's standards. So it was quite common for people, including Jesus and His disciples, to reserve a room for several days before and during the feast. During the three annual feasts, there was usually no room in the inn, but Jesus and His disciples had a providential reservation for their room.

188 *Mark 14:15, Luke 22:12*

189 *During the time of Moses, the location of the place of worship (i.e., the permanent location of the temple) had not been established. Thus, Moses stipulates the location via "at the place where He chooses" (Deuteronomy 14:23), which was later identified as Jerusalem.*

190 *The Feast of Unleavened Bread (i.e., Passover), The Feast of Weeks, and The Feast of Booths (i.e., The Feast of Tabernacles)*

When the disciples prepared the Passover, they were probably preparing the room, assuring that is was swept clean of leaven, arranging the table and dishes, and purchasing sundry items for the week. Recall that during the last supper, Jesus identified Judas as His betrayer and told him to do it quickly. So, Judas went out into the night, but the disciples did not know why he left. They assumed that he left the upper room for the purpose of purchasing "...the things we have need of for the feast..."[191] So, it is safe to infer from this statement that the last supper was not the Passover meal since they had not yet purchased all of the items that would have been needed.

Thus, the date and time of **the last supper was probably just after sundown of Wednesday, Abib 13**, which is actually the beginning hours of Abib 14. Once again, I must emphasize that the last supper was not the Passover meal—it was simply their evening meal on the night before the Passover. Perhaps the simplest and most compelling argument that the last supper was not the Passover meal is that it would have placed Jesus' crucifixion on the next day, Abib 15, the first day of the Feast of Unleavened Bread. As you know, that day is a high Sabbath, and the Jews would not have prosecuted Jesus and handed Him over for crucifixion on a Sabbath day. Furthermore, the Jewish leadership had determined that Jesus must be killed before the festival (i.e., feast) in order to prevent the people from rioting in response.

Arrest in the Garden

It was during their time together in the upper room that Jesus washed the disciples' feet and solemnly explained profound truths to them, many of which they did not understand. He told them that He would be leaving them, and He comforted them, telling them that His Father's house has many places for them to live and He was going to prepare a place for them and would return to take them there. But they did not understand. The air was filled with sorrow and uncertainty, and Jesus continued to comfort and pray for them. It was nighttime,[192] and after they sang a hymn together, they went out to the Mount of Olives, across the Kidron ravine, to a garden to pray.

You may know the story. Jesus took His three closest disciples, Peter, John, and James, and went a distance from the others. But the three were exhausted from sorrow, and He later found them fast asleep.[193] Soon afterward, Judas the betrayer entered the garden, accompanied

191 John 13:29

192 John 13:30 – "...and it was night."

193 Luke 22:45 "When He rose from prayer, He came to the disciples and found them sleeping from sorrow..."

by the Roman cohort (about 600 soldiers[194]), along with officers from the chief priests, and some of the Pharisees; they came with lanterns, torches, and weapons. And after Judas identified Jesus by greeting Him with a kiss, they bound Jesus and took Him away to be tried.

Further Inspection of the Lamb

It was during the nighttime hours of Abib 14 when the small army that arrested Jesus presented Him for trial, first to the father-in-law of the high priest and then to the high priest in the presence of the Sanhedrin. The purpose of the trial was to interrogate Jesus and hear testimony from anyone who would step forward with a charge against Him—anyone. The goal of the interrogators was to find a charge that would bring the sentence of death. Learning the truth was not part of their agenda, since they considered Jesus to be very dangerous for their nation. It was necessary for Him to die, regardless of His innocence, to prevent a rebellion that Rome would ruthlessly crush.[195]

During Jesus' trial in front of the Council,[196] many witnesses rose up to testify against Him, but their testimonies were so flawed and inconsistent that even the chief priests and elders had to reject them.[197] Finally, the high priest stood up and said,

"I adjure You by the living God,
that You tell us whether You are the Christ,
the Son of God."

Matthew 26:63

Jesus' response left no doubt about His claims in the minds of His accusers. He replied,

"You have said it yourself;
nevertheless I tell you, hereafter you will see
the Son of Man sitting at the right hand of Power,
and coming on the clouds of heaven."

Matthew 26:64

194 *A battalion – about 600 men - (Freedman 2000). "Cohort" p268*

195 *John 11:48–53, 18:14*

196 *The Council is actually the Sanhedrin in this context. The Greek word is συνέδριον or synedrion.*

197 *Matthew 26:59–60 and Mark 14:55–56*

Some critics have suggested that Jesus did not actually say, "Yes, I am," and therefore He did not actually claim the title of the Christ, the Son of God. But His words that followed, "...sitting at the right hand of Power, and coming on the clouds of heaven," make His point exceedingly clear, that He did indeed claim to be the Christ. Furthermore, the high priest responded by tearing his robes and saying that Jesus had blasphemed, so there was no further need of witnesses against Him.

Jesus' words gave the Council all the evidence they needed to charge Him with a capital offense under Jewish law. In their minds He had blasphemed in the presence of the court by claiming to be the Son of God, an offense that demanded the death penalty. Thus, "**When morning came...** they bound Him, and led Him away and delivered Him to Pilate the governor,"[198] who had the authority to impose the death penalty.

It is very important to note the words of John, however, when he said,

"Then they led Jesus from Caiaphas into the Praetorium, and it was early; and they themselves did not enter into the Praetorium so that they would not be defiled, ***but might eat the Passover.****"*

John 18:28 (Emphasis added)

Did you see that? The religious leadership wanted to remain ceremonially clean so they could eat the Passover meal later that evening. Recall that the Passover meal was eaten after sundown on Abib 14, and they had not yet partaken of the meal, **which confirms that Jesus' trials occurred on the morning of Passover**, which is also called the day of preparation.[199]

Why were the Jewish leaders concerned about becoming defiled by entering the Praetorium? It was because Pilate was a Gentile, a Roman, and they would have become ceremonially unclean if they had entered the residence or headquarters of a non-Jew.[200] The Law of Moses is clear that everyone who partakes of the Passover meal must be ceremonially clean. Their desire to be clean for eating the Passover is good, but it is strange that the malicious intentions of their hearts—bearing false witness, condemning the innocent, and murder—did not seem to faze the accusers. "But they have done this to fulfill the word that is written in their Law, 'They hated Me without a cause.'"[201] On the other hand, Jesus' accusers believed they were doing the will of God by killing Him for the sake of the nation.

---

198 *Matthew 27:1–2 (Emphasis added)*

199 *Refer to the Tracking Time in Israel compendium to learn more about Passover as a day of preparation.*

200 *The idea of becoming ceremonially unclean by entering the residence of a Gentile is not found in the Bible.*

201 *John 15:25*

Pilate was a reluctant magistrate who did not find any guilt in Jesus, so he repeatedly sought ways to release Him. His first attempt was to transfer Jesus' case to King Herod, since he learned that Jesus was a Galilean and therefore in Herod's jurisdiction. King Herod was in Jerusalem at that time, so it could have been an easy way out for Pilate.

Herod was glad to see Jesus since His fame had spread into his courts; he wanted Him to perform some sort of sign. He questioned Jesus at length, and when He did not answer, he and his soldiers mocked and abused Him. Herod then sent Him back to Pilate in a beautiful royal robe to mock His claim as King of the Jews.[202]

After Jesus was returned to the Praetorium, Pilate summoned the chief priests and the rulers of the people and told them that he had examined Jesus and neither he nor Herod found any guilt worthy of death. Therefore, "I will punish Him and release Him."[203] But the angry crowd erupted, demanding that he crucify Jesus. They argued back and forth until Pilate finally gave into their demands and washed his hands of their mockery of truth and justice.

Right in the middle of this dramatic dialogue, John interjects the following statement:

*"Now **it was the day of preparation for the Passover;***
*it was **about the sixth hour**.*
And he said to the Jews, 'Behold, your King!'"

John 19:14 (Emphasis added)

Now it was the day of preparation for the Passover...

"The day of preparation for the Passover"[204] looks like an incidental comment, and it can easily be overlooked. But don't miss it, because it is pivotal for understanding how the timing of Jesus' death coincided exactly with the death of the Passover lamb. Notice that John was very specific about the day. It was the day of preparation, specifically for the Passover—not the day of preparation for a weekly Sabbath day, but specifically, "it was the day of preparation for the Passover," which once again confirms the date as Abib 14. It was about the sixth hour, which is the noon hour, when Pilate handed Jesus over to the executioners.

202 *Luke 23:11 – "And Herod with his soldiers, after treating Him with contempt and mocking Him, dressed Him in a gorgeous robe and sent Him back to Pilate."*

203 *Luke 23:16 & 22*

204 *Refer to the Tracking Time in Israel compendium to learn more about the day of preparation.*

So they crucified Jesus between two other men, one on either side of Him. The cross of Jesus, however, had a sign above it which said, "Jesus the Nazarene, the King of the Jews."[205] The Roman soldiers who crucified Him cast lots (similar to rolling dice) as a way of dividing His clothing among themselves, once again fulfilling prophesies about the Messiah.[206] After suffering on the cross for several hours, Jesus cried out, "It is finished!"[207] And He bowed His head and gave up His spirit and died.

"That Sabbath Was a High Day"

In the very next verse, John includes a seemingly small detail, but it is a **golden key** for unlocking one of the mysteries of the Appointed Times. Read the following verse carefully:

205 *John 19:19*

206 *John 19:24, Psalm 22:18 – "They divide my garments among them, And for my clothing they cast lots."*

207 *John 19:30*

Chapter 10: Abib 14- The Lord's Passover

"Then the Jews, because it was the day of preparation,
so that the bodies would not remain on the cross[208] on the Sabbath
(for that Sabbath was a high day),[209]
asked Pilate that their legs might be broken,
and that they might be taken away."

John 19:31 (Emphasis added)

Once again, John tells us that it was the day of preparation, but he emphasizes that the imminent Sabbath was a *high* day—**it was a *high* Sabbath.** Recall that high Sabbaths can fall on any day of the week, rather than occurring on a specific day of the week, as do the weekly Sabbath days.

What are the implications of the next day being a *high* Sabbath? It means that the crucifixion did not necessarily happen on a Friday, since this was the preparation for a high Sabbath and not necessarily for a weekly Sabbath. **The day of preparation for the Passover can fall on any day of the week.**[210] It is likely that the crucifixion took place on the afternoon of Thursday, Abib 14, which means the first high Sabbath of the Feast of Unleavened Bread would have begun at sundown on that same day.

Just as the Passover lamb died on Abib 14
during the year of the exodus,
Jesus died on Abib 14
almost 1,500 years later.

When the gospel accounts are viewed together, they paint a vivid picture of the events that surrounded the crucifixion: darkness fell over the whole land, the dead came out of the tombs, a strong earthquake shook the region, and a Roman centurion exclaimed, "Truly, this was the Son of God!"[211] Luke describes the event as a spectacle, saying that the crowds left beating their breasts in grief and remorse.

Within this spectacle atmosphere, Jesus fulfilled the prophesies of the Appointed Times. The Roman soldiers did not break His legs, because He was already dead. Do you remember Moses' instructions about the Passover lamb? *"...you are not to... break any bone of it."*[212] John

208 *It was necessary to remove Jesus from the cross since the Law teaches that leaving a corpse on a tree all night will defile the land. Deuteronomy 21:22–23*

209 *Refer to the Tracking Time in Israel compendium to learn more about high or great Sabbath days.*

210 *If the day of preparation falls on a Sabbath day (i.e., Saturday), then the preparation tasks are completed on the preceding day (i.e., Friday) because of the laborious tasks that were required.*

211 *Matthew 27:54 and Mark 15:39*

212 *Exodus 12:46*

confirms that this was an intentional fulfillment, "For these things came to pass to fulfill the Scripture, 'Not a bone of Him shall be broken.'"[213]

Time of Death

John did not record the time of Jesus' death, but Matthew, Mark, and Luke clearly state that **He died at the ninth hour,**[214] which is around 3:00 in the afternoon.[215] Do you remember when the Israelites were told to kill the Passover lamb? It was at twilight, which is literally between the evenings, between 3:00PM and sundown. **Jesus died during the same timeframe that the Passover lamb was to die.** Once again, the timing of His death aligns perfectly with the Appointed Times.

Therefore, it is appropriate to place the crucifixion on our timeline in place of the death of the Passover lamb. In the same way that the Passover lamb's blood was displayed as a sign for God to spare the firstborn from judgment, so the blood of Jesus was displayed publicly so that God would spare from judgement all those who look to Him for salvation and eternal life.[216]

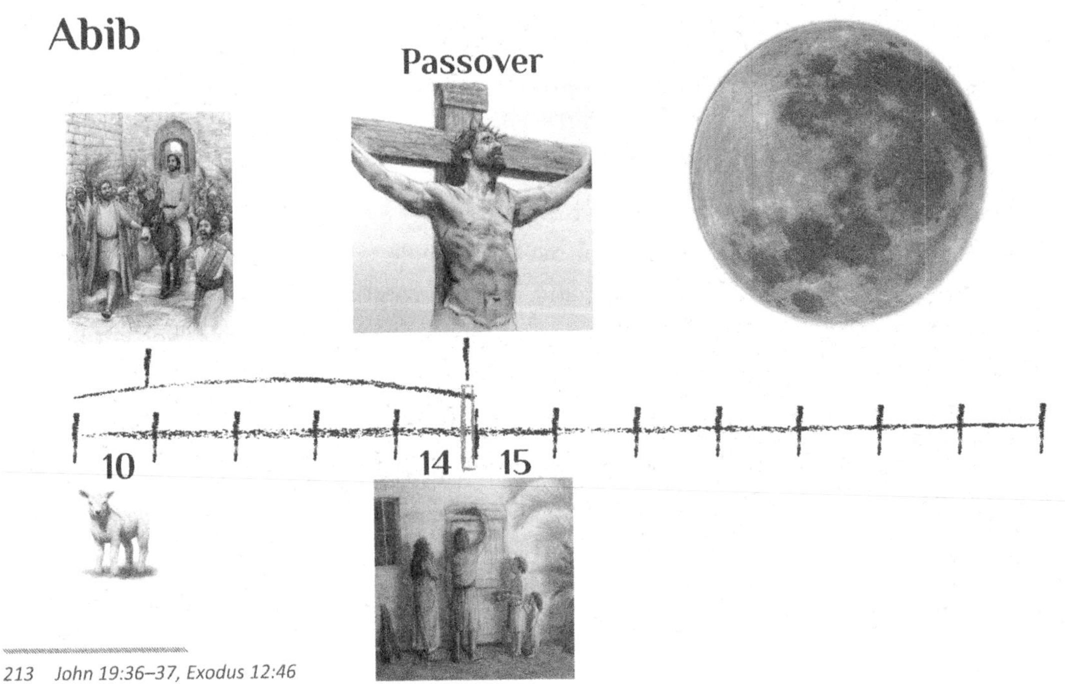

213 John 19:36–37, Exodus 12:46

214 Matthew 27:46–50, Mark 15:34–37, Luke 23:44–46

215 Refer to the Tracking Time in Israel compendium to learn how the ancient Israelites counted the hours of the day.

216 John 3:14–15 "As Moses lifted up the serpent in the wilderness, even so must the Son of Man be lifted up; so that whoever believes will in Him have eternal life."

Understanding the Synoptic Gospels

The gospel of John is quite clear about the chronology of Jesus' final days in Jerusalem, and it aligns perfectly with the Lord's Appointed Times in Leviticus 23. The synoptic gospels, on the other hand, might lead a person to conclude that Jesus ate the Passover meal with His disciples on the evening of Abib 14 and was crucified on the following day, which would have been Abib 15. But Abib 15 is the first high Sabbath of the Feast of Unleavened Bread, and the Lord made it very clear to Moses that it is to be a day of rest, which would prohibit activities such as prosecuting and executing someone.

My strong conviction is that all four gospels were inspired by the Holy Spirit and are consistent in their message. So let's take a closer look at the difficult passages of the synoptic gospels and consider how they actually harmonize with John's account, rather than conflict.

The Chronology of the Synoptic Gospels

The synoptic gospels harmonize with the gospel of John regarding the Triumphal Entry occurring on Abib 10. Although they do not give an indication of the date, we can take our cue from John that the Triumphal Entry occurred on Sunday, based on his *"six days before the Passover"* comment in John 12:1.

The events of Jesus' final week in Jerusalem are also in harmony with John's account. Matthew and Mark both confirm that the crucifixion was to take place *before* the Passover, since the chief priests and elders were determined to kill Jesus *before* the festival (i.e., the Feast of Unleavened Bread); otherwise a riot might occur.[217] So, once again, the chronology is consistent with that of John.

Matthew and Mark also provide specific timing for some events that occurred during the week, saying *two days before the Passover.*[218] Were they simply indicating that Passover was two days away, or should we understand that the events that followed in their narratives actually occurred on Tuesday, Abib 12, two days before Abib 14? Did a key event occur two days before the Passover? Let's take a closer look by examining the difficult statements in the synoptic gospels.

217 Matthew 26:2–5, Mark 14:1–2

218 Matthew 26:2, Mark 14:1. Luke 22:1 simply says "...the Passover, was approaching."

Difficult Statements

We encounter the difficulty in the chronology of Matthew, Mark, and Luke in the verses below. These verses are probably the most challenging to address when trying to harmonize their chronology with that of John, since they paint a very different picture than John's gospel when viewed at a superficial level. So, let's take a closer look at the synoptic gospel passages:

"Now ***on the first day of Unleavened Bread*** *the disciples came to Jesus and asked, 'Where do You want us to prepare for You to eat the Passover?'"*

Matthew 26:17 (Emphasis added)

"On the first day of Unleavened Bread,
when the Passover lamb was being sacrificed, *His disciples said to Him,*
'Where do You want us to go and prepare for You to eat the Passover?'"

Mark 14:12 (Emphasis added)

"Then came the first day of Unleavened Bread
on which the Passover lamb had to be sacrificed.
And Jesus sent Peter and John, saying,
'Go and prepare the Passover for us, so that we may eat it.'"

Luke 22:7–8 (Emphasis added)

Are we understanding these passages correctly? Are they actually saying that the day of the Passover, Abib 14, had already come and gone? After all, the first day of Unleavened Bread is the 15th of Abib. If the day was truly the first day of the Feast of Unleavened Bread, then the Passover lamb would have been sacrificed on the day before, which is Abib 14, so it would not make sense to discuss where they should prepare it.

It is important to note, however, that the Scriptures frequently use the terms Passover and Unleavened Bread interchangeably, which is clearly the case in the Mark and Luke passages above. Since they indicate that the Passover lamb was to be sacrificed on the first day of Unleavened Bread, they are probably referring to Abib 14 rather than the 15th. Even so, it is unlikely that they would have waited until the 14th to prepare for the Passover, since there would not have been enough time to make preparations for that same evening.

Furthermore, according to John's account, Jesus had already been tried and was on the cross on the afternoon of Abib 14, rather than giving instructions about where He and His disciples would eat the Passover, as the synoptic gospels seem to indicate. If Jesus truly met the criteria for being the Passover lamb, then He would have died during the afternoon of the 14th, as John clearly states, so how should we understand these verses in light of John's teaching?

Since you now understand the timing of Passover and the Feast of Unleavened Bread, the above passages should raise some questions in your mind. Specifically, all three synoptic passages suggest that Passover (aka. the first day of Unleavened Bread) had arrived, yet the disciples were instructed to prepare the Passover.

The original language of these passages (i.e., Greek) does not really help when trying to resolve the timing differences between John's gospel and the synoptics. It actually seems to confirm the contradictory timing, that this interaction between Jesus and His disciples was indeed on Abib 15. So, once again, it sounds like a true contradiction with John's gospel, doesn't it?

Fortunately, this *apparent* contradiction can be reconciled when it is viewed within the bigger picture of language translation methodology. Consider this: When translating from one language to another, there are multiple layers that must be considered in order to accurately convey the intended meaning of the original writer or speaker. Certainly, at the very least, we must understand the letters, words, vocabulary, grammar, syntax, and terms.

The translations for the above verses are good translations at these levels, but there is yet another aspect to consider, which involves the colloquial[219] and idiomatic usage of words and phrases. According to The Anchor Bible commentary regarding Matthew 26:17,

"It is possible to translate the Greek by
***'With reference to** the first day of Unleavened Bread…'*
—i.e., the disciples were asking Jesus for guidance about the procedures…"[220]

The author of the commentary explains that the same confusion over the dating is also found in Mark and Luke, which we see in the above verses. But, if we understand these passages in their idiomatic sense, meaning something like "*regarding* the upcoming feast, where should we prepare the Passover?" then the perceived conflict between the synoptic gospels and John simply disappears. Although these passages in the synoptic gospels appear to be definite statements regarding the date, they are actually an idiomatic way of referring to a subject (i.e., the Passover) with a related question about it.

219 *Colloquial refers to casual or informal speech.*

220 *Matthew – A New Translation with Introduction and Commentary (Albright W. F. 1971) p 319 (Emphasis added)*

Please reread the above verses (*Matthew 26:17, Mark 14:12, and Luke 22:7–8*) as if the disciples were asking for Jesus' guidance about the feast preparations, rather than as statements that the date had already arrived. For example, regarding "the first day of Unleavened Bread the disciples came to Jesus and asked, 'Where do You want us to prepare for You to eat the Passover?'"

Further Confirmation – The Day of Preparation

There are other reasons to believe that the above verses are not indicating that the day was actually the first day of Unleavened Bread, Abib 15. Recall that Passover, Abib 14, is the day of preparation for the Passover. Yet, each of the synoptic gospels contains a comment about the day of preparation in a way that precludes the above verses from being literal references to the first day of the Feast of Unleavened Bread.

Matthew 27:62

In **Matthew's** account, after Jesus was crucified, we read, "on the next day, *the day after the preparation,* the chief priests and the Pharisees gathered together with Pilate"[221] in order to request a guard to secure the grave. Their meeting with Pilate took place on the day after the preparation, which is the first day of Unleavened Bread. Thus, it is not possible that Matthew 26:17 (cited in the previous section) could have occurred on the first day of Unleavened Bread.

The phrase "the day after the preparation," is in perfect harmony with John's chronology that Jesus was on the cross on the afternoon of Passover, the day of preparation. Once again, Matthew 26:17 is probably an idiomatic way of asking for guidance about that day.

221 *Matthew 27:62 (Emphasis added)*

Mark 15:42

Mark also relates how Joseph of Arimathea obtained permission from Pilate to remove Jesus' body from the cross and place it in his own tomb.[222] Mark 15:42 provides the timing of the conversation with Pilate by saying, "When evening had already come, *because it was the preparation day, that is, the day before the Sabbath...*"[223] Thus, the chronology of this passage is perfectly aligned with that of John's gospel, that Jesus was crucified on the afternoon of Abib 14, the day of preparation, the day before the high Sabbath.

In light of this, it is not possible that Mark 14:12 (cited in the previous section) could literally be referring to the first day of Unleavened Bread, since this verse tells us that Jesus died on the cross on the day before the first day of Unleavened Bread, which is Passover, the preparation day. The best way to interpret Mark 14:12 is that he was speaking in the Hebrew idiom and essentially saying, "***regarding** the first day of Unleavened Bread, when the Passover Lamb was being sacrificed,*" rather than saying that the first day of Unleavened Bread had already arrived.

Luke 23:54

Luke 23:50–56 also relates how Joseph of Arimathea asked Pilate for the body of Jesus so he could move it into his own tomb. Verse 54 provides the timing as "*It was the preparation day, and the Sabbath was about to begin.*" Thus, if the Sabbath was about to begin, that is, if the first day of Unleavened Bread was about to begin, and Jesus had already died, then Luke 22:7–8 (cited in the previous section) must be understood as an idiomatic reference to the first day of Unleavened Bread, rather than saying that it had already arrived. Simply stated, Jesus was giving instructions to Peter and John about that day which was yet to come.

The chronology of the synoptic gospels can easily be harmonized with the chronology of John if we watch for the Hebrew idiom and are careful to consider the day of preparation as we reckon the timing. The *day of preparation* is a key term, specifically, the day of preparation *for the Passover*, as we seek to harmonize the gospel accounts of the crucifixion. If we interpret these verses in a literal manner, then the synoptic gospels are self-contradictory, which presents a problem of an entirely different nature. But when understood properly, in their idiomatic usage, we find that all four gospels are in perfect harmony.

---

222 Mark 15:42–47

223 Mark 15:42 (Emphasis added)

I Have Earnestly Desired to Eat this Passover

There is one more verse that should be addressed that might mislead the reader regarding the chronology. In Luke 22:14–16, we find Jesus in the upper room, reclining at the table with the apostles. He said to them, "I have earnestly desired to eat this Passover with you before I suffer..." Does this statement mean that Jesus and the apostles were actually eating the Passover together? Does it imply that Jesus' intent was to eat the Passover?

The answer to both of these questions is *not necessarily.* Imagine, for example, that you went to visit a friend in another town. During your conversation, you said, "I have earnestly desired to be with you to celebrate your birthday." Does that mean that you will actually be with your friend to celebrate his or her birthday? Is it possible that the birthday celebration will be on Thursday night, but you must leave on Wednesday? Of course it is possible; you may have simply been expressing your wish or desire, even though you knew it was not going to happen.

The same is possible, even likely, that Jesus was expressing His desire to eat the Passover with His friends, even though He was fully aware that it would not happen since He would be in the grave while other people ate the Passover. So we should not infer from this verse that the last supper was actually the Passover meal; the last supper most likely took place on the evening before the Passover.

Jesus is our Passover. He was sacrificed at the ninth hour on the day of preparation—He became the Lord's Passover. Paul alludes to this in 1 Corinthians 5:7, *"For Christ our Passover also has been sacrificed."*

Chapter 11 – Unleavened Bread and the Bitterness of Death

What images come to mind when you think of the bread of affliction, bitter herbs, and the death of a lamb? When the Israelites walked out of the city of Rameses during the nighttime hours of Abib 15, they knew it would be a difficult journey with great hardship. Moses explained that their journey would be remembered by a meal, the bread of affliction, also known as unleavened bread. Furthermore, bitter herbs and the death of the lamb speak for themselves, creating powerful imagery of suffering.

In the same way, the Feast of Unleavened Bread is a shadow of the Messiah, the Lamb of God, tasting death and being laid in the tomb, which also occurred on Abib 15. The death of the lamb, the unleavened bread, and the bitter herbs create a powerful metaphor of the death of Christ and His burial. Let's look at some of the details about this Appointed Time as they relate to the death of Jesus.

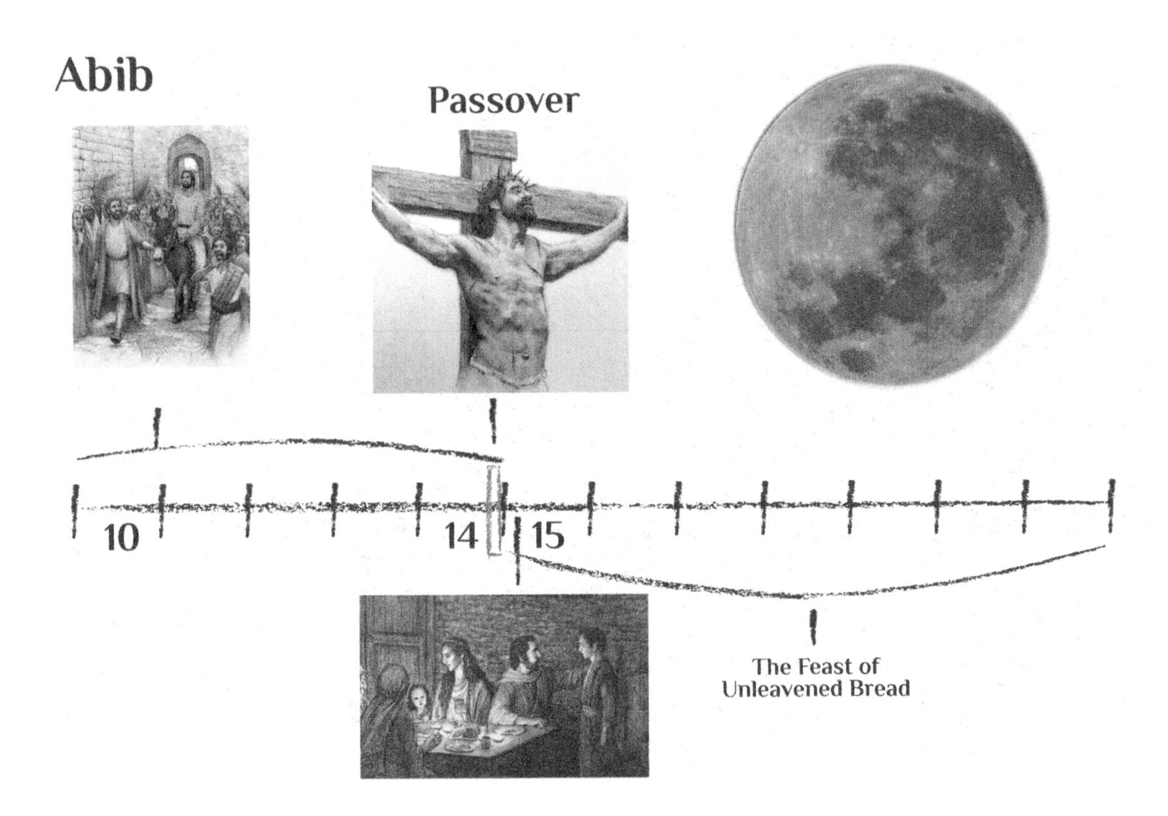

In the previous chapter, we were introduced to Joseph of Arimathea, a rich man, a secret follower of Jesus, and a prominent member of the Council who was waiting for the Kingdom of God.[224] After Jesus was pronounced dead by the centurion,[225] this Joseph gathered his courage and asked Pilate for the body of Jesus. They removed the body from the cross, and Joseph and his friend, Nicodemus, took the body, bound it in linen wrapping, and laid it in a new tomb that was in a garden near the cross of Jesus.[226]

*"**When it was evening**, there came a rich man from Arimathea, named Joseph, who himself had also become a disciple of Jesus. This man went to Pilate and asked for the body of Jesus. Then Pilate ordered it to be given to him. And Joseph took the body and wrapped it in a clean linen cloth, and laid it in his own new tomb, which he had hewn out in the rock; and he rolled a large stone against the entrance of the tomb and went away."*

Matthew 27:57–60 (Emphasis added)

224 *Matthew 27:57, Mark 15:43, Luke 23:51, John 19:38*

225 *Mark 15:44–45*

226 *John 19:38–42*

Matthew and Mark tell us that evening had already come[227] when Jesus' body was laid in the tomb, meaning that, the date had become Abib 15, the first day of the Feast of Unleavened Bread. Once again, we see perfect alignment with the Appointed Times and these significant events of the Messiah's life. Let's place the burial of Jesus on our timeline on Abib 15, which is the first high Sabbath of the Feast of Unleavened Bread.

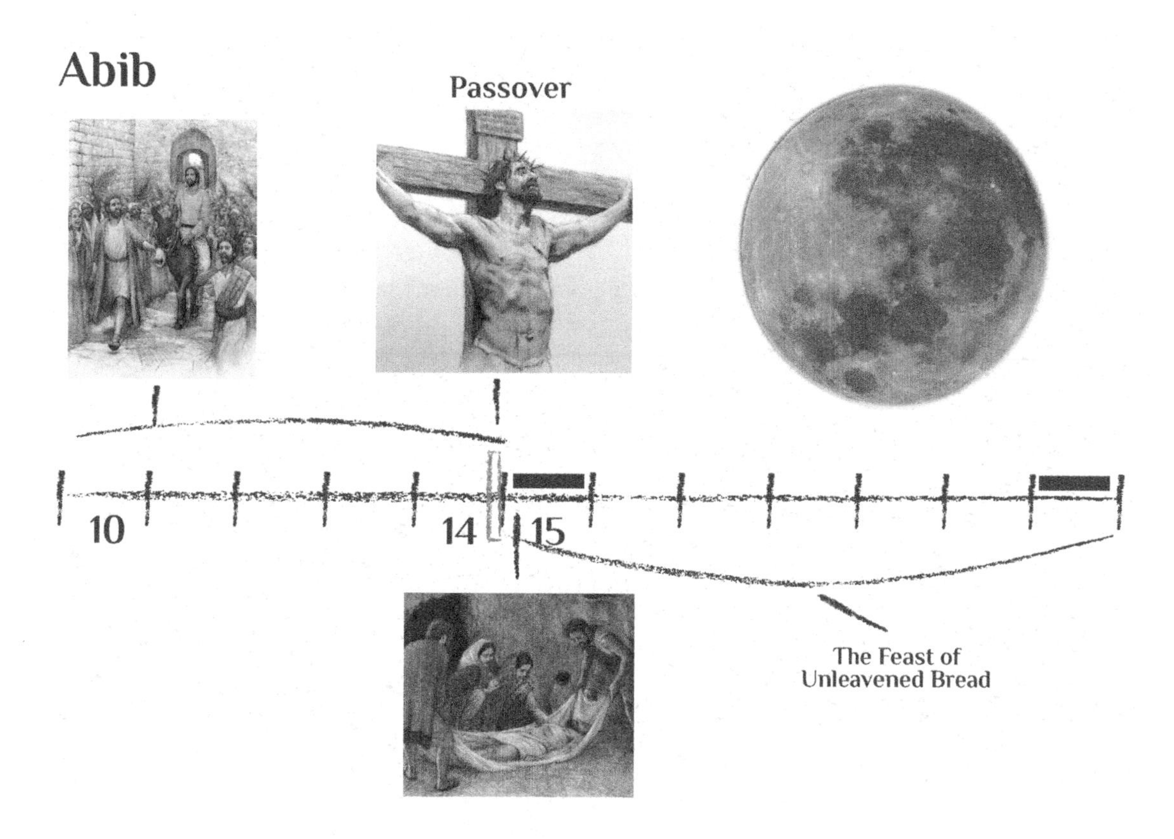

How Long Was Jesus in the Tomb?

The Feast of Unleavened Bread lasts for seven days, but Jesus was not in the tomb for seven days. Most of the relevant Scripture passages simply say that He rose from the grave on the third day.[228] There is, however, a passage in Matthew that records a heated discussion

227 Matthew 27:57, Mark 15:42, Luke 23:54

228 "On the third day" occurs ten times, "after three days" occurs one time (Matthew 27:63), and "in three days" occurs one time (John 2:19). Matthew 12:40 ("three days and three nights") appears to be an idiomatic usage and should probably not be interpreted literally - (Bullinger 2012 - First Published in 1898) page 846.

between Jesus and the scribes and Pharisees, wherein they demanded a sign from Jesus to as proof of the authority behind His words and works. But He told them,

> *"An evil and adulterous generation craves for a sign;*
> *and yet no sign will be given to it but the sign of Jonah the prophet;*
> *for just as Jonah was three days and three nights*
> *in the belly of the sea monster,*
> ***so will the Son of Man be three days and three nights***
> ***in the heart of the earth."***
>
> *Matthew 12:39–40 (Emphasis added)*

I imagine Jesus' opponents had a perplexed look on their faces after hearing His response—what was He talking about? But they certainly understood after His death, when they requested a guard from Pilate, saying, "Sir, we remember that when He was still alive that deceiver said, 'After three days I am to rise again.'"[229] So let's return to our timeline in Figure 12 to see if we can find three days and three nights during Jesus' stay in the tomb.

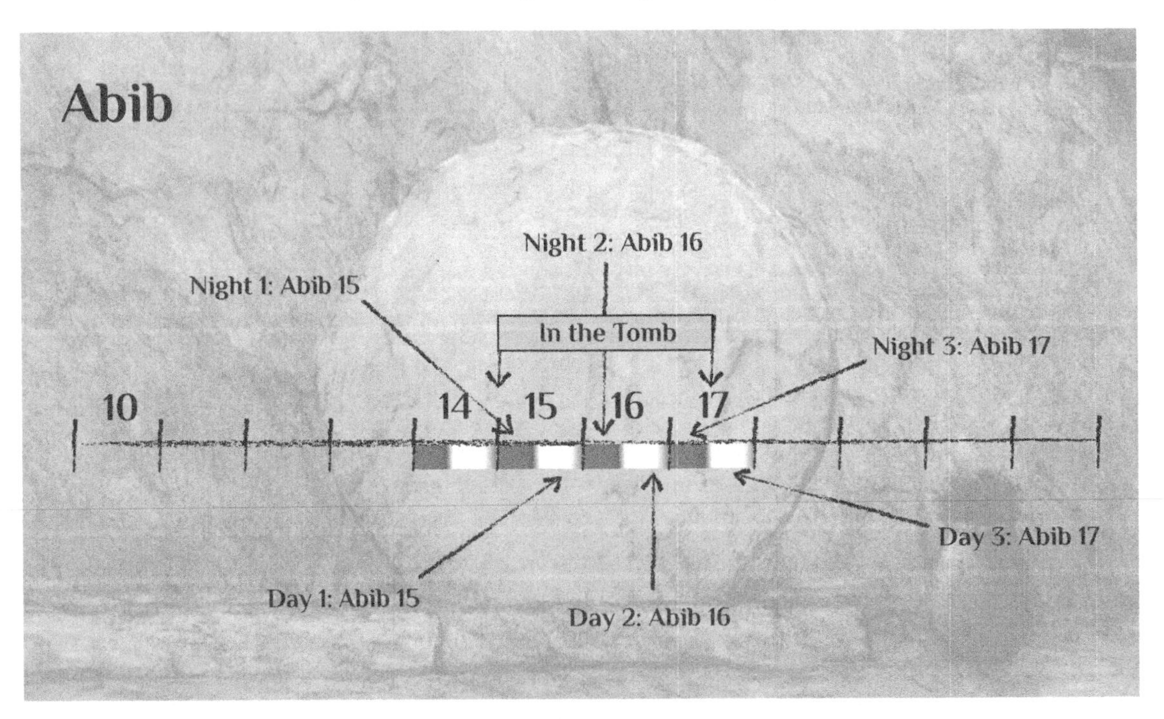

Figure 12

229 *Matthew 27:63*

Referring to the diagram in Figure 12,

- the three nights include the **hours of darkness on Abib 15, 16, and 17,**
- the three days include the **daylight hours of Abib 15, 16,**
- **and a very small portion of Abib 17th.**

Can a Partial Day Be Reckoned as a Full Day?

Some people are bothered by the fact that the third day is only a small portion of the daylight hours. But if Jesus was in the grave for a literal three days, a full 72 hours, then the time of His resurrection would have occurred at exactly the same time that He was laid in the grave, which was clearly not the case since He was laid in the tomb at evening and rose from the dead around dawn. As the Scriptures teach, He died at the ninth hour and rose from the grave sometime during the early morning hours on the first day of the week.

A more realistic and widely accepted perspective is that the Jewish people considered any part of a day to be reckoned as a full day. This is simply a way of speaking in the Hebrew idiom, or *cultural* way of speaking. It is not a literal statement that necessitates three full days and three full nights.

The Bible contains two other stories that demonstrate this same reckoning of partial days as *whole* days, specifically mentioning three days and three nights. To interpret them literally would require a fourth day, making them self-contradictory. The stories can be found in 1 Samuel 30:11–13 and Esther 4:15–5:1.

Regarding the idea of a partial day being reckoned as a *full* day, E.F. Bullinger, the author of *Figures of Speech Used in the Bible*, says, "It may seem absurd to Gentiles and to Westerners to use words in such a manner, but that does not alter the fact... the New Testament is for the most part Hebrew in idiom, but Greek in language."[230]

Indeed, Jesus was in the tomb for three days and three nights, but it would not be reasonable for us to expect the biblical writers and speakers to always convey their thoughts in a literal manner, demanding a 72-hour stay in the tomb. We must give them the latitude to write and speak via their own idioms and colloquialisms, as we do the same in our own writing and speaking.

---

230 (Bullinger 2012 - First Published in 1898) p 846

The Shadow of the Feast of Unleavened Bread

Jesus' body was placed in the tomb around sundown on Abib 15, exactly when the Feast of Unleavened Bread began. The shadow that is cast by consuming a lamb whose blood was shed, consumed with the bread of affliction and bitter herbs, clearly proclaims that the substance of this Appointed Time is the Lamb of God whose blood was shed, as He endured affliction and the bitterness of death, as His body was laid in the tomb.

Chapter 12 – The First Fruit of Many Brethren

It was in the evening,[231] the beginning hours of Abib 15, when Joseph and Nicodemus laid Jesus' body in the tomb. Several women, who were followers of Jesus, looked on so they would know where He was buried.[232] The women rested on the Sabbath, but when they returned to the tomb at early dawn on the first day of the week with the burial spices they had prepared, they found the large stone that had sealed the tomb had been rolled away, and the body of the Lord Jesus was gone.

"It was the preparation day, and the Sabbath was about to begin. Now the women who had come with Him out of Galilee followed, and saw the tomb and how His body was laid. Then they returned and prepared spices and perfumes. And ***on the Sabbath they rested*** *according to the commandment. But* ***on the first day of the week, at early dawn****, they came to the tomb bringing the spices which they had prepared. And they found the stone rolled away from the tomb, but when they entered, they did not find the body of the Lord Jesus."*

Luke 23:54–24:3 (Emphasis added)

Isn't that interesting? **It was the first day of the week**. Based on your knowledge of the Appointed Times, you are probably thinking *that would have been the day of First Fruits*, since it is the Sunday during the week of the Feast of Unleavened Bread. And once again, I would commend you for your grasp of the subject!

Jesus rose from the grave on the day of First Fruits!

231 *Matthew 27:57*

232 *Luke 23:55*

Abib

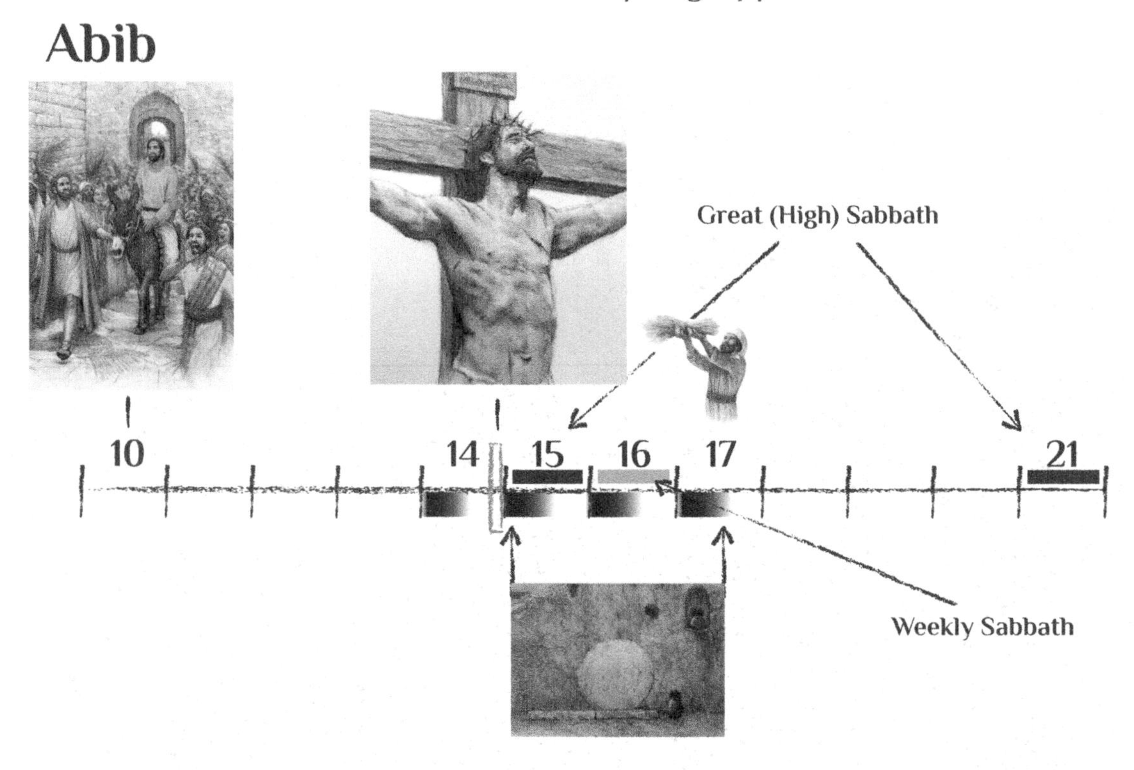

Figure 13

Referring to the timeline in Figure 13, Abib 15 and Abib 21 are the two high Sabbaths of the Feast of Unleavened Bread, and Abib 16 is the weekly Sabbath that occurred during the feast. Since the weekly Sabbath fell on Abib 16 in that year,[233] it means that the day of First Fruits, which is the day *after* the weekly Sabbath, would be the next day, Sunday, Abib 17.

Assuming that our timeline is correct, then Abib 17 would have been the Sunday that Jesus rose from the dead. He was crucified on Abib 14, buried on Abib 15, and in the grave until the morning of Sunday, Abib 17. The Apostles' Creed states it very succinctly: "He suffered under Pontius Pilate, was crucified, died and was buried, ... on the third day he rose again."[234]

233 Refer to the "The Amazing Journey" section of Chapter 6 - The Feast of Unleavened Bread, for information about the day of Passover during the year of the exodus.

234 The Apostles' Creed - (The Episcopal Church 1979)

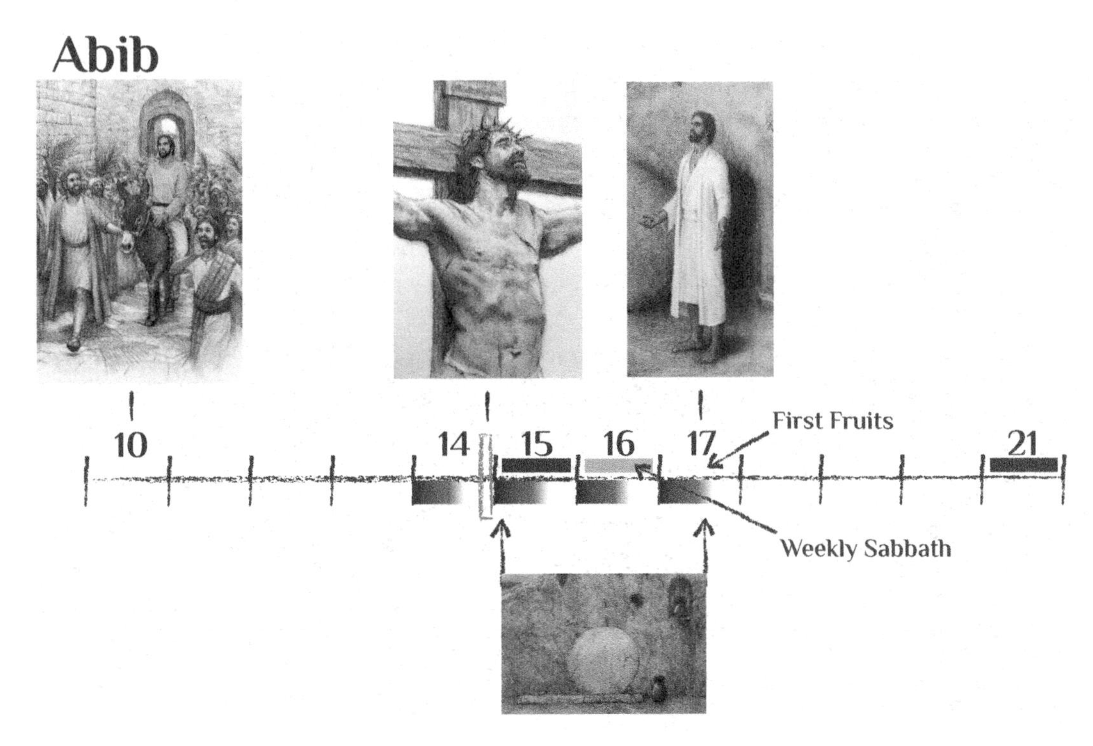

Figure 14 - First Fruits - The Day After Weekly Sabbath

Paul the apostle affirms that Jesus is the First Fruits of the resurrection, saying, "But now Christ has been raised from the dead, the first fruits of those who are asleep." He continues explaining the resurrection of the dead, saying, "But each in his own order: Christ the first fruits, after that those who are Christ's at His coming..."[235] He makes it very clear that the concept of First Fruits applies to Christ and the subsequent resurrection of those who belong to Christ. Do you remember what is implied by the term first fruits? Recall from Chapter 7:

The First Fruits offering is not suggesting that this is the first of many offerings ***to*** *the Lord. Instead,* ***the First Fruits sheaf is the first of many sheaves that will come from the Lord*** *and it expresses an expectation that He will provide more fruit in the coming harvest.*[236]

Thus, Christ was the first to rise from the dead, and there is an expectation that God will raise others from the dead, as well. The others who will be raised are those who belong to Him because they believe in Him for their salvation. Paul makes a very clear connection between First Fruits and the resurrection of the dead, and he is simply heralding the words of Jesus that those who have died will live again.

235 *1 Corinthians 15:20–23 (Emphasis added)*

236 *Refer to the section "Think about It... What Is Meant by First Fruits?" on page 93*

Do you remember Jesus' words from John 6:39? "This is the will of Him who sent Me, that of all that He has given Me I lose nothing, but raise it up on the last day." Jesus is the first fruits of those who will rise from the dead, and those who believe Him are the subsequent fruits whom God will raise from the dead.

The Time of Jesus' Resurrection

At what time did Jesus rise from the dead? The Scriptures do not explicitly tell us the time of day, but it is clear that He had already risen when the women arrived at the tomb at early dawn. Let's see if the events from Israel's exodus from Egypt might shed some light on the timing of this event.

Recall from the narrative of the exodus that the Israelites departed from the city of Rameses sometime in the night of Abib 15. Moses recorded three encampments during their journey, before Pharaoh and his army began pursuing them through the corridor in the sea—that date was Abib 17.

*"**At the morning watch**, the Lord looked down on the army of the Egyptians through the pillar of fire and cloud and brought the army of the Egyptians into confusion. He caused their chariot wheels to swerve, and He made them drive with difficulty; so the Egyptians said, 'Let us flee from Israel, for the Lord is fighting for them against the Egyptians.'"*

Exodus 14:24–25 (Emphasis added)

Does the phrase *morning watch*[237] sound familiar? The morning watch was the last watch of the night, which ended with the dawning of the morning. As you can see from the passage below, it was at the morning watch or daybreak that Israel emerged alive from the sea, which gives insight into the time signature of the Messiah and may shed light on the timing of Jesus' resurrection from the dead.

Then the Lord said to Moses,

"'Stretch out your hand over the sea
so that the waters may come back over the Egyptians,
over their chariots and their horsemen.'
So Moses stretched out his hand over the sea,
and the sea returned to its normal state at daybreak,

237 Refer to the Tracking Time in Israel compendium for more information about the watches in the night.

while the Egyptians were fleeing right into it;
then the Lord overthrew the Egyptians in the midst of the sea.
The waters returned and covered the chariots and the horsemen,
even Pharaoh's entire army that had gone into the sea after them;
not even one of them remained.
But the sons of Israel walked on dry land through the midst of the sea,
and the waters were like a wall to them on their
right hand and on their left.*"*

Exodus 14:26–29 (Emphasis added)

Is it possible that the Lord Jesus rose from the grave at the morning watch on Abib 17, mirroring the Israelites rising from the sea at the morning watch some 1,500 years earlier? Since there is such a strong linkage between the exodus and the events of the Messiah, I believe that is a perfectly reasonable suggestion.

First Fruits – Shadows and Substance

The Israelites rose alive from the sea during the morning watch on Abib 17, so it is quite probable that Jesus rose from the grave at the same time on Abib 17, almost 1,500 years later. The Israelites' rising from the sea was the fulfillment of the shadow of First Fruits, but Jesus' rising from the dead is the significance, the substance that the Lord intended in First Fruits Appointed Time.

The First Fruits shadow is cast by the priest waving the barley sheaf, giving thanks for the crop that is being formed in the fields, while expressing faith by anticipating further blessings from the Lord. The substance that belongs to Christ is Jesus' resurrection from the dead, the first fruit of the great harvest of believers who will also be raised from the dead at the sound of the last trumpet. Thus, we will place Jesus' resurrection on our timeline in Figure 14 as the fulfillment of the day of First Fruits.

The Resurrection of the Dead

Are we really, seriously suggesting that someone returned to life after He was dead? Someone who was brutally tortured and suspended from a wooden structure by nails in His hands and feet, bleeding, suffocating, and gasping for breath? His heart stopped beating, His blood stopped flowing, and His brain was deprived of oxygen? Are we suggesting that this man, a dead man, came back to life?

Recall that these events were orchestrated by God—the same God who created the heavens and the earth. The same God who created the galaxies and our planet and all life therein. The same God who formed the man and woman in the garden, breathed life into them, and pronounced them good. This same God is the one who ordained the Messiah's abuse and death from heaven, so is it too fantastic to believe that He raised Him from the dead?

The resurrection of Jesus is not a fanciful, figurative hope; instead, it is the fleshly, physical resurrection of His body—not just His soul or spirit. And His resurrection is indeed, the basis of magnificent hope for all who believe—the fact that He was resurrected means that we can also be resurrected from the dead.

So, my response is absolutely "Yes." We believe in the supernatural, in the God who created and sustains all creation. He brought Jesus back to life from the dead, since He is the author of all life. I once heard it said, "If you believe Genesis 1:1, then believing the rest of the miracles in the Bible is easy." So it is with believing in the resurrection of the dead.

Furthermore, if there is no resurrection from the dead, then those who believe it would be truly pathetic people. But after weighing the testimonies of those who beheld and touched the resurrected Christ, who changed the world as a result of what they had seen, we can say that our belief is founded on a case that is far beyond a reasonable doubt. Our faith is not blind; it is objective and fully rational.

Chapter 12: The First Fruits of Many Brethren

His Resurrection and Ours

What are the implications of Jesus' resurrection for you and me? Indeed, being raised from the dead and given an immortal body is just the beginning. Sometime after that event, we will be escorted to the dwelling places that the Messiah has prepared for us,[238] and we will be with Him forever, [239]living as immortals in paradise, as the friends and children of God—completely reconciled to Him.

Our resurrection from the dead will bring us into a life of immortality, living in splendors and pleasures that are beyond our earthly imaginations. Everyone senses that there is more to this world than the eye can see. And even though some would suppress the inner voice with skepticism and doubt, it is my belief that everyone believes in their deepest parts that our lives do not end with death. In this world, we live with misery and death, but the pages of the New Testament are alive with the prospect that we will attain everlasting life in the Messiah. Indeed, the eye has not seen, the ear has not heard, and the heart of man cannot imagine all that God has prepared for those who love Him.[240]

The idea of the resurrection of the dead has been our longing since the death of Abel, but through the Messiah, the resurrection from the dead has become the most celebrated hope that has captivated the hearts of humanity. Even more fantastic is the idea that we will continue to live as youthful immortals for all eternity, with no death, no mourning, no crying, and no pain.

The toxin of sin will no longer flow in the veins of men. And what has long been a wish will soon be reality; it is the promise of God, the magnificent hope of all who believe. The misery and despair of this world have been transformed into an incorruptible hope for those who believe. "O DEATH, WHERE IS YOUR VICTORY? O DEATH, WHERE IS YOUR STING?"[241]

---

238 John 14:2–

239 1 Thessalonians 4:17

240 1 Corinthians 2:9

241 1 Corinthians 15:55

Chapter 13 – The Feast of Weeks – Pentecost

Jesus rose from the dead on the day of First Fruits, and **exactly fifty days later...**

"When the day of Pentecost had come,
they were all together in one place.
And suddenly there came from heaven a noise like a violent rushing wind,
and it filled the whole house where they were sitting.
And there appeared to them tongues as of fire distributing themselves, and
they rested on each one of them.
And they were all filled with the Holy Spirit
and began to speak with other tongues,
as the Spirit was giving them utterance."

Acts 2:1–4 (Emphasis added)

The giving of the Holy Spirit, which occurred on the day of **Pentecost**, has ramifications that run far deeper than enabling the apostles to speak the varied languages of the crowds of Jerusalem—that amazing act was only the tip of the iceberg. The gift from the Father forever changed the nature of believers in profound ways. Rather than being self-reliant in their thoughts, meditations, and prayers, the Wonderful Counselor was given to guide them from within, not as a dictator or possessor of their minds, but as the still, small voice that would lead them as they would listen.

Recall that Pentecost is an alternative name for the Feast of Weeks. The timing of this event is exceedingly clear in Acts 2:1—it was the day of Pentecost, an Appointed Time, a day that was appointed by the Lord to host a profoundly significant work of the Messiah. Jesus had ascended to heaven only ten days prior,[242] and now the Holy Spirit, who is also referred to as the *Spirit of Christ*,[243] descended into the upper room, not to simply visit the apostles, but to indwell them forever. Indeed, Jesus kept His word that He will be with them always, even to the end of the age.[244]

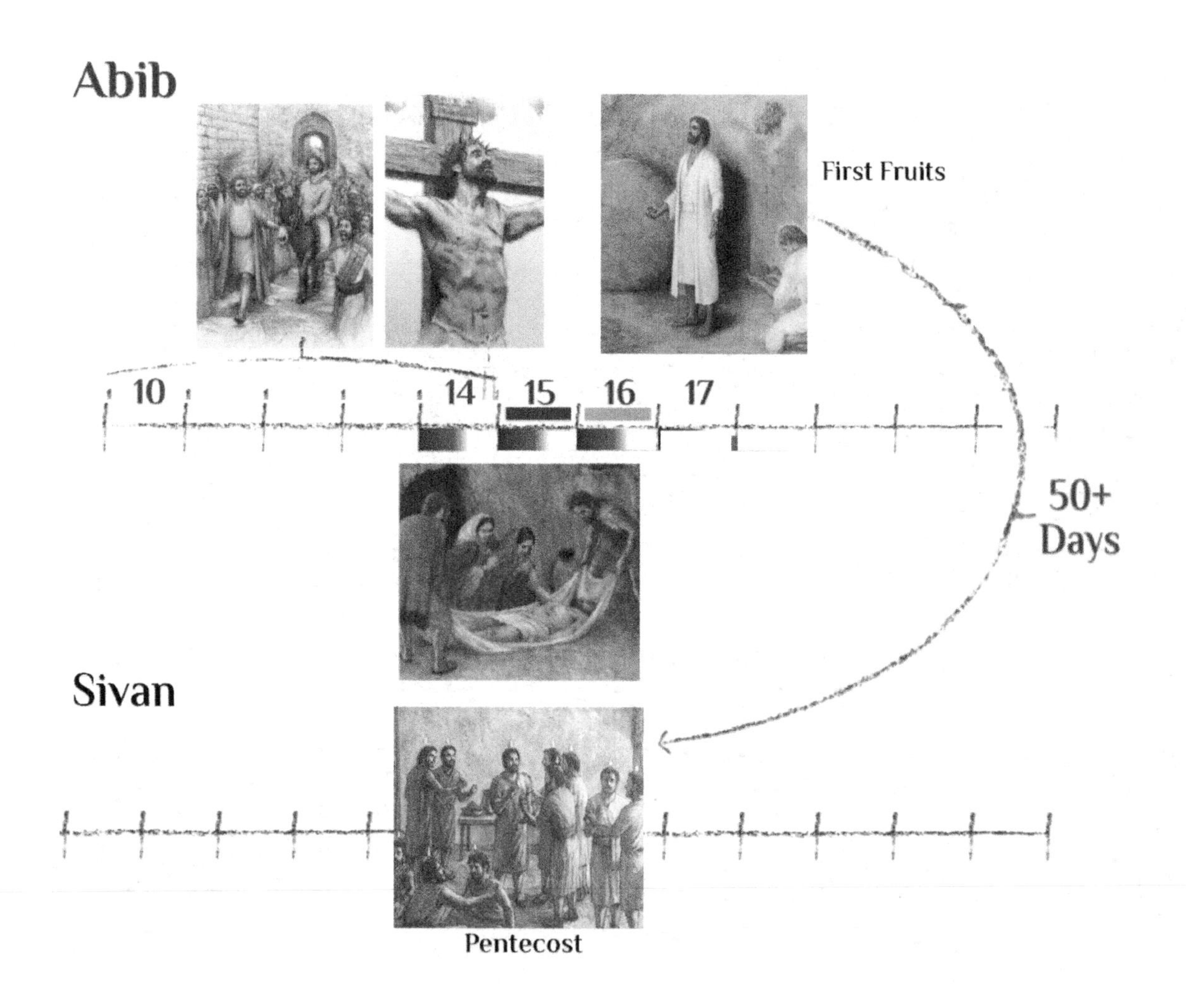

242 Acts 1:3 provides the timing of Jesus' ascension, which is recorded in Acts 1:9.

243 The Spirit is referred to as the Spirit of Christ in Romans 8:9, Philippians 1:19, and 1 Peter 1:11. Acts 16:7 refers to the "Spirit of Jesus."

244 Matthew 28:20 – "...teaching them to observe all that I commanded you; and lo, I am with you always, even to the end of the age." (Emphasis added)

The Giving of the Spirit – the Work of the Messiah

You may be wondering if the giving of the Holy Spirit is truly an act of the Messiah, or if it was perhaps the Father sending the Holy Spirit, without the involvement of the Son—an excellent question. Jesus told His disciples that He would send the Helper to them from the Father, the Spirit of truth who proceeds from the Father.[245] Clearly it was Jesus, the Messiah, who orchestrated this event as the substance of this Appointed Time—it was truly a messianic event. Recall also that John the Baptist told the crowds that he baptizes them with water, *but He (i.e., the Messiah) will baptize you with the Holy Spirit,*[246] once again clarifying that the baptism of the Holy Spirit is the work of the Messiah.

Forty days after His resurrection from the dead, Jesus instructed His disciples not to leave Jerusalem, but to wait there for the promise of the Father.[247] He then affirmed John's words, saying,

"...for John baptized with water,
but you will be baptized with the Holy Spirit not many days from now."

Acts 1:5

Indeed, when the Holy Spirit descended on those in the upper room, it was at the direction of the Messiah, at His request to the Father to send the Helper to the disciples and to those who will believe in Him through their word. As we learned from Paul in Colossians 2:17, the substance of this Appointed Time truly belongs to Christ.

The Events of the Day of Pentecost

What actually happened on that day? Why were the apostles given the ability to speak with other tongues? What did it mean to speak with other tongues?

Recall that all the men of Israel were required to travel to Jerusalem three times per year to participate in the annual feasts of Moses (i.e., the Feast of Unleavened Bread, the Feast of Weeks, and the Feast of Booths). Because of this influx of worshippers, Jerusalem was inundated with people on the day of Pentecost. The visitors included residents of Jerusalem and

245 *John 15:26 – "When the Helper comes, whom I will send to you from the Father, that is the Spirit of truth who proceeds from the Father, He will testify about Me."*

246 *Matthew 3:11, Mark 1:8, Luke 3:16, John 1:33*

247 *Acts 1:4*

visitors from every nation under heaven,[248] including:

> *"Parthians and Medes and Elamites, and residents of Mesopotamia, Judea and Cappadocia, Pontus and Asia, Phrygia and Pamphylia, Egypt and the districts of Libya around Cyrene, and visitors from Rome, both Jews and proselytes, Cretans and Arabs."*[249]

When these people heard the noise of the rushing wind and the multi-lingual apostles, a large crowd quickly formed to try to make sense of it. They were astonished because these men were simple Galileans, yet they were confidently speaking in the languages and dialects of their native lands. *How can this be? We hear them in our own languages, speaking of the mighty deeds of God.* They were amazed and perplexed by this spectacle.

In order to reach the people of these diverse nationalities and languages, the Holy Spirit supernaturally enabled the apostles to speak in the native languages of these visitors to Jerusalem. This group of uneducated Galileans miraculously became fluent in other languages of the world as the Spirit enabled them.

In the midst of this spectacle, Peter addressed the crowd and explained the wonders of Jesus the Messiah, proclaiming that *"everyone who calls on the name of the Lord will be saved."*[250] He went on to tell the crowd that this Jesus was delivered over by the predetermined plan and foreknowledge of God, allowing godless men to nail Him to a cross and put Him to death, but God raised Him up again, since it was impossible for Him to be held in the power of death. Peter then directed his point to each individual in the crowd, saying, *"...know for certain that God has made Him both Lord and Christ—this Jesus whom **you** crucified."*[251]

248 *Acts 2:5*

249 *Acts 2:9–11*

250 *Acts 2:21*

251 *Acts 2:36 (Emphasis added)*

The crowd was pierced to the heart and convicted of their guilt in the death of God's Anointed One, so they asked Peter and the other apostles, "What shall we do?" And Peter responded,

"Repent, and each of you be baptized in the name of Jesus Christ for the forgiveness of your sins; ***and you will receive the gift of the Holy Spirit."***

Acts 2:38 (Emphasis added)

In this statement, Peter made it clear that the gift of the Holy Spirit was not just for the apostles, but it was for all who would believe in the name of Jesus Christ. Peter's words crystalized the message of the gospel—for the crowd in Jerusalem and for all races and generations of humankind throughout history, all the way to you and to me and to *as many as the Lord our God will call to Himself.*[252]

Does this mean that anyone who believes, even in our modern world, will receive the gift of the Holy Spirit? The answer is a resounding "Yes!" Does it mean they will immediately become fluent in other languages? The answer is "Probably not." But it is certain that the Holy Spirit is not given to people who do not believe in Jesus Christ for the forgiveness of their sins.

The gift of the Spirit is a precious treasure—He is an intimate friend to believers. Jesus even told the disciples that it was to their advantage that He go away so that the Spirit would come to them.[253] Imagine their amazement at the thought that the presence of the Spirit in their lives could be better than the physical presence of the Messiah. But it is true—the Spirit is perhaps the most understated, underappreciated gift that man could ever possess.

252 Acts 2:39

253 John 16:7

The Feast of Weeks

How does the giving of the Holy Spirit relate to the Feast of Weeks? Recall that this feast is characterized by a first fruits offering of loaves of leavened bread to the Lord. Were the apostles, on whom the Holy Spirit first descended, the first fruits of this gift from the Father? Was their new vitality and life in the Spirit symbolized by the leaven of the first fruits offering? The imagery of first fruits and leavened bread certainly corresponds with the events that unfolded in the giving of the Holy Spirit.

In accordance with the concept of first fruits, the Lord fulfilled the expectation for additional fruit. For on that same day, 3,000 souls were enrolled in heaven after they believed Peter's words.[254] The harvest that began on the day of Pentecost was abundant, and the Lord has been faithfully adding souls to the roster of heaven daily, even to our day.

---

254 Acts 2:41 – "So then, those who had received his word were baptized; and that day there were added about three thousand souls."

The book of Acts is filled with accounts of additional fruit from fields that were white for harvest. Soon after the day of Pentecost, Peter once again proclaimed the good news of the Christ, and more than five thousand came to faith.[255] The number of believers grew rapidly and expanded to neighboring Samaria, to Asia minor, and to the farthest reaches of the world. The believers would eventually come from every race and nationality of the globe as the church grew to worldwide proportions. Indeed, the first fruits from Pentecost, and the subsequent harvest of souls as directed by the Messiah, are the substance of this Appointed Time.

The Shadow of the Feast of Weeks

Based on Paul's words that the Appointed Times are shadows of things to come, we surmised in Chapter 8 that the Feast of Weeks was a shadow or commemoration of the giving of the Law at Mount Sinai. Recall that fifty days after Israel arose alive from the sea, on the day of First Fruits, they met the Lord, who descended on Mount Sinai to claim them as His people and give His law. The experience terrorized the people with fire and smoke as the mountain quaked, along with thunder and lightning, and the increasing sound of a ram's horn. The people pleaded with Moses to speak to the Lord on their behalf, because they would die if He spoke to them.[256]

The substance of the Feast of Weeks, however, was revealed some 1,500 years after the Law was given, when the Lord once again visited mankind. On this occasion, however, He did not present Himself in terror and fear, but to lovingly empower His people and proclaim amnesty and adoption to all who turn to His Messiah. It is the giving of the Spirit that is the substance of the Feast of Weeks. The event has profound significance to everyone who repents and believes, as their minds, hearts, and bodies immediately become the temple and dwelling place of the Spirit of God—their adoption into the family of God is sealed for all eternity by this living pledge.[257]

255 *Acts 4:4*

256 *Exodus 20:19 – "Speak to us yourself and we will listen; but let not God speak to us, or we will die."*

257 *Ephesians 1:13 "...you also, after listening to the message of truth, the gospel of your salvation—having also believed, you were sealed in Him with the Holy Spirit of promise..."*

What Does it Mean to Receive the Holy Spirit?

The world was changed on the day of Pentecost. Before that day, the Spirit of God was only given to people on certain occasions at the Lord's directing, but as a general rule, neither the righteous nor anyone else was able to consistently experience the guidance of God's Spirit. The apostle John explained that the Spirit had not been given before Jesus was glorified,[258] no doubt because the heavenly counselor and guide could only indwell those who had been purified by the atoning work of the Messiah.[259]

Sadly, many people do not understand or appreciate the gift of the Holy Spirit. Some believers are indifferent toward Him and deny His presence and influence in their lives, while others simply view Him as a tool to provide rudimentary proofs and evidences of spirituality.

Referring to the Spirit, Jesus said that rivers of living water will flow from the innermost being of those who believe in Him.[260] The New Testament has much to say about the hope and joy that comes from the Holy Spirit—hope and joy that cannot be taken away by the world. The Spirit Himself testifies with our spirit that we are children of God,[261] which produces a confidence, hope, and joy that are completely foreign to those of the world.

For those who live by the teaching of Christ, the Spirit will fashion their character

---

258 John 7:39 – "But this He spoke of the Spirit, whom those who believed in Him were to receive; for the Spirit was not yet given, because Jesus was not yet glorified."

259 We will explore the atonement of the Messiah in Chapter 15.

260 John 7:38

261 Romans 8:16

and person by manifesting His fruit in their lives, filling them with love, joy, peace, patience, kindness, goodness, faithfulness, gentleness, self-control, and more.[262] But we must always be mindful that resisting the ways of Christ grieves the Holy Spirit and prevents Him from bringing fruit to maturity in our lives. It is through obedience to Christ's ways, with the assistance of the Holy Spirit, that the Father is glorified.[263] Our character becomes more like that of the innocent Adam and Eve before they ingested the toxin, the Knowledge of Good and Evil. Indeed, it is through our obedience to the Holy Spirit that we are conformed to Christ.

The Scriptures exhort us to be filled with the Spirit, to be led by the Spirit, to walk by the Spirit, and to be taught by the Spirit. He especially leads us into the truths of God's ways, which helps to protect believers from the corrupt inclinations of natural man—our own natural ways.[264]

We are not suggesting that believers will become supernatural know-it-alls who are exempt from error, but that the Holy Spirit will give believers an awareness or feeling of angst when they encounter untruths while giving them a sense of confidence when they are in the truth. It is certainly possible for believers to be drawn into false teaching, but we must continually grow in our understanding of God's Word as our anchor against the winds of apostasy.

How Do We Receive the Holy Spirit?

The Holy Spirit comes to live within a person when he or she comes to faith in Christ—by believing that Jesus is the Messiah. The Spirit is the gift of God, given to us at the time we believe, and He is with us forevermore, never to leave us.

No magic words or incantations are required; just simple, sincere faith, believing in Jesus for the forgiveness of sin. A person can come to faith in a large gathering or in quiet solitude or in any situation they may find themselves. You see, the salvation of Christ takes place in the heart—it does not require mediation or the intervention of a preacher, priest, rabbi, guru, or any spiritual guide. It does not require membership in any church or organization. Coming to faith in Christ enrolls a person in the universal church, which is citizenship in heaven.

When the Spirit indwells us, He seals us in our salvation and leads, guides, teaches, prompts, and counsels us. Perhaps His greatest gift is that He helps us as we pray. When believers pray, their words, thoughts, and emotions are often inadequate to express themselves to God the Father. But the Spirit intercedes for us with groanings too deep for words, according to God's desires. [265]

---

262 *Galatians 5:22–23*

263 *John 15:8*

264 *1 Corinthians 2:11–13*

265 *Romans 8:26–27*

And in this world of darkness and trouble, the Spirit gives us the peace of God, even in the midst of the rage of the evil one. The peace of God is an amazing gift. When situations are overwhelming and calamity seems inevitable, believers are able to reach out to God in their spirits and trust Him for deliverance. It is His Spirit who assures our spirits that we are children of God,[266] as He fills us with the peace of God. Indeed, the gift of the Holy Spirit is not just significant, it is magnificent!

The gift of the Holy Spirit is not just Significant...

it is Magnificent!

Reflecting on the Spring Appointed Times

Take a moment to consider the correlations between the spring Appointed Times and the key events in the life of Jesus. Do you see it? The parallels are stunning. Clearly, God had already planned to redeem mankind, even at the time of the fall into sin. He mysteriously intimated that His salvation would be accomplished through His Messiah[267] almost at the outset of creation. And, if you are able to accept it, the Bible further teaches that this salvation was planned by God, even before the creation of the world.[268]

The correlations and the continuity of the message are even more impressive when we consider that the shadows of the Appointed Times were conveyed by the Lord hundreds of years before they were fulfilled by Jesus. The Bible was written over a span of 1,500 years, by about 40 authors of differing backgrounds, yet the message of the Messiah unfolded mysteriously and flawlessly throughout the centuries and revealed in mysteries from God that would be understood only *after* Jesus completed His earthly ministry.

Indeed, God designed the *spring* Appointed Times to teach about the key events of the Messiah's work that purchased salvation for all mankind. He made it unmistakably clear by incorporating a unique time signature into these shadows—shadows that could be fulfilled only

266 *Romans 8:16 – "The Spirit Himself testifies with our spirit that we are children of God."*

267 *In Genesis 3:15, the Lord God told the serpent (i.e., Satan) that the offspring of the woman would deliver a deathblow on him by crushing his head.*

268 *Ephesians 1:3–4 – "Blessed be the God and Father of our Lord Jesus Christ, who has blessed us with every spiritual blessing in the heavenly places in Christ, just as He chose us in Him before the foundation of the world, that we would be holy and blameless before Him."*

by the true Messiah. The Appointed Times provide a divine confirmation that Jesus is truly the Messiah.

So, what does it mean to you and me? The implications are enormous. The hand of God is clearly behind the prophetic shadows and substance of the Appointed Times. As we consider these sacred events and examine the evidence, we see that the message about the Messiah is true beyond a reasonable doubt—beyond a shadow of doubt. For this reason, it is not only prudent, but it is imperative that we give close attention to the messages of the *fall* Appointed times so we can know God's plans for humanity and creation through His Messiah.

The Spring and the Fall

Before we turn our attention to the *fall* Appointed Times, it may be helpful for you to review the table that is entitled *The Spring Appointed Times on page 11 in Part 1*, to reinforce your understanding of the timing and substance of each *spring* event. A solid understanding of the spring events and their messianic substance will increase your confidence that all of the Appointed Times, including those in the fall, are messages from the Lord about His Messiah.

We can infer from the evidence of the *spring* shadows that the *fall* shadows are also the message of the Lord and must be thoughtfully examined. We cannot afford to ignore them, especially since the *fall* shadows speak of the might and power of the Lord's Messiah in future events that will literally shake the heavens and the earth.[269] This same Jesus who, 2,000 years ago, came to suffer and die as a humble servant, will ascend the throne of the universe as the king and judge of all mankind. Everyone will stand before His throne to be judged based on their deeds—believers and unbelievers alike.[270]

It seems that one of the primary purposes of the *spring* Appointed Times is to provide a way to clearly identify the Messiah, as they call us to learn more about this exceedingly special individual and gain deeper insights into His work. In the chapters ahead, we will explore the might and strength of the Messiah, His atoning work before God the Father, and His abundant blessings for those who receive Him—you will find ample reason to give close attention to the words of the gospel of Jesus Christ.

269 Hebrews 12:26

270 Romans 14:10–12, Revelation 20:11–15

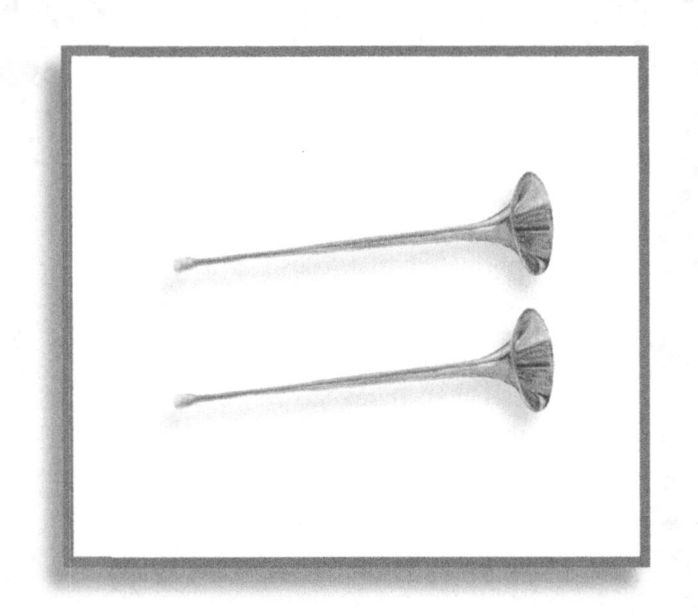

Part 4 – The Fall Appointed Times

Introduction

Like the *spring* Appointed Times, the *fall* Appointed Times also cast shadows of the Messiah's work, adding new dimensions and insight into His role in God's plan for restoring humanity to Himself. The substance of their message is profound, as they teach about Christ's return and ascension to the throne of the Kingdom of God, the resurrection of the dead, judgment and reward, His atoning work, and receiving His redeemed children into the eternal dwellings that He prepared for them.

It is much easier to connect the message of the *spring* Appointed Times to the life events of the Messiah, since it is a matter of connecting prophesies from the past with events that have already occurred. On the other hand, since the *fall* Appointed Times are shadows of events that are yet to be fulfilled by the Messiah, we must exercise the greatest care as we hypothesize and make conclusions about their fulfillment.

The Timing of the Fall Appointed Times

All of the fall Appointed Times take place during the month of Tishri, which is in the September–October timeframe.[271] *Figure 15 - The Timing of the Fall Appointed Times*, illustrates when these sacred events occur on a timeline. If I were to tell you that these Appointed Times refer to the return of the Messiah, His atoning work, and our entry into heaven, could you imagine some sort of significance in their order? I certainly can. But before we speculate about a possible meaning that the Lord instilled within their order, we must first examine each Appointed Time on its own and then step back so we can consider the bigger picture. I can tell you at this point that the answer is not as obvious as we would like it to be.

As you would expect, the Jewish religious leaders have developed a comprehensive theology about the fall Appointed Times, which is based on their timing and order. It is tempting for Christians to simply adopt the Jewish understanding and intermix it with New Testament revelations. But it is essential that we evaluate the fall Appointed Times afresh, with the goal of understanding their messianic substance in light of the teaching of Jesus, the apostles, and the prophets that preceded them.

---

271 *Refer to the Tracking Time in Israel compendium to see a diagram of how the Gregorian and Hebrew months relate to each other.*

Part 4: The Fall Appointed Times

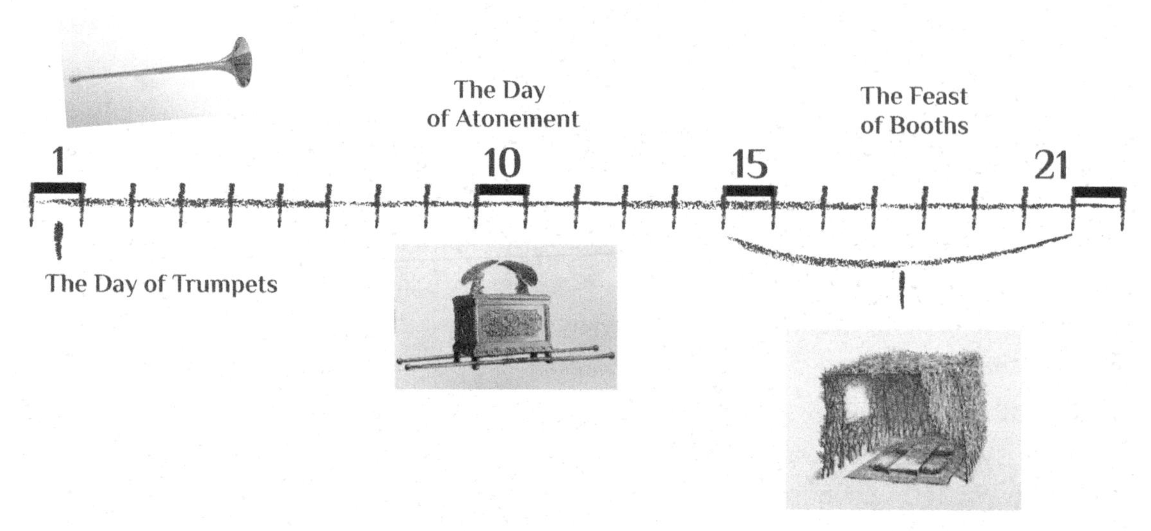

Figure 15 - The Timing of the Fall Appointed Times

Indeed, the Jewish teachings hold some rich truths, many of which were affirmed by Jesus and the apostles, including the weighty truth of our guilt before the Lord, our need for repentance, reconciliation with others, and a profound awareness that everyone must stand before the holy Judge. But, once again, we must study the Appointed Times in light of the teaching of Jesus and the apostles. We have included a very brief overview of the Jewish teachings regarding the *fall* Appointed Times in *Appendix C – Judaism and the Fall Appointed Times* for your review.

For our part, however, we will take a fresh look at the fall Appointed Times. We will examine each of these holy days as they were prescribed by Moses and then evaluate relevant passages in the Hebrew Scriptures, the gospels, and the writings of the apostles to form our understanding of the intended meaning of these mysterious edicts. Let's begin our exploration by looking into the Day of Trumpets.

Chapter 14 – The Day of Trumpets

Speak to the sons of Israel, saying,
*"In the **seventh month** on the **first of the month** you shall have a rest,*
***a reminder** by **blowing of trumpets**, a holy convocation.*
You shall not do any laborious work,
but you shall present an offering by fire to the Lord."

Leviticus 23:24–25 (Emphasis added)

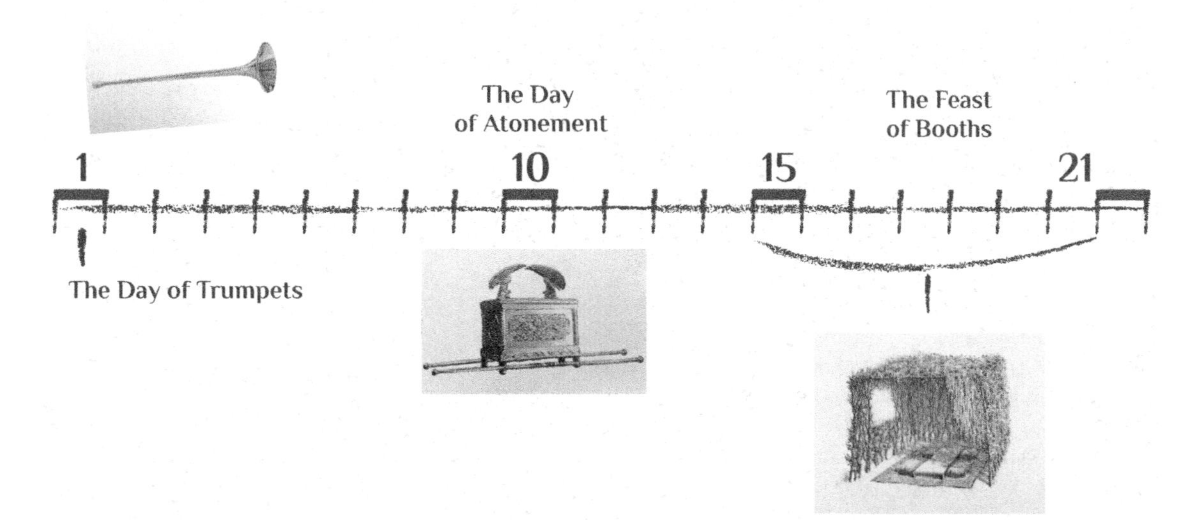

The Day of Trumpets is the first of the *fall* Appointed Times. We are in the September–October timeframe, and autumn is upon us. The silver edge moon is in the night sky, signaling the beginning of the month of Tishri[272] on the Hebrew calendar. The Day of Trumpets is observed on the first day of this month, casting shadows of events that will literally be earth-shaking, announcing the moment when the Lord Himself will descend from heaven with a shout, with the voice of the archangel, and with the trumpet of God.[273] It will be a wondrous day for those who have embraced the Messiah, but those who have defied Him must meet Him face to face, kneeling before Him as their fearsome, holy Judge.[274]

The day on which the last trumpet sounds will be a great day, a magnificent day, filled with wonders and miracles that are beyond our imaginings. Even the dead will return to life from the dust, the seas, and ashes—not as decayed, mindless zombies, but as beautiful, magnificent human beings in the perfection of health and vitality, raised to immortality. As C.S. Lewis fancied, if you saw these resurrected creatures, *you would be strongly tempted to worship*[275] them because of the beauty and glory that God will recreate in His beloved children. On the other hand, those who spurn the call of the Messiah during their stay on this earth will be raised to judgment, disgrace, and everlasting contempt.[276]

What is this day? The Lord gave very little information about the Day of Trumpets, very little information about the activities, and almost no information about its meaning and significance. As you can see in Leviticus 23:24–25, Moses was given the date on which this Appointed Time was to be observed, and he was also told that it was to be a rest, a reminder by blowing of trumpets, and a holy convocation or gathering. The date that the Lord appointed is the first day of Tishri, which is the seventh month.

272 *Refer to the Tracking Time in Israel compendium to learn more about Hebrew months.*

273 *1 Thessalonians 4:16*

274 *The Day of Trumpets Quick Facts table can be found in Appendix E.*

275 *The Weight of Glory – CS Lewis – 1977 - William B. Eerdmans Publishing Company – p15*

276 *Daniel 12:2 - "Many of those who sleep in the dust of the ground will awake, these to everlasting life, but the others to disgrace and everlasting contempt."*

The first aspect of this holy day is a rest, a high Sabbath—the people were required to rest on this day, to honor it as a Sabbath. So, we will add the Day of Trumpets to our list as the fourth of the seven high Sabbaths of the Appointed Times.

A Reminder

But what about the other aspects of this event? What is the reminder that is mentioned? Are the people to be reminded of something, perhaps be reminded of their God? Or is the Lord to be reminded of the people? It may sound strange that the Lord would need a reminder, but we will explain the concept later.

Teruah – Shout to the Lord!

Another question that arises about this day is the phrase *blowing of trumpets*. Strangely, the underlying Hebrew word, *teruah*,[277] does not necessarily mean to blow a trumpet, even though that is certainly one way to observe it. Teruah is a Hebrew word that can mean a trumpet blast, a blast of a ram's horn, or a loud shout such as a command to attack. The word can also mean a cry of the voice with loud sounds, including loud shouts of joyful acclamation. It is even used to refer to the clashing and crashing of percussion and loud cymbals.

Based on this understanding, it would be more accurate to refer to this Appointed Time as the Day of Teruah or Yom Teruah as the Hebrews call it. You may be thinking that this distinction is merely academic, but it actually provides a valuable clue as we trace the outline of the shadow of this Appointed Time. After all, if we are studying a shadow that is not clearly defined, then we may not recognize the fulfillment when we encounter it in the Scriptures.

The Pentateuch contains one additional passage about the Day of Trumpets; it is recorded in Numbers 29:1–6. This passage provides information about the sacrifices that the Lord prescribed for this day, but it offers little or no additional information about the significance of the day or how it was to be observed.

---

277 (Swanson 1997) **9558** תְּרוּעָה (tᵉrû·ʿā(h)): *... 1. blast, ... i.e., the sound of an ancient trumpet as a signal ... 2. ... cry of the voice, loud sounds, i.e., the loud shout of the voice as a signal but no particular focus on content of the sounds ... 3. ... shouts of joyful acclaim, i.e., loud, shouting sound, likely with some meaningful words of acclaim, ... note: in context usually joyful words; 4. ... clashing, crashing, i.e., the resounding percussion sounds of large cymbals" (Emphasis original).*

"Now in the seventh month, on the first day of the month, you shall also have a holy convocation; you shall do no laborious work. It will be to you a day for blowing trumpets."

Numbers 29:1

Notice that the Numbers 29 passage also includes the requirements for a **holy convocation**, a **rest** from work (i.e., a high Sabbath), as well as stipulating that it will be **a day for blowing trumpets**. Once again, the underlying Hebrew language does not actually mention trumpets—the word that is used here is also *teruah*, which was used in Leviticus 23:24. This passage does not, however mention the idea of a reminder. So, even with the additional information, we still do not have any new insight into the meaning of this Appointed Time or how it is to be observed. It is almost as if the Lord is saying, *just wait, the meaning will become clear for you*. And it does become clear when we consider the teachings of the Psalms, Prophets, and Jesus and His apostles.

Trumpets or Shofars?

A ram's horn, which is called a shofar, was a very common instrument for signaling in ancient times. In fact, shofars, trumpets, bugles, and drums were commonly used for communication and signaling in the time of battle until the relatively recent invention of radio communication. Does the Day of Trumpets involve trumpets or does it involve shofars? The answer is *both*—let's take a look...

There is a very interesting passage about trumpets in Numbers 10:1–10, which provides a clue regarding the messianic fulfillment of the Day of Trumpets. In this passage, the Lord instructed Moses to *"make yourself two trumpets of silver, of hammered work you shall make them."* He explained how they should be used for signaling and for sounding alarms for the Israelites:

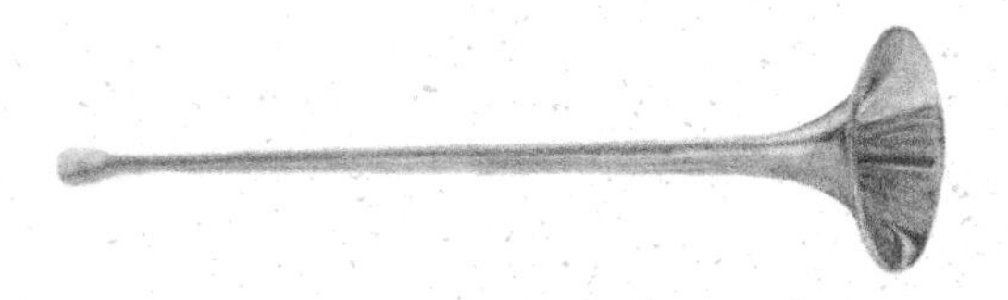

Silver Trumpet

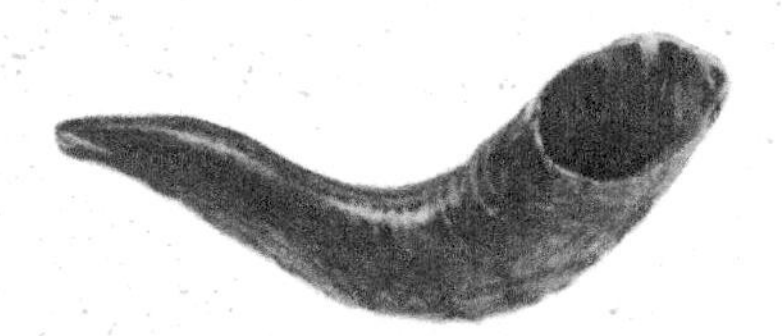

Ram's Horn: Shofar

Chapter 14: The Day of Trumpets

"The Lord spoke further to Moses, saying,
'Make yourself ***two trumpets of silver****, of hammered work you shall make them; and you shall use them for summoning the congregation and for having the camps set out...*

When you go to war in your land against the adversary who attacks you, then you shall sound an alarm with the trumpets, ***that you may be remembered*** *before the Lord your God, and be saved from your enemies.*

Also ***in the day of your gladness*** *and in your* ***appointed feasts,***
and on the first days of your months,
you shall blow the trumpets over your burnt offerings,

and over the sacrifices of your peace offerings;
and they shall be ***as a reminder of you*** *before your God.*
I am the Lord your God.'"

Numbers 10:1–2, 9–10 (Emphasis added)

Notice that, among other things, the silver trumpets are to be used in *the day of your gladness and in your appointed feasts and on the first days of your months.* It is very important to be aware that these silver trumpets were to be used in the feasts of the Appointed Times and on the first day of the month, when the silver edge moon is in the night sky. Now it becomes clear that trumpets are part of the *teruah* that was sounded on the Day of Trumpets, since it also begins on the first day of the month.

Trumpets are part of the teruah that was sounded on the Day of Trumpets

A Reminder – That You May Be Remembered before the Lord Your God

Another important purpose of the silver trumpets is that *they shall be as a reminder of you before your God.* Very interesting... a *reminder* of you before your God, rather than reminding you about God. The idea is that God will hear the trumpet sounds and be reminded of the people.[278] This passage provides additional insight into Leviticus 23:24, when the Lord told Moses that this day, the Day of Trumpets, would be for a *reminder* by blowing trumpets.

Why does the Lord need to be reminded? Does He forget about His people? In the Hebrew idiom, *remember* does not necessarily imply that someone had forgotten something. Remember can also carry the idea of giving attention to something, rather than recalling it from memory. For example, after Noah and his family had been in the ark for five months, God *remembered* Noah and all the beasts and all the cattle that were with him,[279] and He did something about it. He did not forget about Noah and just happened to remember him later. Remember simply means that He turned His attention to Noah and his situation in the ark. Similar usages of *remember* are listed below:

- When God destroyed the cities of the valley, He remembered Abraham, and preserved his nephew, Lot, from the destruction.[280]
- He *remembered* Rachel in her desire to have a child and enabled her to conceive.[281]
- When the Israelites were in agony while enslaved under Pharaoh, God heard their groaning and remembered His covenant with their forefathers Abraham, Isaac, and Jacob,[282] so He raised up Moses as their deliverer.

When the trumpets sound and the teruah rises, God will be reminded of His people and turn His attention to them.

When the trumpets sound and the teruah rises,
God will turn His attention to His people.

The Progressive Revelation of the Day of Trumpets

In order to understand the Day of Trumpets, we will explore passages in the Bible that include trumpets or *teruah*. We will give special attention to passages that offer a view of the future or *last days*, which are referred to as *eschatological* passages, as well as to those which

278 An interesting example of sounding the silver trumpets as an alarm is found in 2 Chronicles 13:13–19. In this historical event, the priests blew the trumpets and raised a war cry when their army was surrounded by the enemy. When they did so, God intervened and routed the enemy army.

279 Genesis 8:1

280 Genesis 19:29

281 Genesis 30:22

282 Exodus 2:24

seem to convey *heavenly* or *transcendent* scenes.

As God gave His Word to the Jewish people throughout the ages, the concept of *the Lord as King* began to appear in the Psalms and Prophets—a concept that was seldom mentioned in the writings of Moses.[283] The Hebrew Scriptures are filled with prophesies about the Messiah, which we mentioned when we introduced the concept of *progressive revelation* in Chapter 2, but we also find that the Psalms and Prophets are very explicit in proclaiming God as the great King.

Psalms 47 and 98 direct their praise to God our King with the trumpet, singing, shouting praises, and expressions of great joy—exclamations that clearly fall into the realm of teruah. Could these Psalms be suggesting that their events might be related to the Day of Trumpets or the Day of Teruah? Notice the different loud expressions—the teruah—as you read these two Psalms below.

*"O **clap your hands**, all peoples; **Shout to God with the voice of joy**.*
*For t**he Lord Most High** is to be feared, **A great King over all the earth**.*
***He subdues** peoples under us And **nations** under our feet.*
*He chooses our **inheritance** for us, The glory of Jacob whom He loves. Selah.*
***God has ascended** with a **shout**, The Lord, with the **sound of a trumpet**.*
***Sing** praises to **God**, sing praises; **Sing** praises **to our King, sing praises**.*
*For **God is the King of all the earth; Sing** praises with a **skillful psalm**.*
***God reigns** over the nations, **God sits on His holy throne**.*
***The princes of the people have assembled themselves** as the people of the God of Abraham,*
*For the shields of the earth belong to God; **He is highly exalted.**"*

Psalm 47:1–10 (Emphasis added)

*"O sing to the Lord a new song, **For He has done wonderful things**,*
*His right hand and His holy arm have gained the **victory** for Him.*
The Lord has made known His salvation;
*He has **revealed His righteousness in the sight of the nations**.*
*He has **remembered** His lovingkindness and His faithfulness to the house of Israel;*
All the ends of the earth have seen the salvation of our God.
***Shout joyfully** to the Lord, **all the earth**;*
*Break forth and **sing for joy** and **sing praises**.*
Sing praises** to the Lord with the **lyre**, With the **lyre** and t**he sound of melody**. With **trumpets

283 *Explicit references to the Lord as a king are found only three times in the Pentateuch: Exodus 15:18, Numbers 23:21, and Deuteronomy 33:5. The Psalms and Prophets expanded on the idea as the Scriptures unfolded.*

and ***the sound of the horn***
Shout joyfully before the King, the Lord.
Let the ***sea roar*** *and all it contains,* ***The world and those who dwell in it****.*
Let the ***rivers clap their hands****, Let the* ***mountains sing*** *together for* ***joy*** *Before the Lord, for* ***He is coming to judge the earth****;*
He will judge the world *with* ***righteousness*** *And the peoples with* ***equity****."*

Psalm 98:1–9 (Emphasis added)

Truly, the writers of these psalms were declaring the power and majesty of the Lord—power and majesty that evokes spontaneous praise and worship from all creation. In addition to associating trumpets, shouts, and general teruah before God the King, the following themes are also conveyed in these psalms:

1. The Lord is a **Great King over all the earth** (Psalm 47:2, 7)
2. He **subdues** the people and the nations (Psalm 47:3), victorious (Psalm 98:1)
3. He has revealed His **salvation** and His **righteousness** (Psalm 98:2, 3)
4. He has **remembered** His lovingkindness and faithfulness to Israel (Psalm 98:3)
5. He chooses (*gives*) an **inheritance** (Psalm 47:4)
6. He has **ascended** (Psalm 47:5)
7. ...with a **shout**, with the sound of a **trumpet** (Psalm 47:5, 98:6)
8. He sits on **His holy throne** (Psalm 47:8)
9. The **princes have assembled** themselves before Him (Psalm 47:9)
10. He is **coming to judge** the earth and the world (Psalm 98:9)

These themes certainly sound like a divine King ascending to His throne, victorious over His enemies, rewarding His servants with an inheritance, and judging those who opposed Him. And don't overlook the nobles (i.e., princes) participating in the ceremony in Psalm 47:9—a coronation?

Trumpets in the New Testament

With these ideas in mind, let's follow the theme of trumpets from the Hebrew Scriptures into the New Testament to see what Jesus and His apostles taught about them. We will focus on four key eschatological passages that feature one or more trumpets:

- Matthew 24 & 25
- 1 Corinthians 15
- 1 Thessalonians 4:13–5:11
- Revelation 8, 9, 10, and 11

And He Will Send forth His Angels with a Great Trumpet
Matthew Chapters 24–25

Two days before Jesus' Passover, the disciples came to Him privately while He was sitting on the Mount of Olives and questioned Him about future events. They asked about His comment that the Temple would one day be totally destroyed, about the sign of His return, and about the end of the age.

His response is recorded in the 24th and 25th chapters of Matthew's gospel; I encourage you to carefully read both chapters in their entirety. Among other things, Jesus warned the disciples about false messiahs who would come to deceive. But the primary focus of this two-chapter response is about the return of the Son of Man—the Messiah—coming on the clouds of the sky with great power and great glory, and how we should be ready for His return.

"For just as the lightning comes from the east and flashes even to the west,
so will the coming of the Son of Man be.

Wherever the corpse is, there the vultures will gather.

But immediately after the tribulation of those days the sun will be darkened,
and the moon will not give its light, and the stars will fall from the sky,
and the powers of the heavens will be shaken.

And then the sign of the Son of Man will appear in the sky,
and then all the tribes of the earth will mourn,
and they will see the Son of Man coming on the clouds of the sky
with power and great glory.

And He will send forth His angels with a great trumpet
and they will gather together His elect from the four winds,
from one end of the sky to the other."

Matthew 24:27–31 (Emphasis added)

As part of this great apocalyptic event, the Son of Man (i.e., the Messiah) will send His angels with the sound of a great trumpet to gather His chosen ones from every place on the planet. Did you get that? The great trumpet is the signal to begin the gathering of Christ's chosen ones—a messianic event that must be completed before the final judgment on the world. The righteous must be evacuated before the wrath begins. Does the gathering include the resurrection of the dead or are the angels only gathering the believers who are alive? This passage does not explicitly answer that question, but we will look into some other passages that make the answer very clear.

It is fascinating that the purpose of the trumpet is to signal the angels to begin their work of gathering those who belong to Christ. There is no power in the universe, satanic or earthly, that can hinder them—this is the work of the Messiah of God.

Let's take a closer look at some of the teaching and events that accompany the coming of the Son of Man. In Matthew chapter 24, Jesus began His response to the disciples by telling them that the major events of humanity, such as wars, speculations of war, famines, and earthquakes, will not be the sign of His return. No, He said, life will be moving along as usual, and these things will simply be the beginning of the events that will lead to His return.

A strange phenomenon will exist, however, and it has existed all through history, that people will hate those who follow Christ, even though His ways are loving and peaceful. Why would that be? Nonetheless, the gospel of the kingdom will be preached in the whole world as a testimony to all nations, and then the end will come. People will betray each other, many will fall away from the Faith, and many will be misled by false Christs. The world will be a real mess, and as lawlessness increases, people's love toward each other will grow cold, continuing the downward spiral of lawlessness and diluted love.

It is difficult to tell which of Jesus' comments are related to the destruction of the Temple, which occurred some 30-40 years later in AD 70, and which are related to the end times; some of His statements may apply to both. One statement that certainly applies to the end times is this:

"For then there will be a great tribulation,
such as has not occurred since the beginning of the world until now, nor ever will. Unless those days had been cut short, no life would have been saved; but for the sake of the elect[284]
those days will be cut short."

Matthew 24:21–22

It is in this context that the Son of Man will return. Do not be misled by false messiahs who deceive and mislead with their miniscule signs and wonders. When the Son of Man returns, it is going to be a cataclysmic, global event—no tricks, simply the great power of the Lord. When He returns, it will be like lightning flashing across the sky—instantaneous and wholly effective.

Jesus made it very clear that no one knows when He will return—no one knows the day or the hour; only the Father knows.[285] Will He return on the Day of Trumpets? I don't know—only the Father knows. But if the *fall* Appointed Times form a precise chronology-map in the same way as the *spring* Appointed Times, then I would believe it is so. On the other hand, I have no idea *which* Day of Trumpets would bring His return, nor do I know the time of day for His return. We are simply told to be on the alert and to be ready, because He could return at any time.[286]

Within this same context, Jesus used a parable to explain that His followers should store up treasure in heaven until He returns. The parable tells of a man who was preparing for a journey, but before he left, he called his own servants and entrusted his possessions to them so they could conduct business and give him a return on his investment.

I recommend that you study this parable carefully within its context, because the man in the parable represents Jesus before He left earth.[287] He entrusts gifts to His servants (you and me) so they can give Him a return on His investment when He returns. It is referring to the day of rewards, which follows the gathering of His chosen ones at the sound of the trumpet—a fascinating thought.

284 *"Elect" means "chosen ones"*

285 *Matthew 24:36 – "But of that day and hour no one knows, not even the angels of heaven, nor the Son, but the Father alone."*

286 *Matthew 24:42*

287 *Matthew 25:14–30*

The obvious question, of course, is, "What does it mean to gain a return on Jesus' investment in us?" That is another excellent question, and fortunately He answered it within this same context in the very next paragraph in His teaching about the Sheep and the Goats in Matthew 25:31–46. Please read this insightful passage in your Bible from this perspective.

At first glance, it is tempting to consider the Sheep and the Goats passage as a parable since Jesus used animals as metaphors. But a closer look reveals that it is not a parable—it is direct teaching from Jesus wherein the sheep and the goats represent the people who obeyed Him versus those who did not.

The celestial setting of this scene follows the sounding of the great trumpet in Matthew 24:31. Here, the Son of Man takes His place on His glorious, heavenly throne and joyously reveals the enormous inheritance for His chosen ones, which is eternal life in the kingdom that was prepared for them from the foundation of the world.[288] On the other hand, those on His left are immediately and unceremoniously sent away into eternal punishment,[289] never to be heard from again—no second chances and no opportunity for pardon.

The passage about the sheep and the goats naturally follows the parable of the man who went on a journey. Both passages teach about reward and punishment, which are themes that are also found in Psalms 47 and 98, as well as in other eschatological passages that accentuate trumpets.

What have we learned from this context which features the great trumpet? Does its teaching seem to coincide with the teaching of Psalms 47 and 98? Jesus spoke of the Son of Man sitting on His glorious throne as a great King. He spoke of gathering His chosen ones from every place on the planet—He *remembered* them and turned His attention to them, as is implied by the *remembrance* of the Day of Trumpets. He spoke of a great trumpet, angels, and events of apocalyptic magnitude, and He also spoke of eternal reward for His chosen ones and eternal punishment for those who did not obey Him. It is certainly part of the thread that began with the Day of Trumpets.

---

288 Matthew 25:34

289 Matthew 25:41

In the Twinkling of an Eye, at the Last Trumpet
1 Corinthians 15

The following words were penned by the apostle Paul, inspired by the Spirit of God:

"Behold, I tell you a mystery; we will not all ***sleep,***
but we will all be ***changed, in a moment,*** *in the* ***twinkling of an eye,***
at the ***last trumpet;*** *for* ***the trumpet will sound,***
and the ***dead will be raised imperishabl****e, and* ***we will be changed."***

1 Corinthians 15:51–52 (Emphasis added)

The context begins in the first verse of 1 Corinthians 15 and continues through the end of the chapter. It seems that doubters had arisen in the church of Corinth who were causing others to waiver in their faith. But Paul, the apostle and shepherd over this Gentile body of believers, reiterated and underscored the truth of the resurrection and its foundational place in the Faith.

"If we have hoped in Christ in this life only, we are of all men most to be pitied...
If the dead are not raised, let us eat and drink, for tomorrow we die."

1 Corinthians 15:19, 32

But in fact Christ has been raised from the dead, the ***first fruits*** *of those who are asleep.*[290] He appeared to Peter, to the twelve, to five hundred believers at one time, and to James and to all the apostles.[291] Paul continues to connect the points of the Scriptures; he refers to Adam, the first man, and how he introduced the knowledge of good and evil into the human race, which brought death to all, but in Christ, all will be made alive.[292]

And how will all be made alive? Something is about to happen—something marvelous and magnificent and unparalleled in the imagination of mankind. It is the work of the Messiah. A miraculous, instantaneous, universal event that will be initiated at the sound of the trumpet of God.

---

290 1 Corinthians 15:20
291 1 Corinthians 15:5–7
292 1 Corinthians 15:20–22

The Last Trumpet

In this passage, the eschatological event occurs *at the sound of the trumpet*, and specifically at the sound of the ***last*** trumpet. What does he mean by the *last* trumpet? Clearly, if there is a *last* trumpet, then there must be multiple trumpets or a series of them. When the Lord gave instructions to Moses about the Day of Trumpets, He said it will be a *day of teruah*, suggesting that there would be sounds and shouts throughout the day. Yet, He did not provide any information to Moses about the sounds or their order and timing. You might say that it is a mystery—*behold Paul is unveiling the mystery*.

In the book of Revelation, the apostle John describes his experience in heaven, wherein seven trumpets were given to seven angels[293]—each angel sounded in his proper order. Could it be that the last trumpet of 1 Corinthians 15:52 is referring to the seventh and final trumpet of this series? I believe it is, especially since the events that are initiated by the seventh trumpet of Revelation involve themes from Psalms 47 and 98, regarding the Lord beginning His reign, the judgment of the dead, and the time of reward for the servants of God, which are events that are highlighted in other eschatological passages about trumpets.

293 *Revelation 8:1–2*

The heavenly scene of the seven trumpets in Revelation, chapters 8–11, is the only eschatological event in the Bible where a series of trumpets is mentioned.[294] Each trumpet signals the start of an event of apocalyptic magnitude, events that could only be of divine origin. Is the seventh trumpet of Revelation revealing the messianic substance of the Day of Trumpets? We will explore the events of the seventh trumpet later in this chapter. For now, however, let's continue to learn from Paul's words in 1 Corinthians 15.

What Will Actually Happen When the Last Trumpet Sounds? We Will Not All Sleep, but We Will All Be Changed.

A euphemism? Yes, Paul is using a figure of speech that we call a euphemism, which refers to the use of a somewhat pleasant word to describe something that is not as pleasant. In this case, he is using the word sleep to describe death. It is clear that he is using sleep to refer to death, otherwise his discussion of the resurrection of the dead would not make sense. Jesus used the same euphemism about Lazarus, when He said, "Our friend Lazarus has fallen asleep," but the disciples did not understand until He plainly told them that Lazarus was dead.[295]

Paul is saying that we will not all die. Did you get that? It means that some people will still be alive when the trumpet sounds to signal the start of this magnificent event. And all who are believers in Jesus the Messiah will be miraculously changed, *gathered* by His angels, and immediately taken to meet the Lord. Not only will those who are alive be changed, but the dead will also come to life—they will be changed from lifeless, decaying corpses and skeletons into imperishable heavenly bodies that will never die.

What did Paul mean when he said we will all be changed? He is revealing one of the most amazing mysteries of the Faith—that our bodies will be miraculously changed from mortal to immortal, from perishable to imperishable. The physical, atomic structure of our bodies will be fundamentally changed in an instant by the power of God, and we will be created anew—we will never again experience pain or death. In Paul's words, the dead will be raised imperishable, and we will be changed—we were born into natural bodies, but we will be raised as a spiritual body.[296] Reintroductions will be necessary when you see your parents, children, and friends—they will look like gods and goddesses—but you might be able to recognize them by their eyes!

In Jesus' words, "...those who are considered worthy to attain to that age and the resurrection from the dead... cannot even die anymore, because they are like angels, and are

294 *Note: A series trumpets are used in the conquest of Jericho, which was a historical event, rather than eschatological.*

295 *John 11:11–14*

296 *1 Corinthians 15:44 – "it is sown a natural body, it is raised a spiritual body."*

sons of God, being sons of the resurrection."[297] Jesus was raised from the dead and given a glorified body, and all who believe will also be resurrected and given perfectly healthy, celestial bodies—we will become immortal and outlive the stars and the galaxies of the heavens. *"Beloved, now we are children of God, and it has not appeared as yet what we will be. We know that when He appears, we will be like Him."*[298]

These words of resurrection from the dead are not mere poetry or wishful thinking or pleasant sayings on a wall calendar or coffee mug that have no substance—these words are truth. The resurrection from the dead is the promise of heaven, from God Himself, to all who receive His Messiah. Now it becomes clear why Moses abandoned all of the wealth and riches of Egypt in exchange for what the Messiah offered.[299] The motivation of the martyrs also becomes clear—they saw and believed something that was far more desirable than their earthly comfort and their lives.

It sounds too fantastic to be true, doesn't it? But, once again, this will be the work of the Creator, the Author of life who originally created the man from dust. It is fantastic, but fully true. New life and living again are themes that are trumpeted throughout the entire body of the Scriptures, and they will come to pass at the sound of the last trumpet.

297 Luke 20:35–36

298 1 John 3:2

299 Hebrews 11:23–29 – especially verse 26

With the Voice of the Archangel and with the Trumpet of God 1 Thessalonians 4:13–5:11

"For the Lord Himself will descend from heaven ***with a shout,***
with ***the voice of the archangel*** *and* ***with the trumpet of God,***
and the dead in Christ will rise first."

1 Thessalonians 4:16 (Emphasis added)

As we continue to trace the thread of trumpets through the fabric of the Scriptures, we find another passage in 1 Thessalonians that speaks of something that sounds like *teruah*: the *shout* from the archangel and the sound of the trumpet of God. These words were written by Paul in his first letter to the Thessalonian church. Once again, it resounds with the certainty of the resurrection of the dead, and we find the same elements, including angels, trumpets, a gathering, and the resurrection of the dead.

Who is the archangel? What does the term *archangel* mean? The apostle Jude tells us very plainly that his name is Michael.[300] He is the chief angel, a warrior angel who heads the armies of the Lord's hosts, the highest angel in the service of God. Be aware, however, that he is not the most powerful angel; there is another majestic angel who is more powerful, but he is not in service of God. He is known as the prince of darkness, the son of the morning, the son of the dawn, the devil, and Satan, among other names.

Paul continues, telling us that the resurrection of the dead will begin with a shout from the archangel, along with the trumpet of God. The underlying Greek word for shout carries the idea of a *cry of command*. It appears that the mighty warrior of heaven is commanding the armies of the Messiah to gather His chosen ones from the four winds, from one end of the sky to the other, in a moment, in the twinkling of an eye. Will there be an angelic fight when the signal is given to gather the holy ones? Will the prince of darkness try to oppose the forces of the Lord?

We also learn from this passage that the Lord Himself will descend from heaven. Christ the King has been anticipating the arrival of His beloved children for millennia, and He will be there to joyously embrace and welcome them to their new lives. Once the believers are safely gathered into His fold, however, there are some other celestial, apocalyptic events that must be accomplished.

300 Jude 9 – "But Michael the archangel, when he disputed with the devil and argued about the body of Moses, did not dare pronounce against him a railing judgment, but said, 'The Lord rebuke you!'"

The Order of the Resurrection

Paul makes several subtle yet very important points in this passage. The first explains the order of the resurrection. The resurrection of the dead will occur immediately before the *living* believers are changed and gathered to Christ. He makes it very clear that the *dead in Christ will rise first*. He is referring to the believers in Christ who have already died—they will be raised from the dead and gathered into the sky—in the clouds—*before* the living believers.

*"**Then** we who are alive and remain*
*will be **caught up together** with them in the clouds **to meet the Lord in the air,***
and so we shall always be with the Lord.
Therefore comfort one another with these words."

1 Thessalonians 4:17–18 (Emphasis added)

Immediately after the resurrected dead are safe, then the believers who have survived to that time will be caught up together with them in the clouds. With that, the greatest hopes and joys that anyone could imagine will be realized—we will meet the Lord in the air and we will always be with Him. I can only imagine what this will be like. Nothing will ever be the same—all of the sorrows and evil that we have ever known will be gone. Looking forward from that moment onward will be the most radical paradigm shift of all time. Nothing will ever be the same.

Caught up Together

I must mention another very interesting point in Paul's words in 1 Thessalonians 4:17:

*"...we who are alive and remain will be **caught up** together with them in the clouds..."*

What does it mean to be *caught* up? The underlying Greek word[301] carries the idea of seizing and carrying off by force, or to seize something to eagerly claim it for one's self, or to snatch out or away. All of these uses of the word describe an action that is abrupt and even aggressive.

Some Christian groups refer to this catching-up event as the *rapture*, even though they concede that the word does not occur in the original languages of the Bible. But regardless of which word is used to describe the event, we must still seek to understand what Paul meant when he taught that believers are going to be *caught up together* when the trumpet sounds.

Clearly, some type of being *caught-up* or *catching-up* is going to happen to those who are in Christ, causing earthbound people to suddenly be snatched up or caught up into the clouds. Who will do the catching-up? It seems that there are only two options here. The first is that it could be an action of God or Christ resurrecting and changing the chosen ones and transferring them upward. Or it could be the *angels* of the Son of Man that Jesus spoke of in Matthew 24:31, which were called into action at the sound of the trumpet.

301 The Greek word that is translated "caught up" is ἁρπάζω (harpazo). STrong's G726

Of course, there are those who will propose a third option, which would be to deny the catching-up and the resurrection of the dead altogether, suggesting that Paul is simply speaking figuratively and not teaching a literal transition from earthly to heavenly bodies. But Paul has already addressed that idea, saying that our faith is worthless if the resurrection from the dead is not real. He went on to tell the Corinthians that the hardships and struggles that he endured would be meaningless if the dead are not raised.[302] No, Paul is not speaking figuratively—he is speaking as literally and as frankly as he can.

Comfort One Another with These Words...

We certainly grieve when death takes our loved ones. Grieving is an important part of recovering from sorrow. But grief need not be debilitating forever, we are able to comfort one another with these words of hope, and we will be able to see our loved ones again and live with them forever. The hope of resurrection is one of the crown jewels of our Faith—without it we are nothing, but with the correct perspective, there is nothing that can stand against us in this life.

Indeed, if God is for us, who can be against us? Paul encouraged us to comfort each other with these words of our imminent resurrection to eternal life, being steadfast, immovable, always abounding in the work of the Lord, knowing that our labor for Him is not in vain.[303]

The Seven Trumpets of Revelation
Setting the Stage – Revelation 8:1–2, 10:7

The fifth chapter of Revelation tells of a book in the hand of the one who sat on the heavenly throne, a book that was sealed with seven seals. No one was found who was worthy to break the seals and open the book—no one except the Lamb who stood before the throne. As the Lamb broke the seals, one by one, the events of the apocalypse began to unfold—the four horsemen of the apocalypse, the souls of the martyrs crying out for vengeance for their blood, and global terrors on planet earth.

When the Lamb broke the seventh seal, there was silence in heaven for about half an hour. Then, seven trumpets were given to the seven angels who stand before God, thus setting the stage for yet more terror and chaos on the planet and on those who did not repent of their godless deeds.[304]

---

302 *1 Corinthians 15:12–32*

303 *1 Corinthians 15:58*

304 *Revelation 9:20–21*

After the first six trumpets had sounded and their terrors filled the earth, a strong angel, who was standing on the sea and on the land, lifted his right hand up to heaven and swore by Him who lives forever and ever, Who created heaven and the things in it, and the earth and the things in it, and the sea and the things in it, that there will be delay no longer. And the angel continued:

> *"...but in the days of the voice of the* ***seventh angel,***
> ***when he is about to sound****, then* ***the mystery of God is finished,***
> *as He preached to His servants the prophets."*
>
> *Revelation 10:7 (Emphasis added)*

With these words, the Spirit makes certain that we grasp the significance of the last trumpet. Watch carefully when the seventh trumpet sounds, because this is not just signaling another disaster on the earth. Instead, it announces the fulfillment of the mystery of God as He preached to the prophets. What is the mystery of God that He preached to the prophets?

The Greek word that was translated as preached in the above passage is rooted in the same word that is translated as *gospel*. It can literally be translated as "He preached the gospel to His servants the prophets." Now the meaning starts to come into focus.

The angel refers to the sounding of the seventh trumpet as the completion of the mystery of God. As we read through the New Testament, we find that the term mystery is most often applied to Christ—the Messiah and everything He entails. The *mystery* of the Christ—the gospel—includes the virgin birth, His death, burial, and resurrection, the atonement and forgiveness of sin, the resurrection of His chosen ones, the Kingdom of God, judgment of the living and dead, life everlasting, and His reign on the heavenly throne. The mystery has been a slowly unfolding secret for long ages past,[305] but it will be fully accomplished when the seventh trumpet sounds.

305 Romans 16:25

Then the Seventh Angel Sounded
Revelation 11:15–19

*"**Then the seventh angel sounded;***
and there were loud voices in heaven, saying,
'The kingdom of the world has become the kingdom of our Lord and of His Christ;
and He will reign forever and ever.'

And the twenty-four elders, who sit on their thrones before God,
fell on their faces and worshiped God, saying,
***'We give You thanks, O Lord God, the Almighty,** who are and who were,*
because You have taken Your great power and have begun to reign.

*And **the nations were enraged**, and **Your wrath came,***
*and **the time came for the dead to be judged,***
*and t**he time to reward Your bond-servants** the prophets*
and the saints and those who fear Your name, the small and the great,
and to destroy those who destroy the earth.'

And the temple of God which is in heaven was opened;
and the ark of His covenant appeared in His temple,
*and there were **flashes of lightning and sounds and peals of thunder***
***and an earthquake and a great hailstorm.**"*

Revelation 11:15–19 (Emphasis added)

Every aspect of the gospel will be fully accomplished in the events that are initiated by the seventh trumpet blast.[306] In this passage, we clearly see teruah in the trumpet blast and loud voices in heaven. Was the teruah that was to be offered every year on the Day of Trumpets a shadow of this heavenly teruah? The fantastic events that will occur at the sound of the seventh trumpet are the messianic substance of this Appointed Time. What could be a greater act of the Messiah than His ascension to the throne as the King of the universe, establishing His eternal kingdom, rewarding His beloved followers, and judging those who opposed Him?

306 *Revelation 10:7*

The Kingdom of the World Has Become the Kingdom of Our Lord and of His Christ

When the Pharisees asked Jesus when the Kingdom of God was coming, He answered, "the kingdom of God is in your midst."[307] Certainly, the King was among them in their midst, as they were speaking with Him. But citizens of the Kingdom of God were also in their midst, including the disciples and all who had received Jesus as the Christ. These same citizens, both the living and the dead, comprise the kingdom of the world, and their souls will be united with heavenly bodies and transferred to the heavenly realm, into the kingdom of our Lord and of His Christ. He will be installed by God as the eternal King, Who will reign forever and ever, and His kingdom will be everlasting.

The Twenty-Four Elders, Who Sit on Their Thrones before God

After the seventh trumpet sounds, signaling the transition of the kingdom of the world to the kingdom of our Lord, the twenty-four elders who sit on their thrones before God will fall down in worship before Him. There is much debate about the identity of the twenty-four elders. Perhaps the most common understanding is that they are the twelve heads of the tribes of Israel and the twelve apostles of Jesus. Determining their identity is somewhat out of the scope of this book, but it is important to note that they are highly esteemed in the sight of God. According to Revelation 4:4 the elders are clothed in white garments and have golden crowns, and their thrones are positioned before the throne of God—they are nobility of the divine order.

Perhaps it would enhance your visual image if you had a better understanding of the of the ambiance surrounding the elders' thrones. When the apostle John was taken up to heaven to receive this revelation, he saw a throne standing in heaven and one sitting on the throne. He was like a jasper stone and sardius in appearance, and there was a rainbow or halo around the throne; its color was like emerald. Out of the throne came flashes of lightning and sounds and peals of thunder, and there were seven flaming lamps burning before the throne, which are the seven spirits of God.

Before the throne was something like a sea of glass, like crystal. And circling all around the throne and the sea were four living creatures full of eyes in front and behind. The first creature was like a lion, and the second creature like a calf, and the third creature had a face like

307 Luke 17:20–21

that of a man, and the fourth creature was like a flying eagle. And the four living creatures, each one of them having six wings, are full of eyes around and within; and day and night they do not cease to say, "HOLY, HOLY, HOLY IS THE LORD GOD, THE ALMIGHTY, WHO WAS AND WHO IS AND WHO IS TO COME."[308]

It was before this throne and before this glory that the twenty-four elders fell on their faces and worshiped God. This will be the scene in the throne of heaven after the seventh angel sounds. The elders will fall on their faces, saying, "We give You thanks, O Lord God, the Almighty, who are and who were, because You have taken Your great power and have begun to reign."

And the Nations Were Enraged, and Your Wrath Came

"And the nations were enraged, and Your wrath came,
and the time came for the dead to be judged..."

Revelation 11:18

Hundreds of years before Jesus walked the earth, a psalmist penned the following words,

"Why do the nations rage and the peoples plot in vain? The kings of the earth set themselves, and the rulers take counsel together, against the Lord and against his Anointed..."

Psalm 2:1–2 (ESV)

The psalmist continues, explaining that the nations are enraged because they do not want to be under the rule of God and His Anointed, saying, "Let us break their chains and throw off their shackles." Psalm 2:3 (NIV)

Why do the nations rage and why will they be enraged at the sound of the seventh trumpet? It is because their minds and hearts are tainted by sin and the knowledge of good and evil. Rather than abandoning godless passions and submitting to the ways of God, they cling to their own ways and seethe in rage against the Lord and His Messiah; their defiant ways and desires test the patience of God and will ultimately evoke His wrath. Their rebellion and unwillingness to heed the warnings of His prophets will result in a resurrection to judgment and eternal punishment.

308 The description of the throne was taken from Revelation 4:1–11 and Ezekiel 1:4–28

The coming judgment is sure, but the compassion of the Lord is great. Until the seventh trumpet sounds, He waits with open arms, offering forgiveness, amnesty, and adoption to everyone who comes to Him and receives His Messiah. Through the prophet Isaiah, He says,

"Seek the Lord while He may be found;
Call upon Him while He is near.

Let the wicked forsake his way
And the unrighteous man his thoughts;
And let him return to the Lord,
And He will have compassion on him,

And to our God,
For He will abundantly pardon.

'For My thoughts are not your thoughts,
Nor are your ways My ways,' declares the Lord."

Isaiah 55:6–8

Ezekiel echoes the compassion and mercy of the Lord saying,

"...I take no pleasure in the death of the wicked,
but rather that the wicked turn from his way and live."

Ezekiel 18:23

Those who received the Messiah, His prophets, the saints, and those who fear His name, will be honored and rewarded by the Son of Man beyond their wildest imaginings. His reward will be granted to His chosen ones in the same swift manner as the other events that follow the seventh trumpet. Some of Jesus' final words in the book of Revelation are, *"Behold, I am coming quickly, and My reward is with Me, to render to every man according to what he has done."*[309]

---

309 Revelation 22:12

The Messianic Substance of the Day of Trumpets

The events of the last days were choreographed long ago, in ages past. Does the Day of Trumpets foreshadow the final trumpet of God that will signal the culmination of our world's history and the beginning of the eternal Kingdom of God? I believe it does. On that day, the actors in the apocalyptic scene will step onto the celestial stage, eager to carry out their parts in the Lord's plan, and the mystery of God as He preached through His prophets will be completed. Indeed, the substance of the Day of Trumpets belongs to the Messiah—the sovereign player in the final events of that great day.

Chapter 15 – The Day of Atonement

The Lord spoke to Moses, saying,
*"**On exactly the tenth day of this seventh month** is the **day of atonement;***
it shall be a holy convocation for you,
and you shall humble your souls and present an offering by fire to the Lord.
You shall not do any work on this same day, for it is a day of atonement, to make atonement on your behalf before the LORD your God."

Leviticus 23:26–28 (Emphasis added)

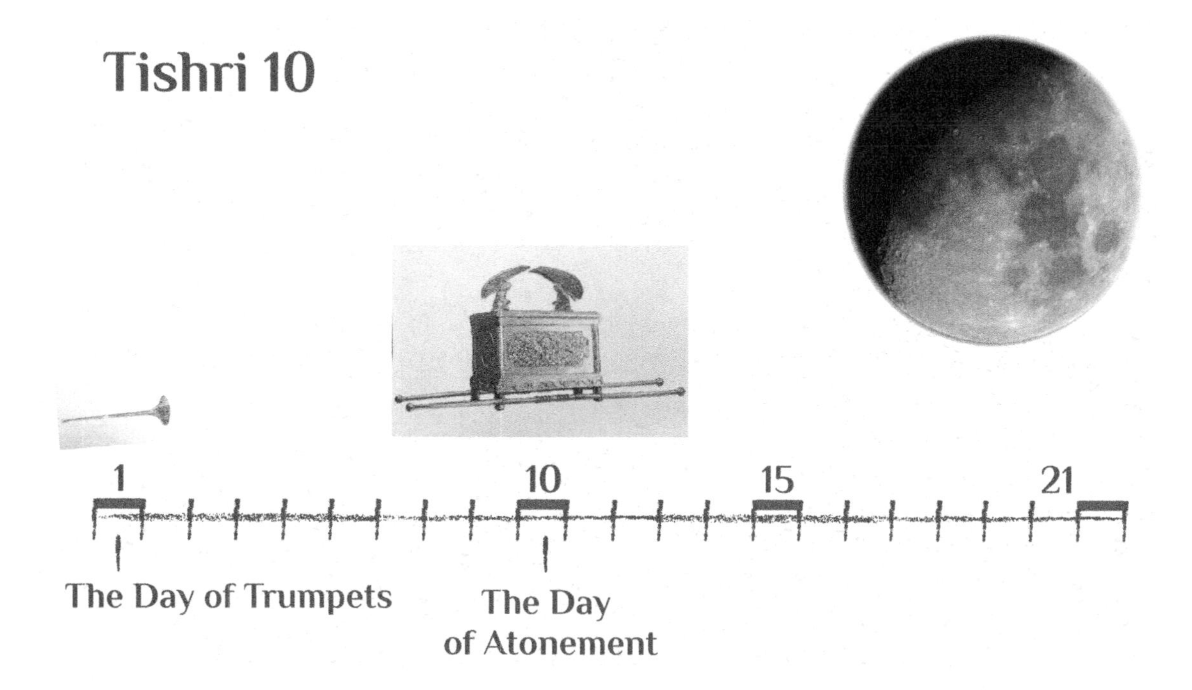

Have you ever wondered about the events that occurred between the time that Jesus died on the cross until He rose from the dead on the third day? How did He purchase men, women, and children from every tribe, tongue, people, and nation for God?[310] How did He mediate our salvation with God?

The answer to this question is found in the shadow of the Day of Atonement. As you would expect, a messianic event of this magnitude would certainly be revealed through the shadow of an Appointed Time, and it becomes obvious very quickly that there was more to Jesus' sacrifice than can be seen by the human eye.[311]

The Day of Atonement

The Day of Atonement is observed in the fall on the tenth day of Tishri, soon after the Day of Trumpets. As you see from the Lord's instructions in Leviticus 23:26–28, it is a very holy day and a Sabbath day; **it is the fifth high Sabbath day of the Appointed Times.**

There is something austere and ominous about the Day of Atonement. The Lord gave very stern warnings to those who refuse to humble themselves on this day. Those who will not humble themselves will be cut off from their people, and He will destroy those who do any work on this day; it is a Sabbath of complete rest.

"If there is any person who will not humble himself on this same day,
he shall be cut off from his people.
As for any person who does any work on this same day,
that person I will destroy from among his people.
You shall do no work at all. It is to be a perpetual statute
throughout your generations in all your dwelling places."

Leviticus 23:29–31

310 Revelation 5:9 – "And they sang a new song, saying, 'Worthy are You to take the book and to break its seals; for You were slain, and purchased for God with Your blood men from every tribe and tongue and people and nation.'"

311 The Day of Atonement Quick Facts table can be found in Appendix E.

Chapter 15: The Day of Atonement

The holy convocation on the Day of Atonement centers around a ceremony that is conducted by the high priest in the tabernacle. Every Israelite attends this ceremony, gathered around the tent of meeting; they are participants through their attendance, humility, and obedience. The high priest carefully follows the ceremonial ritual, which was defined by the Lord and is recorded in Leviticus 16. Through this ceremony, the priest makes atonement for himself, his household, and all the people of Israel.

The Meaning of Atonement

One of the first items we should address is the meaning of atone and atonement. Atone is a verb that describes the act of making things right with an offended party for an offense or crime that was committed. In order to atone for an offense, a person must make amends or reparations that will satisfy, soothe, or appease the offended party. For example, a judge might tell a person that he must atone for a crime that he committed, and his atonement might involve spending time in prison, paying a fine, or making reparations to the party that was hurt by the crime. *Atonement* is the actual reparation or price that was paid to appease an offended party. For example, a person might say that his atonement was to pay a fine for the offense that he committed.

The Hebrew word that is translated as atonement is ***kippur*** (כִּפֻּר). Thus, **Yom Kippur** is the Hebrew term for the Day of Atonement. The New Testament, however, uses a different word to express this concept; it is propitiation. Propitiation is generally understood to be virtually synonymous with atonement. For example, John tells us *"In this is love, not that we loved God, but that He loved us and sent His Son to be the **propitiation** for our sins."*[312] John is saying that God's Son is the price that was paid—the propitiation—so that we could live.

The Most Solemn Day

The Day of Atonement is the most solemn day of the year for Israel. It is not a feast day or a day of rejoicing; it is a day of solemn reflection about their guilt before the Lord. Indeed, we have seen that the punishment for not humbling themselves was very strict; those who did not humble themselves were to be cut off[313] from their people. The Hebrew word that is translated as humble yourselves is sometimes translated as *afflict* yourselves. Although it is not explicitly

312 1 John 4:10

313 (Hebrew: Kareth) "means not necessarily physical dissolution but extinction of the soul and its denial of a share in the world to come." – (Ehrman 1965) Volume 1

stated, it is widely accepted among Jewish people that this command implies a mandatory day of fasting as a means of self-affliction.

On this day, there was no place for pride or boasting, since all iniquities, transgressions, and sins were confessed before the Lord in a ceremony that would make atonement for their sins. Even the high priest wore plain linen garments instead of his normal ornate, high-priestly garments. He is the primary actor in this ceremony that God designed, entering the most holy place and standing face-to-face with the Lord.

We have seen how the Bible makes it very clear that every person has sinned. Even though an offense might be against another individual, the fact is that all offenses are ultimately against God Himself because we have violated His design for His creation. We have offended the holy God, and amends must be made. The very idea that we need atonement is truly sobering. Even though we might believe that we are good people who have never committed any heinous crimes, we are, nonetheless, guilty in the eyes of the Judge. It is not a matter of simply feeling guilty, we truly have guilt—we are guilty.

As we read Moses' writings about the Day of Atonement, it appears that the ceremony only benefitted the nation of Israel. But as the revelation of the Scriptures unfolded throughout the centuries, it became very clear that the Day of Atonement casts a shadow of a much greater event, which is the Messiah making atonement or *propitiation for our sins; and not for ours only, but also for those of the whole world.*[314] Therefore, the Day of Atonement is a very significant day that has relevance to everyone, including you and me. Because of the atoning work of the Messiah, this most solemn day will soon be celebrated by people from all nations with eternal rejoicing.

Setting the Stage for the Day of Atonement

In order to fully appreciate the ceremony of the Day of Atonement, it is necessary to explain its setting and describe the objects that are involved. I would love to provide a full explanation of the tabernacle and its furnishings, but that is somewhat beyond the scope of this book. Nonetheless, we will explore the items and aspects that relate to the Day of Atonement in order to set the stage so the ceremony can be portrayed before you with the greatest clarity.

In the background of this Appointed Time that follows, we will briefly examine the tabernacle, the veil, the ark of the covenant, the mercy seat, and the significance of the cherubim on the mercy seat. With this as a backdrop, we will follow the steps of the high priest as he leads

314 1 John 2:2

the ceremony of the Day of Atonement, as it was described by the Lord in Leviticus 16.

The Tabernacle

When the Lord conveyed His Appointed Times to Moses, the people were camped in the wilderness, looking forward to moving into the Promised Land. Their encampment was enormous, with more than two million people living in a community of temporary dwellings that were called booths or tabernacles. Soon after the people affirmed their covenant with the Lord at Mount Sinai,[315] He directed Moses to raise a contribution from the people to construct a tabernacle or *"a sanctuary for Me, that I may dwell among them."*[316] This tabernacle also became known as the tent of meeting, where the Lord met with Moses or the high priest. Figure 16 is an artist's concept of the tabernacle.

Figure 16 - The Tabernacle

315 Exodus 24:3–8

316 Exodus 25:8

The contributions for the tabernacle were completely voluntary for the people—they were not required to give anything. But the people were so pleased to have a part in building the Lord's sanctuary that Moses eventually had to tell them to stop giving because they had more than enough to complete the construction.[317] The required materials for the tabernacle included gold, silver, and bronze, along with fabrics of blue, purple, and scarlet. The fabrics were made of fine linen, goat hair, rams' skins dyed red, porpoise skins, acacia wood, oil for lighting, spices for anointing oil and incense, and onyx stones.[318] Where did they get such an abundance of fine materials? Certainly not from the wilderness. They were most likely the riches that were given to them by their Egyptian neighbors before their exodus.[319]

One of the most important aspects about the design of the tabernacle is that it is actually a copy and shadow of the things of heaven. When Moses was about to erect the tabernacle, God warned him to make all things according to the pattern that he was given on Mount Sinai.[320] In a similar way that the Appointed Times are shadows of the Messiah, the tabernacle is a shadow of the things of heaven, and it teaches certain details about heaven that the Lord wants us to know. Since shadows only present an outline of the actual object, we are spared from being distracted by the glorious details that would cause us to miss the point of the teaching.

The tabernacle itself was rather small considering that it was an earthly sanctuary for the God of the universe. Although interpretations of the design vary slightly, it appears that it was a rectangular shape, six cubits[321] wide by twenty cubits long (roughly 9 feet x 30 feet or 2.7 meters x 9.1 meters). It was covered with multi-layered curtains of goat hair, which formed a tent over the top to protect it from the elements.

It was situated within a courtyard that was called the outer court. The outer court was surrounded by a series of large linen curtains and pillars that connected to each other, forming a rectangular court. The outer court was 100 cubits by 50 cubits (150' x 75' or 46 meters by 23 meters), with a curtain that was five cubits high (7.5' or 2.3 meters). The outer court was home to the altar and the laver, which was a large basin for the ceremonial washings for the priests.

317 *Exodus 36:5–7*

318 *Exodus 25:1–9*

319 *Exodus 3:22 and 12:35–36*

320 *Hebrews 8:5*

321 *A cubit is a unit of length that was used by ancient cultures; the length of a cubit varies by culture. Scholars vary in their interpretation of the length of a Hebrew cubit, with estimates ranging from 18 inches or .46 meters to 24 inches or .61 meters. Even though the length is uncertain, it is still possible to visualize the proportions of an object if a consistent length is used for the cubit. In this book, we use the 18 inch or .46 meter estimate.*

The Holy Place

The inside of the tabernacle was divided into two distinct sections that were separated by a thick veil that had two cherubim woven into it. If you walked into the tabernacle through the outer door, you would find yourself in the section that is called "the holy place;" the smaller section on the other side of the veil is called "the holy of holies" or "the most holy place." The holy place consumes about two thirds of the tabernacle's floorspace, and the holy of holies is the remaining one third.

The furnishings of the holy place included three sacred items. The first was an ornate golden table that displayed the bread of the Presence before the Lord. The bread remained on the table at all times and was baked every Sabbath day.[322] The second furnishing was a pure gold ornate lampstand that had seven oil lamps that were continually burning. The lampstand and its base were made of hammered work, with golden cups, bulbs, and flowers that were formed into it. The third furnishing was a small golden altar that was used for burning incense, which was positioned in front of the veil that concealed the holy of holies. An artist's depiction of the holy place is shown in Figure 17.

Figure 17 – The Holy Place

322 *1 Chronicles 9:32*

The Holy of Holies

The holy of holies is the most sacred place of all; it housed only one sacred object, which was the ark of the covenant. The holy of holies was so sacred that no one was allowed to enter it— not even the priests— not even the high priest.. There was one special day of the year, however, when the high priest would enter the holy of holies, taking the blood of a bull and a goat to make atonement for the nation—**this solemn day was the Day of Atonement**.

Figure 17b – A view from the Holy Place into the Holy of Holies

The Ark of the Covenant

Figure 18 – The Ark of the Covenant

The ark of the covenant, which is pictured in Figure 18, was the only object in the holy of holies. It is interesting that it was the first item that the Lord mentioned as He conveyed the design for the tabernacle, perhaps an indication of its central place in Jewish worship. The ark might be compared to a golden box or chest; it is 2.5 cubits long, 1.5 cubits wide, and 1.5 cubits high, (approximately 3′ 9″ x 2′ 3″ x 2′ 3″ or 1.1m x .7m x .7m). Three sacred items were placed in the ark: a golden jar containing manna, Aaron's rod that budded as a confirmation that he was the Lord's chosen priest,[323] and the tablets that had the Ten Commandments inscribed on them.

The ark was designed with four golden rings on the sides. Long poles covered with gold were inserted through the rings so the ark could be carried by the priests on their shoulders. The poles were always to remain in the rings of the ark.

The Mercy Seat

We must address another extremely important aspect of the ark of the covenant—it is the cover, which is also called the mercy seat. The mercy seat was made of pure gold and formed with two golden cherubim molded onto it (refer to Figure 19). The two cherubim were to be on each end of the cover, facing toward each other. Their wings were to be spread upward, covering the mercy seat, and the faces of the cherubim were to be facing downward, perhaps to convey reverence, fear, or adoration of the Lord.[324] The reason for having cherubim on top of the mercy seat is profound and of the greatest importance for understanding the Day of Atonement.

323 *Numbers 17:1–11*

324 *The Lord's instructions for the cherubim on the mercy seat are recorded in Exodus 25:18–20*

Figure 19 – The Mercy Seat

This description of the mercy seat probably raises some questions in your mind. For example, why is it called a *seat*? It does not look like a seat. Do the angelic beings that are pictured in Figure 19 accurately depict cherubim? Did the Israelites worship the ark of the covenant in a similar way that the other nations worshiped idols? These are excellent questions, and the answers become clear in the Scriptures with a little searching. Let's begin by gaining a more accurate understanding of cherubim.

Cherubim

Clarifying the terminology is an essential first step when exploring any subject. Thus, *cherubim* is the plural form of cherub. We could say that our image of the ark shows two cherubim, with one cherub on the right and another cherub on the left.

Are the cherubim in our image accurate depictions? My answer is an emphatic, "No, they are grossly inaccurate likenesses of cherubim." Moses did not describe the cherubim who were to grace the mercy seat; the Lord simply told him to make them of hammered gold and form them as one piece with the mercy seat. Throughout the ages, people have confused cherubim with angels, and produced distorted artistic renderings that look like little babies with wings, or beautiful women or strong men with wings.

The Bible does, however, provide very detailed descriptions of cherubim, but to my dismay, I can hardly visualize them in my mind or draw them on paper or render them on a computer. So, I resorted to using an angelic being of classic style in our rendering of cherubim on the mercy seat. Please pardon my inaccuracy and please do not be misled into believing that my image is an accurate representation of cherubim. Even so, we will use these inadequate images to describe the reason the cherubim are part of the mercy seat.

Ezekiel's Vision of Cherubim

Cherubim are indeed heavenly beings, but they seem to be a different species than angels or perhaps a different class of angels. The prophet Ezekiel was given a glimpse into the heavenly realm where he saw a fantastic vision wherein cherubim were key players. In the first chapter of his prophecy, he explains that the heavens were opened and he saw visions of God.[325] In his vision, he saw an enormous storm cloud approaching from the north. The cloud was flashing with fire and glowing with bright light. In the midst of it was something like glowing metal and figures that resembled four living beings. He continues to describe the cherubim as follows:[326]

» The cherubim were living beings with human form.

» Each of them had four faces and four wings.

» Their legs were straight, their feet were like calves' hooves, and they gleamed like glowing bronze.

» Under their wings, on their four sides, were human hands.

» Their wings touched one another.

» Their faces did not turn when they moved—each went straight forward.

» Each had the face of a man, the face of a lion on the right, the face of a bull on the left, and all four had the face of an eagle.

» Their wings were spread out above (Note: just like the Lord's requirement for the mercy seat).

325 Ezekiel 1:1

326 Although Ezekiel does not identify these beings as cherubim in chapter 1, he clearly makes the connection in Ezekiel 10:20, saying, "These are the living beings that I saw beneath the God of Israel by the river Chebar; so I knew that they were cherubim."

- Each had two wings touching another being and two wings covering their bodies.
- Each went straight forward. Wherever the spirit was about to go, they would go, without turning as they went.
- In the midst of the living beings was something that looked like burning coals of fire, like torches darting back and forth among them.
- The fire was bright, and lightning was flashing from the fire.
- The living beings ran to and fro like bolts of lightning.
- A wheel was on the earth beside each cherub.
- Each wheel was of fine workmanship, like sparkling beryl, as if one wheel was within another.
- The rims of the wheels were lofty and awesome and full of eyes all around.
- Whenever the cherubim moved, the wheels moved with them since the spirit of the beings was in the wheels.
- Whenever the cherubim went, the wheels went, also. Whenever they stood still, the wheels stood still. Whenever the cherubim rose from the earth, the wheels rose with them and stayed close beside them. Whenever they stood still, they dropped their wings.
- An expanse, like awesome gleaming crystal, was spread out over the heads of the cherubim.
- Under the expanse, their wings were stretched out straight, one toward the other.
- Each one had two wings covering its body on each side.
- The sound of their wings was like a roar—like the sound of the waves of the sea, like the sound of an army, like the sound of the Almighty.

Can you picture a cherub in your mind?

Enthroned Above the Cherubim...

As we continue to explore Ezekiel's vision, we should focus on a very important aspect that could be easily overlooked—it is the awesome gleaming crystal expanse over the heads of the cherubim. The expanse was not part of the cherubim—it seems to emanate from above.

Ezekiel continues, saying that above the expanse that was over the cherubim's heads was something resembling a throne, like lapis lazuli in appearance.[327] And on that throne, high up, was a figure with the appearance of a man. From His loins upward appeared like glowing metal that looked like fire all around within it, and from His loins downward was something like fire; and there was a radiance around Him, like the appearance of the rainbow in the clouds on a rainy day. Such was likeness of the glory of the Lord. And when I saw it, I fell on my face...[328]

The prophet Isaiah proclaimed the same concept—that the Lord is actually enthroned above the cherubim.

"O Lord of hosts, the God of Israel, ***who is enthroned above the cherubim,***
You are the God, You alone, of all the kingdoms of the earth.
You have made heaven and earth."

Isaiah 37:16 (Emphasis added)

The Psalmist also exclaimed,

"The Lord reigns, let the peoples tremble;
He is enthroned above the cherubim*, let the earth shake!"*

Psalm 99:1 (Emphasis added)

Do you see the connection to the mercy seat and to the Day of Atonement? When the Lord conveyed the details of the ceremony, He began by saying,

"Tell your brother Aaron[329] that he shall
not enter at any time into the holy place inside the veil,
before the mercy seat which is on the ark, or he will die;
for ***I will appear in the cloud over the mercy seat."***

Leviticus 16:2 (Emphasis added)

During the course of the ceremony, the high priest stands face-to-face with the Lord, who appears in the cloud of smoke above the cherubim on the mercy seat. The high priest is protected only by the atoning blood.

We will explain the cloud in a moment, but it becomes very clear that the cherubim on the mercy seat symbolize the real cherubim that are underneath the throne of God. It also becomes clear how the cover of the ark of the covenant can be called a seat, since the Lord sits

327 *Lapis lazuli is an intensely blue precious mineral.*

328 *Ezekiel 1:26–28 paraphrased by the author.*

329 *Note: Aaron was Moses' brother, and was anointed as the first high priest.*

above the cherubim. Even more so, it is called the mercy seat, because the atonement that was provided by the Lord is the greatest act of mercy that has ever been demonstrated, especially when it was fulfilled by His Messiah. The ark of the covenant was certainly not an idol that the Israelites worshiped—it was a sacred reminder that God the Lord is enthroned above the mighty cherubim in the heavenly realm and could never be typified by an idol that was fashioned by man.

Are You Bothered by the Blood?

I believe it is important to take some time to address this question before we look further into the Day of Atonement. Many people in our modern world are repulsed and even incensed by the idea of sacrifice—especially by the thought of a blood sacrifice. I must admit that the idea is quite foreign to me, and I sometimes turn away from thinking about it.

Is it truly necessary for blood to be shed in order to appease God? Surely, He would not expect or demand a blood sacrifice in order to forgive the sins of 21st century humankind, would He? Wouldn't it please Him if we engage in loving deeds—perhaps if we champion the cause of the lowly and needy and help them by giving alms or leaving groceries at their door?

Do not misunderstand—giving alms and caring for the needy are of immense importance to God. But the fact is that good deeds cannot and do not atone for offenses and cleanse guilt. Let me repeat that—*good deeds cannot and do not atone for offenses and cleanse guilt*. The only thing that can appease God is if the worshipper brings the sacrifice that He stipulates, a sacrifice that is pleasing and acceptable to Him. Our own efforts and ideas about appeasing Him fall far short of His holy demands.

Good deeds cannot and do not atone for offenses or cleanse guilt....

A blood sacrifice seems like a notion of ancient, superstitious, primitive man. On the other hand, a blood sacrifice conveys the stark reality that our sins and trespasses against this holy God are not isolated to the spiritual realm. Indeed, our actions and the wrath that they will incur are very much in the physical realm—it is not merely a spiritual or ethereal issue. A blood sacrifice forces us to connect sin with death—with real, physical death.

Even more so, a blood sacrifice is a mandatory part of atonement; it is an integral component of God's holy character. It is not simply an object lesson to convince us of the gravity of our sin. The Lord told Moses that

> ***"the life of the flesh is in the blood,***
> *and I have given it to you on the altar to make atonement for your souls;*
> *for* ***it is the blood by reason of the life that makes atonement."***
>
> *Leviticus 17:11 (Emphasis added)*

If we seek atonement from God, it must be on His terms, and His terms require the shedding of blood. *According to the Law, one may almost say... without shedding of blood there is no forgiveness.*[330]

Is it possible for us to escape the impending judgement of the holy One? Is it conceivable that we could be released and set free, even though our hearts are pitted with sin? Are our hopes of having someone else stand in for us and bear our penalty simply an invention of man, or did the Lord Himself devise and provide for such a plan? Indeed, He did, and the plan for our substitute and our freedom are intimated through the Day of Atonement.

So, the blood should bother you—it is not a small price to pay, especially since the blood of the Lamb of God was shed in lieu of shedding your own blood. We may squirm inside and even be somewhat repulsed and uncomfortable as we think about it, but we must face and embrace the harsh reality that the shedding of blood is absolutely required for our atonement before God.

The Ceremony – Leviticus 16

On Tishri 10, the two silver trumpets sound, summoning the entire congregation of Israel to the doorway of the tent of meeting.[331] Whether the sun was shining or dark clouds were looming, the ceremony of the Day of Atonement had to be observed on this day. The people came with humble, repentant hearts, deeply aware of their need for cleansing before their God. The ceremony was not lengthy, but it cast shadows of an event that would, one day, be fulfilled in another realm and would be relevant to worshippers of every nation and every era. The ritual that met the eye could only be fully understood after the Messiah completed it in the heavenlies on a day that was yet to come.

330 *Hebrews 9:22*

331 *Numbers 10:3 – "When both are blown, all the congregation shall gather themselves to you at the doorway of the tent of meeting."*

The ceremony began when the entire congregation was gathered around the tent of meeting. The high priest conducted the ceremony as a perilous honor, since his life was truly in danger if he approached the Lord in a way that was not prescribed. Indeed, Moses was given instructions about the Day of Atonement after two of Aaron's sons were consumed by fire for approaching the Lord in their own way, rather than as the Lord stipulated.[332]

We have divided the Lord's instructions into seven steps, and we will follow the high priest through these steps as he officiates making atonement for the sins of the people of Israel, of this most holy Appointed Time. The details are recorded in the 16th chapter of Leviticus, which has been printed in its entirety in Appendix D of this book for your reference.

Figure 20

Step 1 – The Attire – No Place for Pride

The first item of business for this day was the high priest's attire. He did not don his normal, ornate priestly garb, which was designed for glory and for beauty.[333] Instead, he wore the plain white holy linen tunic.[334] It had four parts: linen undergarments that were worn next to his body, the linen tunic, a linen sash, and a linen turban. There is no place for personal pride or self-glorification when approaching the Lord, which is the reason for this humble, plain garb. Refer to Figure 20 – to see a comparison of these priestly garments.

In preparation for making atonement for the sins of the people of Israel, the high priest was to offer a bull as a sin offering to make atonement for himself and his household. According to the Talmud, the bull was to be purchased at his personal expense, rather than being provided by

332 *Leviticus 10:1–7, 16:1*

333 *Exodus 28:2*

334 *(Rodkinson, The Babylonian Talmud 1903) Volume 3, TRACT YOMAH (DAY OF ATONEMENT). CHAPTER IV, p. 66 – The white color of the tunic (garment) is confirmed in this passage of the Talmud.*

the congregation.[335] In addition to the bull, two male goats, preferably of similar color, stature, and price,[336] were also part of the ceremony. They were provided by the congregation of Israel, rather than at the expense of the high priest. One of the goats would be designated as a sin offering and the other would become the scapegoat.

Step 2 – Selecting the Sacrifice

The next step in the ceremony was for the high priest to cast lots, which is similar to rolling dice, to determine which goat would become the Lord's and which would become the scapegoat. The lots remove the human element from the selection process. From the book of Proverbs, we learn that every decision from casting lots is from the Lord,[337] who certainly had His hand in determining the outcome for the Day of Atonement.

335 *(Rodkinson, The Babylonian Talmud 1903) Volume 3, TRACT YOMAH (DAY OF ATONEMENT). CHAPTER I, p. 2 – The cost of the bull was paid by the priest.*

336 *(Rodkinson, The Babylonian Talmud 1903) – Volume 3, TRACT YOMAH (DAY OF ATONEMENT). CHAPTER VI, p. 87 – The goats were to be equal in color, stature, and price, both purchased at the same time.*

337 *Proverbs 16:33 – "The lot is cast into the lap, But its every decision is from the Lord."*

After Solomon's temple was completed, about 487 years after the exodus, the various items of worship became more refined, even though they filled the same function. The lots, for example, became small golden tokens, each about the size of a man's thumb, that were drawn from a lot box (Figure 21 - The Lot Box) by the high priest. One of the golden tokens was inscribed with "To the Lord," to indicate the Lord's goat, and the other was inscribed with "To Azazel," which indicated the scapegoat.[338] A token or lot was randomly selected from the lot box by the high priest and raised above the head of the goat to determine its role in the ceremony, whether it was to be the Lord's goat or the scapegoat.

Figure 21 - The Lot Box

You may be wondering about the term Azazel. It is somewhat of a mysterious name that has caused confusion about the ceremony, and thus caused the purpose and meaning of the scapegoat to become grossly misunderstood throughout the years. Azazel can literally be interpreted as goat of *removal or the sent away*, but it can also be interpreted as a name of a demonic fallen angel that is found in some ancient Hebrew literature.[339]

The distortion in the ceremony arose many years after the instructions for the Day of Atonement ceremony were given to Moses. The people came to believe that the "To Azazel" lot meant that the scapegoat was to be given to the goat demon and, every year, it was led to the edge of the wilderness and pushed off of a high cliff to its death,[340] rather than being released as Moses stipulated. Killing the scapegoat was clearly not in the plan that the Lord conveyed to Moses in Leviticus 16. You will understand how this grossly distorts the intended meaning of the Day of Atonement as we continue to explore the ceremony.

338 *(Rodkinson, The Babylonian Talmud 1903) – Volume 3, TRACT YOMAH (DAY OF ATONEMENT). CHAPTER IV, p. 58 – The goats were chosen by lots from a lot box during the temple period.*

339 *Book of Enoch 8:1, 9:6*

340 *(Rodkinson, The Babylonian Talmud 1903) Volume 3, TRACT YOMAH (DAY OF ATONEMENT). CHAPTER VI, p. 94 – The man who stands in readiness (i.e., the conductor) pushed the scapegoat down a cliff to his death.*

Step 3 – Atone for the Sin of the High Priest and His Household

Now that the stage is set, the atoning ceremony can begin. No one is allowed to be inside the tent of meeting while the high priest is performing this sacred duty.[341] The first step is for Aaron (i.e., the high priest) to slaughter the bull to make atonement for himself and for his household *before* making atonement for the nation of Israel.

Why was it necessary for the high priest to have his sins atoned before making atonement for the people? It makes sense that only a cleansed, innocent person could intercede and ask for cleansing for someone else. Certainly, the intercessory actions of a defiled, unclean priest would not be accepted by God. The Talmud recognizes this fact[342] and the New Testament book of Hebrews also tells us that "it was fitting for us to have such a high priest, holy, innocent, undefiled, separated from sinners and exalted above the heavens."[343]

A Sinful Man Standing Face-to-Face with the Lord

The high priest would then slaughter the bull and put some of the blood in a golden bowl. Before entering the holy of holies, he would take a firepan full of glowing coals from the altar[344] and two handfuls of finely ground sweet incense and then bring them inside the veil that separated the holy place from the holy of holies. After he was inside the veil, the high priest would put the incense on the glowing coals from the altar and allow the cloud of smoke to rise and cover the mercy seat; otherwise he would die.[345] Do you recall the words of the Lord in

---

341 Leviticus 16:17

342 (Rodkinson, The Babylonian Talmud 1903) – Volume 3, TRACT YOMAH (DAY OF ATONEMENT). CHAPTER IV, p. 64 – "The disciples of R. Ishmael taught: So is it right according to the law, for it is better that one guiltless should atone for the sinners than that one not yet purified from sins himself should atone for other sinners. "

343 Hebrews 7:26

344 (Rodkinson, The Babylonian Talmud 1903) – Volume 3, TRACT YOMAH (DAY OF ATONEMENT). CHAPTER IV, p. 64- "MISHNA: He slaughtered it [the bull]... He took the censer, mounted the top of the altar, and cleared the coals on either hand: taking a censerful of the inner glowing coals, then he came down again, and placed it [the censer] on the fourth row of stones in the forecourt."

345 Leviticus 16:12–13

Leviticus 16:2? He said, "***I will appear in the cloud over the mercy seat.***" Thus, a sinful man was standing face-to-face with the living God, protected only by the sacrificial blood. It must have been a terrifying experience for the high priest. He was, no doubt, filled with trepidation and anxiety in the days leading up to the ceremony.

At this point, the blood for the high priest's own atonement was applied. He would take some of the blood of the bull and sprinkle it with his finger on the east side of the mercy seat and also on the front of the mercy seat, seven times.[346] Through these actions, he made atonement for himself and for his household.

Step 4 – Atone for the Nation of Israel – The Lord's Goat

It was now time to make atonement for the people by sacrificing the Lord's goat as a sin offering. The high priest would slaughter the Lord's goat and bring its blood inside the veil. He would then apply it in the same way that he applied the blood of the bull, sprinkling it on and in front of the mercy seat. It is this act that is analogous to the Messiah entering the more perfect tabernacle that was made without hands (i.e., not by humans) and going before God the Father to obtain eternal redemption.

Step 5 – Atone for the Holy Place, the Tent of Meeting, and the Altar

After making atonement with the blood in the holy of holies, it was necessary to make atonement for the holy place, the tent of meeting, and the altar because of the impurities, transgressions and sins of the people.[347] The high priest would do so by taking some of the blood of the bull and the goat and putting it on the horns[348] of the altar on all four sides. Then, as he did with the mercy seat, he was to sprinkle it on the altar seven times with his finger in order to cleanse it from the impurities of the sons of Israel. When he finished, the next step was to offer the live goat.

346 Leviticus 16:14

347 Leviticus 16:16

348 The horns of the altar were probably not like animal horns. They were most likely pointed corners that were formed into the altar's architecture.

Step 6 – Offer the Live Goat – the Scapegoat

Now the time has come to offer the scapegoat. The high priest was to lay both of his hands on the head of the live goat and confess over it all the iniquities of the sons of Israel and all their transgressions regarding all their sins.

I used to think it would have been an impossible task for the high priest to confess the sins of millions of people while standing with his hands on the head of the scapegoat. But the people simply took the Lord at His word. So, the high priest recited the following words, believing that the Lord would be faithful:

I beseech Thee, Jehovah, they have committed iniquities, transgressed, sinned before Thee,
Thy people the House of Israel. I beseech Thee, for the sake of Jehovah, forgive the iniquities,
transgressions, and sins that they have committed, transgressed, and sinned before Thee,
Thy people the House of Israel, as it is written in the Torah of Moses Thy servant, thus:
"For on that day shall he make an atonement for you, to cleanse you,
that ye may be clean from all your sins before Jehovah."

And the priests and people who stood in the forecourt,
hearing the expressed name [of God, i.e., Jehovah]
issuing from the mouth of the high-priest,
used to kneel, prostrate themselves,
and fall on their faces, and say:
Blessed be the name of His kingdom's glory for ever." [349]

The sins of the people were conferred onto the head of the Scapegoat...

After conferring the sins of the people onto the head of the scapegoat, a man who had been designated took the scapegoat outside of the camp and sent it away into the wilderness.

349 *(Rodkinson, The Babylonian Talmud 1903) – Volume 3, TRACT YOMAH (DAY OF ATONEMENT). CHAPTER VI, p. 91 – The high priest's confession for the people over the scapegoat.*

"The goat shall bear on itself all their iniquities to a solitary land;
and he shall release the goat in the wilderness."

Leviticus 16:22 (Emphasis added)

Notice that the scapegoat did not have to die—it was set free.

Do You See It?

Think about the imagery that is portrayed in the ceremony. The scapegoat had all of the sin and transgressions of the nation of Israel conferred onto it; it was grotesquely unclean, but it was set free. The Lord's goat, on the other hand, had no sin, but it was killed and its blood made atonement for the people—the people were cleansed and forgiven by its blood in the sight of the Lord.[350]

Do you see the Messiah in the mosaic of this Appointed Time? Jesus, our high priest and sacrifice, had no sin, yet He died and His blood made atonement for our sins, while sinful people who believe Him for their salvation are cleansed and their transgressions were carried far away. As the psalmist later told us, "As far as the east is from the west, so far has He removed our transgressions from us."

Step 7 – Washings and Offering Burnt Offerings

In the final part of the ceremony, it was necessary for the high priest to care for some final details. After releasing the scapegoat, he went back into the tent of meeting and removed the linen garments and left them there. He bathed his entire body in water and put on his normal attire. He then offered the bull and the Lord's goat as burnt offerings on the altar as a sin offering. The hides of the bull and goat were then taken outside the camp and burned with fire.

The other participants also had to cleanse themselves. The man who released the goat into the wilderness had to wash his clothes, bathe his body with water, and afterward return to the camp. The man who burned the hides of the bull and the goat also washed his clothes and bathed his body with water and came back into the camp. Did you ever wonder about the washings that are mentioned in the book of Hebrews? It mentions washings in the context of the Day of Atonement.[351]

350 Leviticus 16:30

351 It becomes clear that Hebrews 9:10 is referring to the Day of Atonement, since the context, Hebrews 9:6-10, refers to the high priest entering the inner tabernacle once a year, which occurs only during this ceremony.

*"...since they relate only to food and drink and various **washings**, regulations for the body imposed until a time of reformation."*

Hebrews 9:10 (Emphasis added)

It is referring to the washings of these participants in the in this ceremony, teaching that they are rituals for the body (i.e., the flesh) until a time of reformation. That time of reformation occurred when Jesus, the Messiah, made atonement for us with God the Father.

Thus, the ceremony was finished. The Lord said, *"for it is on this day that atonement shall be made for you to cleanse you; you will be clean from all your sins before the Lord."* Indeed, the people were clean because the Lord had spoken and cannot lie. But how long did the cleansing last? Surely, every person in the assembly would have sinned at some point from the time of this cleansing until the next Day of Atonement, which was one year later. It is likely that some people sinned as they were returning to their tents after the ceremony, perhaps by coveting or lusting in their hearts. Full cleansing, eternal cleansing and forgiveness could only be obtained through the perfect sacrifice of the Messiah which was offered some 1,500 years later.

The Messiah's Atonement for Us

Do you recall that the tabernacle is a pattern or even a floorplan of the divine, royal court of God? In the heavens, the Lord is enthroned above the crystal expanse that is above the wings of the mighty cherubim, which is typified by the mercy seat of the ark of the covenant. The seven lamps on the golden lampstand symbolize *seven lamps of fire burning before the throne, which are the seven Spirits of God.*[352] Could it be that the altar of incense that is positioned before the veil represents the altar that is before the throne of God in heaven?

*"Another angel came and stood at the altar, holding a golden censer; and much incense was given to him, so that he might add it to the prayers of all the saints on t**he golden altar which was before the throne**. And the **smoke of the incense, with the prayers of the saints, went up before God** out of the angel's hand."*

Revelation 8:3–4 (Emphasis added)

In the book of Hebrews 9:1–5 the writer provides a brief review of the tabernacle and its furnishings. It is interesting in 9:5 that he describes the cherubim on the ark of the covenant as

352 *Revelation 4:5*

"overshadowing the propitiation," rather than using the term *mercy seat*.[353] His focus is clearly on the propitiating or atoning work of Christ. He continues, explaining the ceremony of the Day of Atonement:

"Now when these things have been so prepared, the priests are continually entering the outer tabernacle performing the divine worship, ***but into the second, only the high priest enters once a year, not without taking blood****, which he offers for himself and for the sins of the people committed in ignorance."*

Hebrews 9:6–7 (Emphasis added)

What is the significance of the veil and the holy place? If I understand the writer of Hebrews correctly, it seems that there is no such veil or an outer holy place in the heavenly courts—it is all one enormous throne room. He tells us that the outer tabernacle, which is the holy place, exists only for this present age in the earthly tabernacle. The purpose of the holy place and the veil are to signify that the way into the presence of the Lord had not been disclosed.

"The Holy Spirit is signifying this, that the way into the holy place has not yet been disclosed while the outer tabernacle is still standing, ***which is a symbol for the present time.****"*

Hebrews 9:8–9 (Emphasis added)

Indeed, now that Jesus, the Messiah, has paved the way into the throne room of God by His atonement, there is no longer a need for an outer tabernacle that is separated by a veil from the presence of God.

When the Messiah appeared, He entered the enormous, divine throne room—the greater and perfect tabernacle that is not of this creation. When the high priest entered the holy of holies with the blood of a calf and a goat, he stood face-to-face with the Lord in the cloud of smoke that rose above the mercy seat. In doing so, he cast a shadow of the Messiah, who entered the heavenly tabernacle and stood face-to-face with the Lord Almighty, enthroned above the living, mighty cherubim. And with His own blood, the blood of the pure and spotless Lamb of God, He obtained eternal redemption. The book of Hebrews states it as follows:

---

353 Hebrews 9:5 – This passage could literally be translated as "overshadowing the propitiation," but most Bible translations render it as "overshadowing the mercy seat," since it was beneath the cherubim.

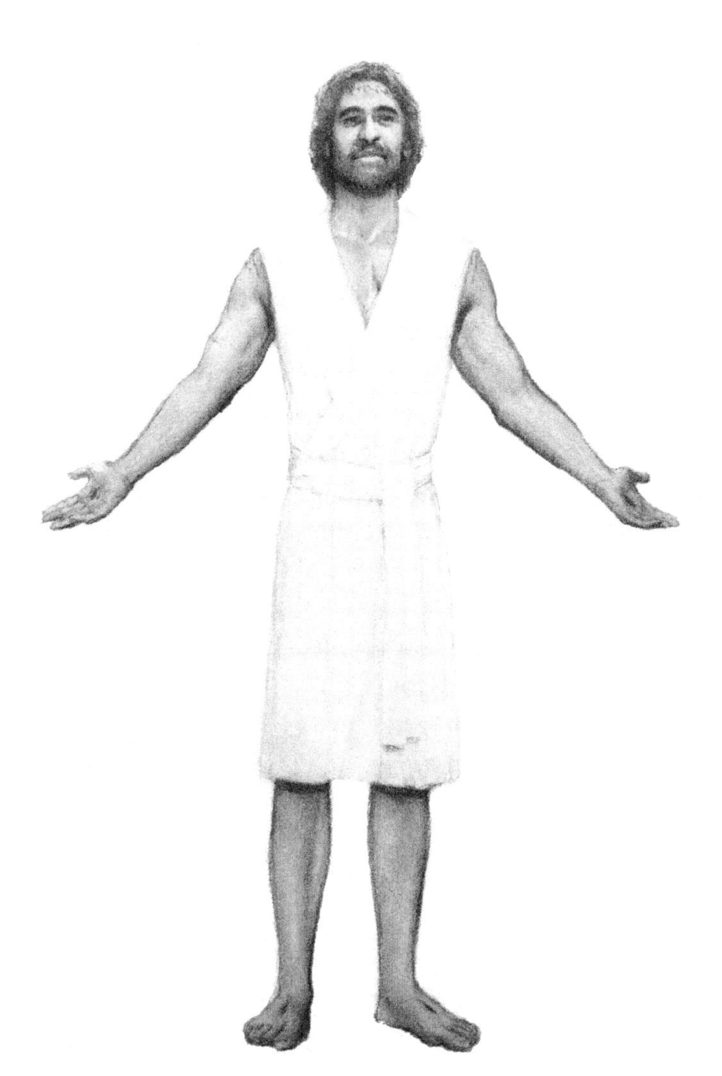

"But when Christ appeared as a high priest of the good things to come, He entered through the greater and more perfect tabernacle, not made with hands, that is to say, not of this creation; ***and not through the blood of goats and calves, but through His own blood, He entered the holy place once for all, having obtained eternal redemption.***

...

For Christ did not enter a holy place made with hands, a mere copy of the true one, but into heaven itself, now to appear in the presence of God for us."

Hebrews 9:11–12, 24 (Emphasis added)

Truly, when Jesus in His dying words said, "It is finished," He meant far more than anyone ever imagined. His atoning work was finished, because it was absolutely perfect and will never need to be repeated.

The Inadequacies of the Shadows

It was absolutely necessary for the Messiah to die to make atonement for sin, because it is impossible for the blood of bulls and goats to take away sins.[354] About a thousand years before the birth of Jesus, King David spoke of the necessity of the sacrifice of the Messiah:

"Sacrifice and meal offering You have not desired;
My ears You have opened;

354 *Hebrews 10:4*

Burnt offering and sin offering You have not required.
Then I said, 'Behold, I come;
In the scroll of the book it is written of me.
I delight to do Your will, O my God;
Your Law is within my heart.'"

Psalm 40:6–8 (Emphasis added)

The writer of Hebrews quoted David's words and continued, saying, "**...a body You have prepared for Me.**"[355] Since the sacrifices and offerings of the Law of Moses were merely shadows, they were unable to eternally forgive sin. After all, they were only intended to be shadows of something far greater. Thus, the Lord prepared a body for His Son, the Messiah, so that He could offer Himself as the perfect sacrifice and thus do the will of the Lord. And it is by this one offering of the Messiah that He has perfected for all time those who are being sanctified.[356] This is a covenant from the Lord Himself—a promise that we can trust. The Holy Spirit also confirms messianic promises to us:

"'THIS IS THE COVENANT THAT I WILL MAKE WITH THEM
AFTER THOSE DAYS, SAYS THE LORD:
I WILL PUT MY LAWS UPON THEIR HEART,
AND ON THEIR MIND I WILL WRITE THEM,'
HE THEN SAYS,
'AND THEIR SINS AND THEIR LAWLESS DEEDS
I WILL REMEMBER NO MORE.'"[357]

Did you see that? In addition to completely erasing our sins from the record, the Lord is going to write His laws on our hearts and minds. That's great news for people who believe they could not live in heaven because they have such a strong bent toward sinning. By this covenant, the Lord is promising to change us by imprinting His ways on our hearts and minds so we will not have the desire to sin anymore. Fortunately, these are not the rigid laws of Moses that no one could keep. The true laws of the Lord are summed up in the essence of love—supremely loving the Lord our God and loving our neighbor as our self. The sacrifice and atonement of the Messiah are the ultimate remedy for weary, sinful souls.

355 *Hebrews 10:5*
356 *Hebrews 10:14*
357 *Hebrews 10:16–17*

The Pure Lamb Standing Face-to-Face with the Father

I have no idea how long ago, in ages past, the meeting between the Messiah and God the Father had been planned, but I would love to have beheld the joy of that reunion as it unfolded. I imagine Jesus the Son, standing before His beloved Father on His throne, bleeding and abused, but smiling triumphantly—they had accomplished the objective that was prophesied back in the garden. The offspring of the woman had been bruised on the heel and He is now positioned to bruise the head of the serpent. Truly, the job was finished—the Son of God, the Messiah, had accomplished the redemption of the world that God so loved. This good news, the gospel, is the means through which God can justly save everyone who believes.[358]

Because of the work of the Messiah, the way into the holy place has been disclosed; it is through the blood of the pure and spotless Messiah, who *through the eternal Spirit offered Himself without blemish to God*.[359]

If the sacrifices of the ancient priests had been perfect, then they would not have been repeated every year. As the people intentionally or unintentionally stepped into sin after the ceremony, then they were, once again, in need of atonement. But the atonement that was completed by the Messiah was perfect, ongoing, and eternal. It will never need to be repeated. Thus, the work of Jesus was finished, even to the extent that He ceased His atoning work after offering one sacrifice, which perfected those who believe for all time. And He then sat down at the right hand of the Father.[360]

The atonement of the Messiah was not just significant... it is the most significant event in all human history.

We are the beneficiaries of the atoning work of the Messiah—we are like the scapegoat, the one who got away. His work was full and thorough and eternal. ***The atonement of the Messiah was not just a significant event—it is the most significant event in all human history***—even greater and farther reaching than the original sin of Adam and Eve. Paul taught us that *the free gift is not like the transgression*.

358 *Romans 1:16 – "For I am not ashamed of the gospel, for it is the power of God for salvation to everyone who believes, to the Jew first and also to the Greek."*

359 *Hebrews 9:14*

360 *Hebrews 10:12–14*

"For if by the transgression of the one the many died,
much more did the grace of God and the gift
by the grace of the one Man, Jesus Christ, abound to the many."

Romans 5:15

Like the scapegoat, we are covered with sin, but we are cleansed and set free because the Lord's innocent one willingly died in our place and made atonement for us with His own blood. The gift excels far beyond cleansing, because those who have been called will receive the promise of adoption and an eternal inheritance.[361] The atoning work of Christ is magnificent, but the judgment of Christ is terrifying. Yet, it is because of His atonement that we do not have to face His judgment. How will we escape if we neglect so great a salvation?[362]

The Offense of the Gospel

The gospel of Christ tends to offend because it claims that Jesus is the only way to God. But, now that we have a clear understanding of Christ's atonement, we can better understand the reason that it is so exclusive. It is not a matter of arrogance, suggesting that one religion is better than another. It all goes back to the precious and unique treasure, which is the blood of Christ—there is nothing else that can appease the wrath and anger of God and bring forgiveness. Giving money to the poor and doing good deeds cannot and do not atone for our offenses. Praying, burning incense, and offering sacrifices cannot and do not atone for our offenses. Indeed, there are no grand gestures that we can perform before God to earn His forgiveness. Forgiveness and cleansing come only through the blood of Christ.

Popular wisdom teaches that all roads and all religions lead to heaven, but they do not. Does it make sense now? It is not a matter of arrogance or a desire to exclude others. But truly, there is absolutely nothing—no wealth, deed, piety, etc.—that can procure forgiveness and cleansing from God. It is not arrogance—it is a matter of humility. What can be offered that is equivalent to the cleansing, appeasing blood of the spotless Lamb of God? It is a sacrifice that cannot be reproduced or equaled in any way.

When Jesus said, "I am the way, and the truth, and the life; no one comes to the Father but through Me,"[363] He was referring to the atonement that He would accomplish; it is the only way to the Father. When He said, "For God so loved the world, that He gave His only begotten

361 *Hebrews 9:15*

362 *Hebrews 2:3*

363 *John 14:6*

Son, that whoever believes in Him shall not perish, but have eternal life."[364] He was revealing how that atonement is applied to a person's life—it is applied to every individual who simply believes in the Son. "The gate is small and the way is narrow that leads to life, and there are few who find it,"[365] but you have found it.

Yes, the gospel tends to offend, but it also brings the greatest comfort and assurance through knowing that the Messiah has already obtained eternal redemption for us. We can cease our labors and striving to be righteous in the eyes of God, since the price that He demands has been paid in full.

The only sacrifice that is acceptable for atonement is the blood of Christ that was offered two thousand years ago. It is an extraordinary gift from God that must be examined and assessed with great care by every person because the way to God is indeed narrow. These are the shadows that are cast by the Day of Atonement.

364 *John 3:16*

365 *Matthew 7:14*

Chapter 16 – The Feast of Booths

Again the Lord spoke to Moses, saying,

"Speak to the sons of Israel, saying,
'On the fifteenth of this seventh month
is the Feast of Booths for seven days to the Lord.'"

Leviticus 23:33–34 (Emphasis added)

The Feast of Booths is the most festive and joyous Appointed Time of all. In this seven-day feast, the Lord commanded the people to celebrate and rejoice—not just the heads of the households, but every native-born in Israel, including the sons, daughters, male and female servants, the Levites (i.e., the priests), orphans and widows, and even people who are strangers in town.[366] *Have a great time—and that's an order*![367]

"On the ***first day*** *is a holy convocation;* ***you shall do no laborious work*** *of any kind. For seven days you shall present an offering by fire to the Lord.*
On the ***eighth day*** *you shall have a holy convocation*
and present an offering by fire to the Lord; it is an assembly.
You shall do no laborious work."

Leviticus 23:35–36 (Emphasis added)

366 Deuteronomy 16:14
367 The Feast of Booths Quick Facts table can be found in Appendix E.

This feast was an outdoor celebration wherein every Jewish household was to build a festive, temporary shelter or booth, complete with a table, food, and drink, and celebrate the blessings of the Lord their God—a perfect time for friends, family, and neighbors to casually visit and enjoy food and friendly times together. The focus of this festive Appointed Time was thanksgiving to the Lord after the ingathering of the fall harvest, but it also had a historical aspect, as the people remembered their forefathers living in booths during the exodus from Egypt.

Strangely, the Lord set the timing for this joyous feast only five days after the very solemn Day of Atonement. Why would He order His Appointed Times in such a way? Why would He so quickly move the people's focus from solemnity to celebration? Wouldn't He want the people to dwell on His forgiving mercies of the atonement and on the meaning of the sacrifices? Wouldn't He want them to muse on the sorrow and solemnity of the atonement?

These are excellent questions, but His reason is also excellent—it is because the atonement of the Lord—the shadow of the Messiah—was absolute and perfect. The atonement was so thorough and complete that the sins of the people were completely eliminated from the Lord's reckoning; all debts were canceled and all sins were forgiven. Truly, the time for celebration had arrived. When the substance of the Feast of Booths is revealed later in this chapter, the reason for celebration will become overwhelmingly obvious.

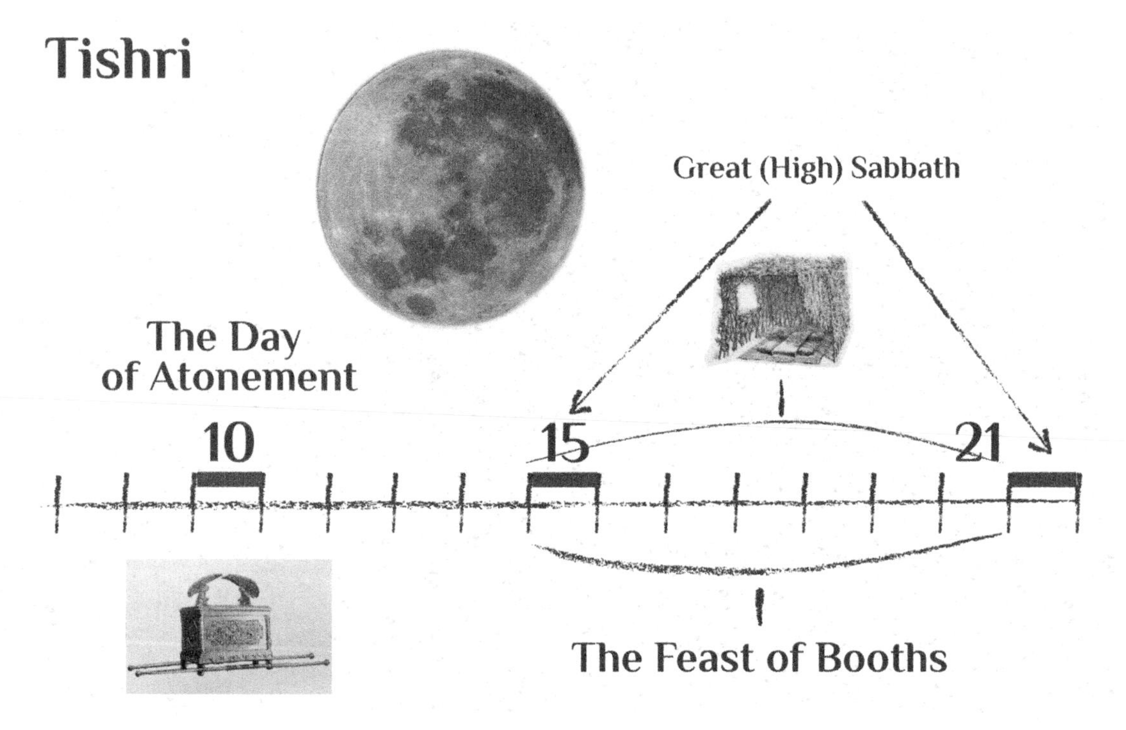

Chapter 16: The Feast of Booths

As with the other Appointed Times, we will begin with the chronological listing in Leviticus 23 and then explore the other writings of Moses to see what we can learn about this feast. The Feast of Booths is described in verses 33–43; let's begin in verse 39:

*"On exactly the **fifteenth day of the seventh month**,*
when you have gathered in the crops of the land,
*you shall celebrate the feast of the Lord **for seven days**,*
*with a **rest on the first day** and a **rest on the eighth day**.*
Now on the first day you shall take for yourselves the foliage of beautiful trees, palm branches and boughs of leafy trees and willows of the brook,
and you shall rejoice before the Lord your God for seven days.
You shall thus celebrate it as a feast to the Lord for seven days in the year.
It shall be a perpetual statute throughout your generations;
you shall celebrate it in the seventh month.
You shall live in booths for seven days; all the native-born in Israel shall live in booths, so that your generations may know that I had the sons of Israel live in booths when I brought them out from the land of Egypt. I am the Lord your God."

Leviticus 23:39–43 (Emphasis added)

The Timing of the Feast of Booths

Notice, first of all, that the Feast of Booths, which is sometimes called the Feast of Tabernacles or the Feast of the Ingathering,[368] occurs in the fall during the seventh month of the year, which is in the September-October timeframe. It begins on Tishri 15 and lasts for seven days, the fifteenth through the twenty-first of the month.

Recall that the Feast of Unleavened Bread began with a high Sabbath on the first of its seven days, and it ended with a high Sabbath on its seventh day. It is interesting, however, for the Feast of Booths, the Lord stipulated a high Sabbath on the first day, but the ending high Sabbath was observed on the *eighth day*, which is *after* the conclusion of the seven-day feast. What is His reason for that? The answer will become obvious as we explore and gain deeper understanding of this Appointed Time.

Since this *outdoor* feast begins on the fifteenth of the month, the people could have the

368 *Exodus 23:16, 34:22*

beautiful and natural illumination of a full moon at the beginning of the feast if the weather permitted. Perhaps the Lord's reason for the timing of this feast was to provide a special accent light in the heavens for His people during this joyous celebration. Notice also in the above passage that this feast was timed after the crops had been gathered in, which provided an additional level of gratification for the people, since they would have rest from their labors and provision for their future needs.

A Historical Commemoration

In addition to being a harvest celebration, the Feast of Booths also has a historical component, commemorating the exodus by having the people live in booths, or temporary shelters, as their ancestors did when they left Egypt. In Leviticus 23:43, the Lord said, "*...so that your generations may know that I had the sons of Israel live in booths when I brought them out from the land of Egypt.*" Thus, in a similar way that the spring Appointed Times were reminders of historical events, so the Feast of Booths was a reminder of the difficult living conditions during the exodus.

Moses included a very important ingredient in the Feast of Booths that occurred every seventh year. In Deuteronomy 31:10–13, we read:

"Then Moses commanded them, saying, 'At the end of every seven years,
at the time of the year of remission of debts, ***at the Feast of Booths,***
when all Israel comes to appear before the Lord your God at the place which He will choose,
you shall read this law in front of all Israel in their hearing.
Assemble the people, the men and the women and children and the alien who is in your town,
so that they may hear and learn and fear the Lord your God,
and be careful to observe all the words of this law.
Their children, who have not known, will hear and learn to fear the Lord your God,
as long as you live on the land which you are about to cross the Jordan to possess.'"

The reason for this commandment is clear—every person in the land, even the alien, must learn the laws of the Lord. They must hear and learn and fear the Lord, observing the details of His ways. Is the idea of fearing the Lord a negative concept? Perhaps, but it is necessary, in the same way that it is necessary to teach people to fear or respect fire, or raging waters or electricity. Thus, the public reading of the Law of the Lord every seventh year was a very healthy thing for everyone in the land of Israel.

What Is a Booth?

Let's begin by clarifying the terminology. The Hebrew word for booth is ***sukkah***, and the plural is ***sukkot***. Thus, people frequently refer to the Feast of Booths as simply Booths or Sukkot.

You may be wondering, what is a *sukkah*? A sukkah, which is sometimes referred to as a tabernacle, is a temporary dwelling or shelter. During the time of the exodus, sukkot were used to provide privacy for the Israelites as they journeyed through the wilderness. Since the people did not have nylon or canvas tents, they constructed shelters from the provisions of nature that were freely available. In the Leviticus 23 passage that we cited earlier, we learn that sukkot were covered with *"the foliage of beautiful trees, palm branches and boughs of leafy trees and willows of the brook,"*[369] which could provide some privacy for each family. During the feast, every household was required to construct a similar temporary dwelling to remind the people of the hardships that their ancestors endured.

You may have noticed in Leviticus 23:41 that the Lord said, *"It shall be a perpetual statute throughout your generations..."* By this, He means that every Israelite must celebrate the Feast of Booths every year, even in our current modern times. Are sons of Israel still following this commandment? Yes, indeed, in various places around the world, you can find these festive booths with obedient people celebrating as the Lord commanded 3,500 years ago. You will find people eating, relaxing, praying, reading, and visiting with each other in their sukkot during the feast. Once again, the focus of this celebration and rejoicing is on the goodness of the Lord—it is truly a feast of thanksgiving to God.

During the time of Nehemiah, people constructed their sukkot on rooftops, in their courtyards, in the public square at the city gates, and even in the courts of the house of God. Everyone who returned from the captivity in Babylon made booths and lived in them for this Appointed Time—it was a time of great rejoicing.[370]

The Talmud teaches that the roof of the sukkah should be made of leafy, organic materials. The Law of Moses allows some latitude for the types of materials, saying the foliage of beautiful trees, and he goes on to provide examples of palm and willow branches. Recall the words from our passage in Leviticus 23.

---

369 Leviticus 23:40

370 (Rodkinson, The Babylonian Talmud 1903) – Volume 4, TRACT SUCCAH, Chapter I, p. 8 – Stipulates that the minimum length of a sukkah wall must be one span. The definition of a span is somewhat ambiguous in in the Talmud, but the width of a hand (palm-width) seems to be typical.

God Reigns

Chapter 16: The Feast of Booths

"Now on the first day you shall take for yourselves the foliage of beautiful trees, palm branches and boughs of leafy trees and willows of the brook..."

Leviticus 23:40

In the eighth chapter of Nehemiah, we read that the people celebrated the Feast of Booths by building their sukkot with various types of olive branches, myrtle, and palm branches.

"Go out to the hills,
and bring olive branches and wild olive branches,
myrtle branches, palm branches and branches of other leafy trees,
to make booths, as it is written."

Nehemiah 8:15

Notice in these two passages that, in addition to allowing latitude regarding the types of branches and boughs, there was also liberty regarding *where* the materials were found—in these cases they were from brooks and the hills. The variety and location of boughs did not seem to be an issue, as long as they were leafy foliage that could provide privacy and protection for the occupants. It does, however, seem to be important that *living* materials were the primary construction material of the booths.

The Substance of the Feast of Booths – Taking up Residence

As we have seen, one of the purposes of the Feast of Booths is for the Israelites to commemorate the difficulties that were faced by their ancestors when they lived in booths during their exodus from Egypt. Since the substance of the Appointed Times are about the Messiah, we must ask: What imagery comes to mind through the Feast of Booths as we see a joyous multitude taking up residence with celebration and giving thanks to God? Is there a similar messianic event on the horizon that has these same characteristics? Indeed, there is—something of messianic significance that is far greater than the annual rehearsal of the actual event. I have come to the conclusion that the Feast of Booths is a shadow of Messiah the King, taking up residence in the heavenly Jerusalem, and those whom He redeemed taking up residence in the eternal homes that He prepared for them.

So you want to build a sukkah...

Yes, I can certainly understand why a person would want to enjoy outdoor feasting and celebration with family and friends for seven days, especially as a way of honoring and giving thanks to the Lord. The Scriptures provide a list of required materials that are to be used for a sukkah, but we can gain some additional information from the Jewish traditions that are recorded in the Talmud.

According to the Talmud, it is not necessary for a sukkah to be constructed entirely from scratch. It is permissible to use two walls of an existing building and then add a temporary third or fourth wall. But you must choose your location carefully, since there must be an unobstructed view of the sky and the stars when you look upward from inside of your sukkah. This means that it must be built outdoors and not underneath a tree or any other structure. After you have built your structure, you may cover the roof and walls with branches and boughs of leafy foliage.

It is necessary for a sukkah to have at least three walls, but the third wall can be very small, approximately three to five inches wide (i.e., eight–thirteen centimeters). The purpose of a sukkah is to provide protection from the sun, wind, and rain, which was also the need for the sojourners during the exodus. One of the primary requirements is that the sukkah provide more shade during the day than the amount of sunlight it allows to enter.

The sukkah must be large enough to accommodate a table and chairs that are large enough for a family, but it is permissible for a single-person sukkah to be much smaller. Since the Feast of Booths is a true celebration, people frequently decorate their sukkah with harvest-themed posters, decorative lighting, and other special accents to make it a festive, temporary home. After all, this is to be their accommodation for seven days, so it is fitting to make it an enjoyable part of their celebration.

The Seventh Sabbath – Eternal Life

There is another clue in the Lord's instructions for this feast that hints at our eternal rest in heaven. Recall that this seven-day feast has a Sabbath on the first day, but the Lord also prescribed a Sabbath day *after* the feast ends. What might He be intimating by this? Is it possible that it represents the eternal rest and eternal life that He promises to the redeemed? The final Sabbath rest begins *after* the feast ends; it does not end with the feast. It is separate from it and, in a figurative way may suggest that this Sabbath rest is on-going and eternal. The Sabbath is the starting place of the eternal rest and eternal life.

The fourth chapter of Hebrews focuses on the eternal rest that the Lord offers to those who believe. As we learned from The Sabbath Shadow section in Chapter 3 – The Sabbath Day, this rest refers to the eternal rest of the Lord. Someone might suggest that the rest was simply referring to the rest that the Israelites found by entering the Promised Land, which Joshua won through the conquest of the land. But the writer of Hebrews reminds us that even after Joshua's conquest, the Lord spoke of another day—another rest even after the time of Joshua.[371] *So there remains a Sabbath rest for the people of God.*[372] It follows that the Sabbath that is observed after the Feast of Booths is a shadow of eternal life and rest in heaven.

The Lord Taking up Residence in the Temple

Do the Scriptures hold other hints that *taking up residence* might be the essence of the Feast of Booths? Consider this: as they journeyed, the Israelites of the exodus took up residence in their sukkot during their years in the wilderness. By observing the Feast of Booths, the following generations were to remember their difficulties by taking up residence in their own sukkot. But what about the earthly residence of the Lord? The tabernacle that Moses built was a temporary dwelling for the Lord until a permanent house could be built,[373] and roughly 500 years after the exodus, King Solomon completed the construction of the Temple and dedicated it as the Lord's dwelling place.[374] The design of the Temple was a similar pattern as the tabernacle which was given to Moses, but it was a permanent, magnificent structure in Jerusalem.

---

371 Hebrews 4:8 – "For if Joshua had given them rest, He would not have spoken of another day after that."

372 Hebrews 4:9

373 Just so you know, the Lord did not take up residence in the tabernacle during the Feast of Booths; Exodus 40:17 clearly sets that date as the first day of the first month (i.e., Abib 1) of the second year.

374 2 Chronicles 6:2 – "I have built You a lofty house, And a place for Your dwelling forever."

When it was completed, Solomon assembled the heads of the tribes of Israel—the elders of Israel—in Jerusalem for the purpose of transferring the ark of the covenant to its new, permanent home. The Scriptures give a very interesting insight about this event:

"All the men of Israel assembled themselves to the king
at the feast, that is in the seventh month.
Then all the elders of Israel came, and the Levites took up the ark.
They brought up the ark and the tent of meeting
and all the holy utensils which were in the tent;
the Levitical priests brought them up."

2 Chronicles 5:3–5 (Emphasis added)

Did you notice the timing?

This event occurred during the feast in the seventh month, which is the Feast of Booths.

The narrative continues, explaining how the ark was placed in the new holy of holies, underneath the wings of cherubim that had been crafted for the Temple. After the ark was in place, King Solomon, along with all the congregation of Israel, sacrificed so many sheep and oxen that they could not be counted.

Then Solomon took his place on a special platform that had been set in the midst of the court of the Temple, knelt, and spread out his hands in prayer toward heaven, to the God of his fathers, in the presence of the entire assembly of Israel. His prayer was genuine and from a humble heart, steeped in God's wisdom; giving praise, confessing sin, and asking that the Lord be attentive to the person who prays toward this house, both the people of Israel and the foreigner, and that He grant their requests.[375] When Solomon had finished praying, fire came down from heaven and consumed the burnt offering and the sacrifices, and the glory of the Lord filled the house.[376] Would it be correct to say that the Lord took up residence in this earthly home **during the Feast of Booths**? Indeed, He did.

When Solomon had finished praying, **fire came down from heaven** and consumed the burnt offering and the sacrifices, and the **glory of the Lord filled the house**.

2 Chronicles 7:1 (Emphasis added)

375 *King Solomon's prayer of dedication for the Temple is recorded in 2 Chronicles 6:12–42 and 1 Kings 8:22–53.*
376 *2 Chronicles 7:1–3*

The Lord took up residence in His house during the Feast of Booths in the year the Temple was dedicated. The Scriptures refer to the Temple as the *house* of the Lord, which also carries the idea of residence. The prophet Ezekiel also records the sad day when the glory of the Lord departed from the Temple because it had been deeply profaned by the iniquities of the people.[377]

In My Father's House Are Many Dwelling Places

Almost one thousand years after the Temple was dedicated by Solomon, the disciples were together in the upper room for the last supper. They questioned Jesus about where He was going, and He responded, *"Where I go, you cannot follow Me now; but you will follow later."*[378] After a brief correction of Peter,[379] Jesus went on to say,

"In My Father's house are many dwelling places; if it were not so, I would have told you; for I go to prepare a place for you. If I go and prepare a place for you, I will come again and receive you to Myself, that where I am, there you may be also."

John 14:2–3

In these words, the Messiah Himself introduced the subject of taking up residence. His words offer insight into two residences: the Father's house and the dwelling places that the Son is preparing for His followers. What is the Father's house and what are the dwelling places that He's referencing? Let's continue to explore...

Revelation 21 and 22

Jesus frequently taught about eternal wealth and how His followers should store up treasure in heaven so they will have an abundance when they arrive,[380] but He did not provide nearly as much information about their eternal dwellings or the paradise in which they would live. After He ascended to heaven, however, He allowed one of His angels to guide the apostle John on a personal tour of the new heavenly home; the fantastic sights are recorded in the 21st and 22nd chapters of the book of Revelation.

377 *Ezekiel 10:1–19*

378 *John 13:36*

379 *John 13:37–38*

380 *Matthew 6:19–21, 13:44–46, 25:14–30, Mark 8:36, 10:28–31, Luke 16:1–14, 19:11–27*

These two chapters were written with a very different tone than the previous chapters of the book. All the apocalyptic nightmares had ended, and a new world had been brought into existence, designed for the ultimate Sabbath rest of peace and righteousness. Without question, the centerpiece of this new world is the throne of God and the Lamb in the tabernacle of God.[381] The throne is situated in the beautiful, magnificent city—the heavenly Jerusalem. Could this pristine dwelling be the fulfillment of the shadow that is cast by the Feast of Booths? Were the dwelling places that Jesus is preparing for His loved ones part of this tabernacle? Let's follow John on his tour of this dwelling and try to imagine the things he beheld.

The scene in John's vision opens immediately after the righteous judgment of God had thrown those whose names were not written in the book of life into the lake of fire—the same lake of fire in which the devil, the beast, and the false prophet had been thrown, to be tormented forever and ever. If you glance back at Revelation 20:11, you will see that our current planet Earth and its heavens had also been completely destroyed, as they fled from the presence of the one who sat on the great white throne. They were gone, but had been replaced with a new, uncorrupted planet Earth that is the dwelling place of the Lord and His people.

Note to the Reader

Dear reader—in the following pages of this chapter, I have presented what I believe to be the fulfillment of the Feast of Booths, which is heaven, as described in the 21st and 22nd chapters of Revelation. I have done my best to present the teaching of these chapters as faithfully as possible, although I have ordered them somewhat differently by combining related subjects, rather than following the order in which they were presented in Revelation. In doing so, I believe that I have maintained the original, intended meanings of the prophecy.

The following pages also contain some speculation and conjecture, which are my own guesswork about how the pieces of the prophetic puzzle might fit together. In these cases, I have indicated when I am guessing or speculating, so you will not be misled into thinking that these are the exact teachings of the Scriptures. We might call these the products of a sanctified imagination within the bounds of the Scriptures. I believe we are on the right track, but I strongly encourage you to study the scriptural account on your own to verify my conclusions. May God bless you as you study.

381 *Revelation 22:3*

As Beautiful as a Bride

Revelation 21 records John's words as if he were approaching this new planet from a distance:

"Then I saw a new heaven and a new earth; for the first heaven and the first earth passed away, and there is no longer any sea. And I saw the holy city, new Jerusalem, coming down out of heaven from God, made ready as a bride adorned for her husband."

Revelation 21:1–2

Doesn't it seem strange that a city was coming down from heaven? Was it levitating in the skies? Nonetheless, at that point, John heard a loud voice from the throne, saying,

*"...Behold, **the tabernacle of God** is among men, and He will dwell among them, and they shall be His people, and God Himself will be among them,"*

Revelation 21:3 (Emphasis added)

What an amazing change from the current relationship between God and man. Imagine the Almighty God, the Creator, dwelling among us and being accessible to us. Once again, we see an event of messianic magnitude that is foreshadowed by an Appointed Time—the Messiah and those whom He redeemed taking up residence in the eternal dwellings.

Do you remember the scene at Mount Sinai, when the people were terrified when the Lord descended on the mountain in a thick cloud of smoke with thunder and lightning? They begged Moses to talk with God on their behalf because they were filled with the terror of His presence.[382] But in the heavenly Jerusalem, everything has changed; the people are actually able to see the face of God,[383] and He will tenderly wipe every tear from their eyes. Because of the cleansing atonement of the Messiah, the redeemed can stand confidently before Him with their souls and consciences washed as white as snow.

Notice that the dwelling of God is referred to as a *tabernacle*. The Greek word for tabernacle, (σκηνή - skēnē), refers to a concept that you already know. In the Greek translation of the Hebrew Scriptures,[384] the same word is used in Leviticus 23 for booth regarding the Feast of Booths. Of course, it can be used to refer to the tabernacle that the Lord instructed Moses to build, but it also can refer to a tent or tabernacle that is *made of green boughs or skins or other materials*.[385] Does the idea of a sukkah come to mind? This is certainly not a conclusive argument, but we will return to it later with some additional information.

Tears in Heaven?

The voice from the throne continues to describe the new world that God created:

"and He will wipe away every tear from their eyes;
and there will no longer be any death;
there will no longer be any mourning, or crying, or pain;
the first things have passed away."

Revelation 21:4

Why would the people have tears in their eyes if there will no longer be any mourning or crying or pain? Tears of joy, perhaps? Or could it be that some of these people are grieving

382 *Exodus 20:18–19*

383 *Revelation 22:4*

384 *The Septuagint, also called the LXX*

385 *(Unger 1957, 1961, 1962, 1982) – p1059*

because they had loved ones from the previous earth who were cast into eternal punishment? The Scriptures do not provide a direct answer to this question, so we can only speculate, but it is clear that God will be a tender, loving Father who will comfort and wipe every tear of His beloved children. Do the words of Jesus make sense in this light? *Blessed are those who mourn, for they shall be comforted.*[386] When you muse on the beatitudes of Jesus in Matthew 5:3–12, you will see that every one of them is fulfilled in the eternal kingdom of God—I recommend that you read them again with this in mind.

Can you imagine a world where there is no death? We will have time in abundance, literally all the time in the world. This will change the way that we live in profound ways. There will no longer be looming thoughts of dying someday, no more dread, no more fear of walking through the valley of the shadow of death. People might spend their days and months enjoying extended visits with loved ones or enjoying excursions to exotic places on the new earth. Don't worry, you will not be leaving your friends forever—they will still be around! The absence of death and pain will also eliminate mourning and the tears that accompany it. Indeed, the first things have passed away—what a beautiful world it will be!

The words of John continue:

"And He who sits on the throne said, 'Behold, I am making all things new.'
And He said, 'Write, for these words are faithful and true.'"

Revelation 21:5

The Lord is making all things new, including a new, uncorrupted planet with a pristine ecosystem in which His people can flourish. All of the damage that has plagued our current planet because of God's judgment and man's folly will be undone.

A Tour of the Dwelling Place of God

Imagine this...

"...you have come to Mount Zion and to the city of the living God,
the heavenly Jerusalem, and to myriads of angels,
to the general assembly and church of the firstborn who are enrolled in heaven,
and to God, the Judge of all, and to the spirits of the righteous made perfect,
and to Jesus, the mediator of a new covenant, and to the sprinkled blood..."

Hebrews 12:22–24

386 *Matthew 5:4*

You are about to enter the city of God, the heavenly Jerusalem. Myriads of angels will be walking among us on the streets of gold. Myriads of believers—those redeemed by the Lamb—will reside here, in their homes, as citizens of this magnificent metropolis. And greatest of all, God, the righteous judge and Father of all, will dwell with us in this celestial tabernacle.

John's tour of the tabernacle of God begins in Revelation 21:9. As we read his words, try to envision what he saw and experienced, and develop an image in your mind:

"Then one of the seven angels
who had the seven bowls full of the seven last plagues came and spoke with me, saying,
'Come here, I will show you the bride, the wife of the Lamb.'
And he carried me away in the Spirit to a great and high mountain,
and showed me the holy city, Jerusalem, coming down out of heaven from God,
having the glory of God.
Her brilliance was like a very costly stone, as a stone of crystal-clear jasper."

Revelation 21:9–11

This passage contains some strange and mysterious words. Are we to understand that the bride, the wife of the Lamb (i.e., the wife of Christ), is a city? Or is it possible that the angel is saying that the wife of Christ resides *within* the city and he will lead us to her on this tour?

Recall that Paul, on several occasions, used marriage to describe the relationship between Christ and the church.[387] For example, in 2 Corinthians 11:2, he said, *"For I am jealous for you with a godly jealousy; for I betrothed you to one husband, so that to Christ I might present you as a pure virgin."* So it is reasonable to understand that the angel is leading John to the bride, to redeemed believers, where they are residing in the magnificent city that Christ prepared for them. We will encounter these people—this bride—in a few verses.

Notice that the angel carried John away in the Spirit to a great and high mountain so he could view the new Jerusalem. Will there really be mountains in heaven? Since we were told that this is a new, physical planet earth, then the idea of having real mountains is quite plausible. From this we can infer that heaven is much more than clouds and harps, as some would have us believe. John is describing a paradise, a very real, physical planet that will be the new home of humanity. As we follow John and the angel on this tour, we will see many more beautiful adornments that will help shape our understanding of heaven.

As he looked upon the city from the mountain, he described it as if there was an aura about her: *"Her brilliance was like a very costly stone, as a stone of crystal-clear jasper."*

387 See also: Ephesians 5:25, 32

Indeed, there is a very real glow that emanates from her, as we will see later. This city is beyond extraordinary. The material of the city was pure gold, like clear glass, and the material of the wall was pure jasper.[388] Can you see it in your mind? Let's join John's tour to get a clearer mental image.

The Holy City

As he approached the outskirts of the city, John was clearly amazed at her immensity and beauty. The heavenly Jerusalem was surrounded by a magnificent wall that apparently astounded him, since he gave us so much detail about it. Let's begin by examining the dimensions of the city, its gates, and its wall.

"The angel who talked with me had a measuring rod of gold to measure the city, its gates and its walls. The city was laid out like a square, as long as it was wide. He measured the city with the rod and found it to be 12,000 stadia in length, and as wide and high as it is long."

Revelation 21:15–16 (NIV)

The city was measured at 12,000 stadia long and 12,000 stadia wide... What are stadia? As always, we will clarify the terms: *stadia* is the plural form of stadion, and one stadion is approximately 600 feet or 183 meters. When you do the math, you will find that the city is a square that is approximately 1,364 miles long and 1,364 miles wide (approximately 2,200 kilometers by 2,200 kilometers). For the purpose of comparison, it is almost half the land area of the United States of America or almost half the land area of the nation of China. And remember that this is a city—it is not a country or a state or a province. It is enormous!

You may be thinking, however, that these measurements must be different than human measurements, but John anticipated that objection. In verse 17, he explicitly says that human measurements are a*lso angelic measurements* (NASB).

388 Revelation 21:18

Can It Be?

But the unimaginable aspect is that the city is as high as it is wide—it extends more than 1,300 miles (2,200 kilometers) from space down to earth, from far above earth's atmosphere. Can you picture that? It is interesting to search the Internet for images of the new Jerusalem. Some artists depict it as a cube or a pyramid or a dome, while others as a tall, pointed structure. But John did not describe the city as actually resting on the surface of the earth. Instead, he described it *as coming down out of heaven from God.*

Does the new Jerusalem actually rest on the surface of the earth? I cannot say for sure, although the wall that surrounds the city most certainly rests on the earth since it has foundation stones. But what is the composition of the city? What extends 12,000 stadia from heaven down to earth?

Perhaps we can learn from the tabernacles (i.e., the booths) that the Israelites constructed as they took up residence during the Feast of Booths. As the material of their booths was comprised of living materials that were made by the hand of God, *such as the foliage of beautiful trees, palm branches and boughs of leafy trees and willows of the brook,*[389] is it possible that the tabernacle of God is also made of living, celestial material? Perhaps it forms a heavenly tabernacle in which the mighty cherubim and seraphim soar and dart around the throne of God.[390] Perhaps it is describing the glowing aura of the living God that will illuminate the entire city.[391] Could it be a building or a complex of celestial buildings? Absolutely, but regardless of its composition, the tabernacle of God will indeed be among men.

Tabernacles and Temples

I should emphasize that this is a tabernacle—a dwelling place where God has taken up residence. It is not a temple. In Revelation 21:22, John explicitly says that he saw no temple in the city, because *the Lord God the Almighty and the Lamb are its temple.* Once again, we need to clarify the terms—what is a temple and what is its purpose?

We already know that a tabernacle is a dwelling place, as was the tabernacle that Moses constructed. But based on this passage, it seems that a temple is a sacred place wherein

389 Leviticus 23:40

390 Cherubim are described in Ezekiel 1 and 10

391 Revelation 22:5 "And there will no longer be any night; and they will not have need of the light of a lamp nor the light of the sun, because the Lord God will illumine them..."

mankind meets and worships an unseen deity. The unseen deity may be represented by an idol in some religions, even though the spirit of the deity remains unseen. But in the heavenly Jerusalem, everything has changed. There will not be a need for a temple in heaven because the One whom we worship will be seated right before us on the throne of heaven. God Himself will be among us, which will negate the need for a temple in the new Jerusalem.

The Wall of Pure Jasper

At this point, it seems that John's tour is still outside the city wall, ready to enter through one of the gates. But John was apparently so captivated by the beauty of the wall that he gave a detailed description of it before entering. Try to envision what he observed:

"It had a great and high wall, with twelve gates,
and at the gates twelve angels; and names were written on them,
which are the names of the twelve tribes of the sons of Israel.
There were three gates on the east and three gates on the north and
three gates on the south and three gates on the west.
And the wall of the city had twelve foundation stones,
and on them were the twelve names of the twelve apostles of the Lamb."

Revelation 21:12–14

"He also measured its wall,
144 cubits by human measurement,
which is also an angel's measurement."

Revelation 21:17 (ESV)

We have already learned that the wall is enormous, since it surrounds a city that is more than 1,300 miles long and wide. The angel measured the wall at 144 cubits, which is approximately 216 feet or 65 meters, but he did not specify whether that refers to the height or the thickness of the wall. We cannot know for sure based on the scriptural text, but I would guess that it is at least 144 cubits high. If it is 144 cubits thick, then the wall would probably be even higher than 144 cubits—**higher than a twenty-story building**. Either way, it is truly a great and high wall as John said.

Notice the layout of the city wall: There will be three gates on each wall, with an angel stationed at each gate. Would the angel be our equivalent of an honor guard, dressed in angelic splendor? Whatever the purpose, all who enter the gates would certainly be filled with awe at the sight of the magnificent, heavenly creature.

In ancient times, the term *gate* often implied much more than a fortified doorway or entryway. It was in the city gates that leaders conducted civic business, and elders, courts, judges, and even kings assembled. In some cases, the Scriptures mention that a square was by the gate,[392] which provides a place for the people to congregate and be involved in the governing process.

Jesus told the apostles, "Truly I say to you, that you who have followed Me, in the regeneration when the Son of Man will sit on His glorious throne, you also shall sit upon twelve thrones, judging the twelve tribes of Israel."[393] In this light, the reason becomes apparent for having the name of each son or tribe of Israel on a gate and the name of each apostle on the foundation stone of the wall.

Imagine, for example, a tall and glorious gate with the name of Judah inscribed on it, and the name of Peter inscribed on the foundation stone that is adjacent to that gate. In this example, the apostle Peter would be seated on his throne in this city gate, judging the people of the tribe of Judah. The people of the heavenly Jerusalem will have their business and legal matters decided by the apostolic judge at the gate for their tribe. Will there be issues and concerns that require judges in heaven? Apparently so, but the nature of those cases will probably be quite different from those in our current world.

"The material of the wall was jasper..."

Revelation 21:18

As you picture this enormous wall in your mind, you should know that it is not made of common stones or clay or concrete—the material of the entire wall is that of a gemstone, of pure jasper. In Revelation 21:11, John describes jasper as being *crystal-clear*, but by modern categorization, jasper is not clear—it is opaque. So, it is likely that John's ancient usage of the word may refer to another type of gemstone that is transparent, able to reflect and refract the light. But the point is that this great and high wall, which spans more than 5,000 miles around the city and is over 200 feet high, will be made from a beautiful gemstone that is probably translucent, so the radiance from the throne of God and the Lamb can pass through it.

392 *Examples of gates with squares are found in 2 Chronicles 32:6 and Esther 4:6*

393 *Matthew 19:28*

The Foundation Stones of the Wall

John's description of the foundation stones of the wall is also astounding. Most modern architects and designers try to hide foundations with various landscaping techniques, covering them with flowers, bushes, lattices, and walls. But the foundation stones of the heavenly wall are the complete opposite, since each stone is a gigantic precious gemstone—objects of immense beauty that will actually be showcased rather than hidden.

"The first foundation stone was jasper; the second, sapphire; the third, chalcedony; the fourth, emerald; the fifth, sardonyx; the sixth, sardius; the seventh, chrysolite; the eighth, beryl; the ninth, topaz; the tenth, chrysoprase; the eleventh, jacinth; the twelfth, amethyst."

Revelation 21:19–20

Each foundation stone is approximately 450 miles long (i.e., over 700 kilometers) and probably at least as thick as the wall. Can you imagine a pure emerald foundation stone of that length and possibly 200 feet (i.e., 60 meters) thick? How high would it rise above the ground? It must be at least high enough for the people to see the name of the apostle that is inscribed on it. In accordance with the grandeur of this city, I would guess that the foundation stones would rise 20–30 feet (i.e., 6–10 meters) above the ground where they are embedded.

"The foundation stones of the city wall were adorned with every kind of precious stone."

Revelation 21:19

In addition to its innate beauty, each foundation stone will be ornamented with every kind of precious stone. Imagine an enormous emerald foundation stone that is arrayed with diamond, ruby, sapphire, topaz, turquoise, and every imaginable gemstone. Walking through the gates of this city would dazzle all who enter, as they stroll through the corridor of the gate, walking on streets of pure gold that are as transparent glass. The radiance from the throne of the Father of lights, reflecting from the street and flashing through the crystalline adornments will create a dreamlike wonder. But it will not be a dream, for the presence of God is the essence of reality.

JUDAH
PETROS

Gates of Pearl

"And the twelve gates were twelve pearls; each one of the gates was a single pearl."

Revelation 21:21a

What is the material of the city gates? You may have heard someone refer to the *pearly gates* of heaven, which conjures mental images of a gate that is made of pearls that are bonded together in some way. But, as you have probably guessed, the gates of the heavenly Jerusalem will be of far more grandeur than a handmade craft project, since each gate will be carved from a single pearl.

How tall will the gates be? Perhaps 50 feet (15 meters)? Possibly 75 feet (22 meters)? My guess is that they will be at least 100 feet tall (30 meters) in order to be proportionate to the wall that is over 200 feet (60 meters) high. Do you think there are some gigantic oysters somewhere in the universe that are currently cultivating the pearls? I am being facetious, but God is certainly able to call them into existence out of nothing or create them in whatever manner He desires. No matter how they will be created, they will be beyond magnificent.

The walls that surrounded ancient cities were much more than a simple barrier that separated and protected the city from the outside world. Obviously, ancient walls were large enough for guards to take their positions to monitor and defend the city, but in addition to having guard houses, they were large enough to host residences, shops, and cafés. As an example, the walls of the ancient city of Babylon were so large that Herodotus[394] described them as having buildings on top that faced each other, and the width of the wall that was between the buildings was wide enough to turn a four-horse chariot.[395] The wall of the new Jerusalem will certainly have such grandeur, but whether it will sport a street on its upper level and host gardens, cafés, shops, or scenic outlooks, is something that I do not know. Nonetheless, it's fun to imagine what our new home will be.

394 *Herodotus was an ancient Greek historian who lived from approximately 484–425 BC.*

395 *(Hutchins 1952, 1989), page 40*

Streets of Gold

"...and the city was pure gold, like clear glass...
And the street of the city was pure gold, like transparent glass."

Revelation 21:18 and 21

Now we enter through the gates and find both the city and its streets are pure gold, like transparent glass. Can the city streets really be made of pure gold? Gold is a very soft metal and would not be suitable for pavement in our current world, but in the new earth and heavens, all things are being made new, meaning it would certainly be possible that gold will have different properties than we now know. It is also possible that John is speaking figuratively or that celestial footsteps will not be as punishing. Regardless of the substance, it is certainly going to be brilliant, reflecting the glories of God.

What would you expect to see as we walk the streets of the dwelling of God? Will it only be stone and metal, or will we find that it is home to the things that we already know and enjoy? Will we find things that give joy, pleasure, and life to humans? Read carefully as John and the angel describe our home-to-be. In addition to the mountain that we already mentioned, you will see rivers, trees with rich foliage, fruit, good kings, nations, wealth, and especially the throne of God and the Lamb. It will certainly be a lush, welcoming habitation for everyone.

Will the throne of God be situated in the center of the city? The text does not tell us explicitly, but I imagine that it will. When the Israelites camped in the wilderness, the Lord stipulated that the tribes camp around the tabernacle of the Lord at a distance—each by their own banner. Three tribes on the east side, three on the south, three on the west, and three on the north side, with the Levites camped in the midst of the others.[396] Could this also be the arrangement of the tribes of Israel in the heavenly Jerusalem, with three gates on each side of the city, with the name of a tribe on each?

As we walk the streets of the heavenly Jerusalem, we will be walking among those who were redeemed by the blood of the Lamb, immortals living in the dwellings that Jesus prepared for them, nestled in the beauty of the city of God. Will some of these redeemed be living in the mountains or hills, while others live in snowy wooded lands, and others live in rich, tropical environs? It is certainly possible—the city will be large enough to span many different climates and terrains. Just as our current earth enjoys a variety of cultures, races, and lands, I suspect that the new earth and heaven will be spiced with similar variety but immersed in a universal

396 *The arrangement of the camps are described in Numbers 2:1–31*

bond of love. Everyone will have the Law of God—the Law of love—imprinted on their hearts, with no inclination to deviate from it.

"And the Holy Spirit also testifies to us; for after saying,
'This is the covenant that I will make with them After those days, says the Lord: I will put My laws upon their heart, And on their mind I will write them.'"

Hebrews 10:15–16

I Saw No Temple in It

"I saw no temple in it, for the Lord God the Almighty and the Lamb are its temple."

Revelation 21:22

As we continue our journey, we are reminded that there is no temple in the city, for the Lord God the Almighty and the Lamb are its temple. So, we come directly before the awesome throne of God and the Lamb, not concealed in a fortress with walls and guards, but in the middle of the street, as if to welcome everyone, inviting them to come and behold His glory and immerse themselves in worship of the timeless, Divine Mystery. Glory will be before us, God Himself—the Deity that we can behold but never comprehend.

Two Life-Giving Elements

"Then he showed me a river of the water of life, clear as crystal,
coming from the throne of God and of the Lamb, in the middle of its street.
On either side of the river was the tree of life,
bearing twelve kinds of fruit, yielding its fruit every month;
and the leaves of the tree were for the healing of the nations."

Revelation 22:1–2

Do we need to explain who the Lamb is? By now, you know that the Lamb is the Messiah. John the Baptist referred to Him as the Lamb of God who takes away the sins of the world.[397] Did John the apostle see two Beings sitting on the same throne—God and the Lamb? Or are God and the Lamb the same Being? The writings of the New Testament resonate with

397 *John 1:29 "The next day he saw Jesus coming to him and said, 'Behold, the Lamb of God who takes away the sin of the world!'"*

the mysterious teaching that God and the Lamb are one in the same, even as explicitly as *"In the beginning was the Word, and the Word was with God, and the Word was God."*[398] Here, in the new Jerusalem, we come face to face with the Divine Messiah. What will your response be when you stand before your Maker—the one who called you into existence and breathed life into your frame?

Notice that there are two life-giving elements around the throne. Being in the presence of God is more than just an experience of musing on His majesty and pondering His timelessness. In His presence, He freely gives us the food and drink of life. The first is the water of life, not in a small vile locked in a vault in an inner chamber and guarded by angels—but a river, freely flowing with the life-giving potion.

What is this water of life? I believe it is none other than the elixir of immortality—the fountain that restores and revitalizes the human frame, giving youthful vigor to the mind and body. At 10,000 years old, the citizens of the new earth will have the vitality and energy of a 25-year-old and the wisdom and beauty of immortality. No wrinkles, no aches and pains, no dementia—perfection in the flesh. O to lay down in that river, in the life-giving flow!

The second life-giving element is the *tree of life* that is growing on both banks of the river that flows from the throne. Is this the same tree of life that Adam and Eve were denied access to because they disobeyed? Is it the same *tree of life* that was guarded by cherubim with a flaming sword so man would not eat of it and subsequently live forever?[399] I believe it is, or some type of tree of life that will have the ability to revitalize our heavenly bodies. Recall from Genesis 3:22, the reason the Lord assigned a guard to the tree was because man *"might stretch out his hand, and take also from the tree of life, and eat, and live forever..."*

Forever Young

Does this really mean that we will live *forever*, as in **never ever** die? Will resurrected humans really outlive galaxies and the stars of the heavens? Please allow me to speculate: It is likely that Adam and Eve had both eaten the fruit of the tree of life before they were banished from the Garden of Eden. They had the powerful elixir of immortality flowing through their veins, which rejuvenated their minds and bodies and greatly increased their lifespans. The effects of the elixir were passed to their descendants until its effects slowly dissipated throughout their generations. How long did some of the early humans live after the fall?

398 John 1:1

399 Genesis 3:22–24

Adam lived 930 years

Seth lived 912 years

Jared lived 962 years

Methuselah lived 969 years

Noah lived 950 years

As an example, let's draw a comparison between Noah and ourselves and assume the average lifespan of the modern human is 70 years old. Halfway through our 70 years, at age 35, we can be quite fit and youthful. In a similar way, when Noah was 475 years old, halfway through his life of 950 years, he was also probably quite fit and youthful. He probably looked like a modern man who is 35 years old. But imagine the wisdom and maturity that he would have from all of his life experience. On the other hand, he would have been energetic and playful, as well!

I sometimes chuckle when I think of 475-year-old Noah meeting a modern group of 35-year-old men who are working out at the gym or playing basketball. If you looked at this group, you would not know that Noah was more than ten times their age; he would blend in perfectly. And because of his wit and experience, he could probably beat them at their own game – they couldn't even tell him a joke that he hadn't heard!

Now, consider yourself as an immortal at the young age of 10,000. You will be perfectly youthful, healthy, and playful, yet mature and wise—the radiance of immortal beauty. Full access to the river of the water of life is available to all who belong to the Messiah. As we will see in a moment, Jesus promised to *give to the one who thirsts from the spring of the water of life without cost.*[400]

Nations in Heaven

Notice in Revelation 22:1–2, the benefits of the tree of life will be available to the nations. Did you know that other nations will exist and thrive on the new earth, the same earth on which the heavenly Jerusalem resides? The trees will produce a harvest every month of the year, so the nations will not have to wait to receive the healing balm. This raises some questions that seem to be contradictory. Why would healing be necessary in a world where there will not be pain? Why don't these nations have dwelling places within the beautiful city? Do they have kingdoms on other parts of the new earth? We will explore these questions very soon and learn

400 *Revelation 21:6*

some things about the kings of these nations. Nonetheless, the trees that grow on the banks of the river will somehow have the ability to heal the nations. Perhaps, as the kings bring their glory into the city, they will return to their people with this healing, life-giving treasure.

No Longer Any Curse

John made a statement in the following passage that could easily go unnoticed.

"There will no longer be any curse;
and the throne of God and of the Lamb will be in it,
and His bond-servants will serve Him;
they will see His face, and His name will be on their foreheads."

Revelation 22:3–4

Do you recall Adam's punishment for eating of the tree of the knowledge of good and evil? The Lord cursed the ground with thorns and thistles so that growing crops would become hard labor for mankind. But in the new earth, there will no longer be any curse—no more thorns and no more thistles.

Can you imagine a place where the ground is not cursed, but is fertile for growing life-giving crops? A land with no weeds or thorns or thistles that would choke the growth before the harvest? I am guessing that hunger and starvation will not exist on the new earth because nutritious food will grow wild. Everywhere we turn, we might find wild melons, grapes, bananas, apples, and oranges—we may even find unknown delicacies that have not survived the perils of our current planet earth. Wild fruits, vegetables, grains, herbs, and treats of all sorts might be freely available to everyone in the paradise that the Lord is creating for those who love Him.

The Bond-Servants

As John looked around the dwelling place of God and observed His throne, the river of the water of life, and the trees of life, he saw the bond-servants of God, those who were redeemed by the blood of the Lamb. Is this the bride, the wife of the Lamb that the angel mentioned in Revelation 21:9? These people will serve God and have the privilege of seeing His face, gazing into the eyes of their Creator, the one who knows them better than they know themselves. They will bear His name on their foreheads, for they are highly esteemed and honored by God.

The thought of being a bond-servant to God for eternity may not immediately appeal to you. Images of peeling grapes and fanning a sovereign with palm branches, or possibly dusting furniture or serving meals might come to mind. Although these things may be possible, it is more likely that being in the service of the Lord would involve the idea of reigning or ruling in some way. In the same context, Revelation 22:5 says that these bond-servants will reign forever and ever, which implies much more than servile labor.

So, rather than envisioning a servant of menial tasks, consider that this role might be like a *servant* or *minister* in a government, such as the *Minister of Foreign Affairs*, a *Minister of Commerce*, or perhaps an *ambassador* to another nation on earth. In a similar way, in Jesus' parable of the nobleman in Luke 19:11–27, the faithful were granted authority over cities; they were elevated to being rulers. Regardless of the type of service, being in the presence of God and the Lamb would be the greatest joy and honor that a person could ever own. As David mused, *How blessed is the one whom You choose and bring near to You To dwell in Your courts,*[401] so will the redeemed of the Messiah be blessed.

The Luminary

John continues to describe the environment of the holy city and its effect on the bond-servants of God and the Lamb.

"And there will no longer be any night;
and they will not have need of the light of a lamp nor the light of the sun,
because the Lord God will illumine them; and they will reign forever and ever."

Revelation 22:5

"And the city has no need of the sun or of the moon to shine on it,
for the glory of God has illumined it, and its lamp is the Lamb."

Revelation 21:23

It is difficult to imagine that this city will not have nighttime because the Lord God will illumine it with the lamp of the Lamb. Will it be a blinding brightness since it will illuminate such an enormous city? I don't believe so—I believe it will be pleasant, gently glowing throughout the transparent city, the clear streets of gold, and even through the great and high wall that

401 Psalm 65:4

surrounds her. It will be a light that will make us constantly mindful of the loving presence of God and the Lamb.

The people of the city will not have need of lamps or the sun or the moon, but John did not say that there will not be a sun or a moon. It is possible that the nations who inhabit other parts of the planet would not benefit from the illumination of the holy city, so they might need a sun and possibly a moon. Their days and nights might be very similar to those on our current earth.

The Nations

"The nations will walk by its light, and the kings of the earth will bring their glory into it. In the daytime (for there will be no night there) its gates will never be closed; and they will bring the glory and the honor of the nations into it; and nothing unclean, and no one who practices abomination and lying, shall ever come into it, but only those whose names are written in the Lamb's book of life."

Revelation 21:24–27

It is fascinating to think that other nations will exist on the new earth, probably with their own cities, civilizations, and societies, but without corruption and sin. Have you heard how kings and queens honored each other with lavish gifts when visiting other nations? That is what John is describing in this passage. The greatest honor that anyone could ever obtain is to have an audience with the King of Kings—the King of the Universe. When the kings of the earth visit, they will be dressed in splendor, accompanied by their servants and royal court, and bring gifts and treasures to the great King. In so doing, they will bring the honor and glory of their nations into the new Jerusalem, before the Lord Himself.

What will these kings and kingdoms be like? Since their hearts and minds will not be tainted with the knowledge of good and evil, they will be benevolent leaders, who seek the good of their people and their kingdoms. The names of all of these kings and their subjects were written in the Lamb's book of life; otherwise they would not have survived the judgment of the great white throne and be allowed to live in the new earth and its heaven. Furthermore, the new Jerusalem and the entire earth will be free of those who practice the ways of darkness—the ways that are opposed to the righteousness of the Lamb.

I would be remiss if I did not emphasize the words from the throne—words about eternal well-being and words of warning.

"Then He said to me,
'It is done. I am the Alpha and the Omega, the beginning and the end.
I will give to the one who thirsts from the spring of the water of life without cost.
He who overcomes will inherit these things, and I will be his God and he will be My son.
But for the cowardly and unbelieving and abominable and murderers
and immoral persons and sorcerers and idolaters and all liars,
their part will be in the lake that burns with fire and brimstone,
which is the second death.'"

Revelation 21:6–8

The Shadows and Substance of Tabernacles

The shadow that is cast by the people of God taking up residence in temporary dwelling places whispers of a future event of messianic magnitude. It is refined even more as we see the Lord God taking up residence in the Temple during the Feast of Tabernacles in the days of Solomon. According to the Lord's instructions about this Appointed Time, the people were also required to observe a Sabbath rest *after* the seven-day festival ended. Is it possible that this Sabbath rest is a shadow of how our ultimate rest in paradise will begin after the activities of this earth end? These three components—the people taking up residence, the Lord God taking up residence, and a crowning Sabbath rest—form the shadows of the Feast of Tabernacles.

We gain a glimpse of the substance of this Appointed Time through Jesus' promise of a future event wherein He would go away to prepare places for His followers in His Father's house and would return to receive them to Himself and be together forever. In the book of Revelation, we are given a detailed look at the magnificent dwelling place of God, the heavenly Jerusalem, on a newly created planet earth.

"Behold, the tabernacle of God is among men, and He will dwell among them, and they shall be His people, and God Himself will be among them, and He will wipe away every tear from their eyes; and there will no longer be any death; there will no longer be any mourning, or crying, or pain; the first things have passed away."

Revelation 21:3–4

It is in this description of the heavenly kingdom that we find the messianic substance

– the fulfillment of the Feast of Tabernacles. The Lord God and the Lamb are seated on the throne as the centerpiece of the celestial city, dwelling among the redeemed, the bride of Christ, in an eternal, joyous rest. This is the great hope of all who place their faith in the Lord Jesus Christ, and this is His final call:

"'I, Jesus, have sent My angel to testify to you these things for the churches.
I am the root and the descendant of David, the bright morning star.'
The Spirit and the bride say, 'Come.' And let the one who hears say, 'Come.'
And let the one who is thirsty come, let the one who wishes
take the water of life without cost."

Revelation 22:16–17

Dreaming of Heaven...

Imagine with me for a moment... What do you think we will do in heaven? Some people think we are going to spend eternity around the throne, praising God forever. One man told me that idea did not sound very appealing to him, so he was not interested nor motivated by the thought of living in heaven. On the other hand, he did not want to spend eternity in torment, so he continued to live as a somewhat depressed and unmotivated Christian.

But I suspect that praising God around His throne will be a very special event that we will be able to do when we are on vacation or holiday each year. It will be a privilege and a thrill that we will anticipate throughout each year—like a special holiday or event on this earth that we get to enjoy with special people. Perhaps it will be like Christmas holiday with friends and family or the Israelites traveling to Jerusalem each year to celebrate the Feast of Tabernacles.

But what activities will engage our time and attention during the other weeks of the year in the new paradise? It seems reasonable that we will spend our time doing the things that God created us to do. Will our new bodies be created with fundamentally different abilities and desires, or is it possible that some of our current human characteristics will be the same in our resurrected minds and bodies?

In order to answer that question, let's examine God's intended design for Adam and Eve before the catastrophic fall. We will then step back and look at the bigger picture of the character, nature, and desires of humanity, while sifting out the aspects that are tainted by the knowledge of good and evil. We may then gain a better understanding of what human beings will be like in the regeneration regarding the desires, drives, and abilities they will have.

The Original Design

Think with me about the original design of mankind and how it might relate to God's design in the regeneration. Brainstorm with me, if you will... Recall that God created man in His own image, creating them male and female.[402] His intention and deep desire was to create these beings in His own image. The Lord was pleased with His work of creation,[403] and He loves the people of His world.[404] Since He is unchanging, I suspect that He will again create our heavenly bodies and minds in His image in the regeneration. If so, humans will again have powerful intellects and deep feelings, along with innate talents, skills, desires, and propensities that are similar to those that we currently possess, but they will be in line with His good ways—in His likeness.

Among His initial commands to the man and woman, God told them to subdue the earth and rule over the fish of the sea and over the birds of the sky and over every living thing that moves on the earth. Clearly, God also equipped the man and woman with the abilities to accomplish the goal of establishing dominion over creation. The Lord equipped them physically, intellectually, and quite possibly with the desire in their hearts to do these tasks. Indeed, they probably found fulfillment and enjoyment in their God-given roles.

The Human Spirit

As the story of humankind unfolded throughout history, it became obvious that men and women were equipped with an unlimited variety of talents, skills, desires, and passions. Perhaps it would be more accurate to say that people were driven from within to pursue their heart's desires—the desires that God instilled in them by design. We might refer to these desires and drives as the human spirit, but it is probably more accurate to say that the human spirit is actually a micro version of the image of God.

What are some of the characteristics of the human spirit? What has God designed into man in our current world? Clearly, He has given us:

» A spirit of curiosity, which we pursue through science, exploration, and discovery

» A quest for adventure—prowess in pushing the boundaries in our pursuits and reaching for the outer limits of creation

402 Genesis 1:27 and 5:1–2

403 Genesis 1:31, Psalm 104:31

404 John 3:16

- » A love of music and the arts, including singing, mastering musical instruments, dance, drama, painting, writing, oration, and so many more
- » A love of sports—the heart and thrill of competition, physical skill, precision in movement, dexterity, speed, and agility
- » Expertise in craftsmanship—sculpture, woodworking, furniture, clothing, jewelry, and so many more
- » A mastery of engineering—architecture, building, and other disciplines
- » Culinary mastery—creating mouth-watering delicacies that literally add spice and sweetness to life, as well as providing life-sustaining nutrition
- » Prowess for invention—using learning and intellectual abilities to create devices for necessity, pleasure, and convenience
- » Compassion and empathy—the ability to convey and recognize beauty, emotion, excitement, and sympathy
- » Appreciation of wisdom, knowledge, beauty, talent, skill, emotion, and grandeur
- » Friendship, companionship, and brotherhood—knowing and needing each other
- » A heart for worship—the innate desire to know and honor the Being that is beyond ourselves and worthy of our worship

Humans are magnificent creatures, fearfully and wonderfully made. But I must emphasize that humans are indeed *creatures*—we are one of the masterpieces of God's endless creativity. The above list is certainly not exhaustive. You may be thinking that I omitted an aspect of the human spirit that captivates your heart, and you are probably right. After all, the diversity and breadth of the human spirit is extremely broad.

Could all of the characteristics in the above list be categorized as good in the sight of God? Might any of them be evil or sinful in themselves? I believe that all of them are good and healthy and stem from the image and character of God. Of course, every one of them can be used in evil and depraved ways, but in themselves, each one of them is good. Would it be correct to suggest that the items in the above list are expressions of the image of God? I believe they are, and it seems logical that He would instill the same abilities into His redeemed, regenerated creatures of His own image.

In that light, it is my guess that most of the pursuits that are common to humans in this age will also flourish in the age to come. So what is the difference? The difference in heaven will be the object and motivation of our pursuits. Rather than going for the gold, we will go for the Glory of God. For example,

» As the cliff-diver leaps from the ledge, he will say in his heart, "Look, Father—this body that You gave me can soar through the air as I dive!"

» The drama team will proclaim in their hearts, "Look, Father – the drama that we wrote and perform speaks of Your greatness and Your love and Your mysteries!"

» The biologist will be overcome with awe, saying, "Look Father—I now understand how You created the human genome structure to define our bodies with the specific characteristics that make us unique and special in Your sight—Your creation is magnificent!"

» When the football player scores, he will drop to his knees and thank the Father for making him in such a magnificent and wonderful way.

» Dancers will joyously proclaim in their hearts, "Father, be honored through our art, for we have composed it for Your glory and Your pleasure—we perform for You!"

As in our current world, every skill and ability that we have comes from God, whether we acknowledge it or not. But in the world to come, everyone will know and acknowledge it and give their thanks and praise to the Giver of life. In the regeneration, when the biologist looks up from the microscope or the astronomer looks down from the telescope, they will drop to their knees in worship and adoration as they observe the magnificent work of the unfathomable Creator. Their hearts will resonate with praise for God, and they will ask, "Who is man that You should be mindful of him? Why have You loved us so?"

So on our holidays, when we have the privilege of standing before the throne of God and the Lamb, to praise Him with other believers from all other nations, languages, and ethnicities, we will proclaim from our hearts with the deepest sincerity, that "blessing and glory and wisdom and thanksgiving and honor and power and might, be to our God forever and ever."[405]

This is heaven. Do you want to be there? I could talk with you and brainstorm about it for days, but I have limited space in which to write. I want to be there—it is my great hope and anchor and the driving force in my life.

---

405 Revelation 7:12

Encouragement for Skeptics

But for the skeptics out there, I feel that I should briefly address some common misconceptions. I have heard people say that they don't want to go to heaven because it's boring, or because they won't have their earthly pleasures, including romance and sensual pleasures. But my response is, "Don't be so sure." God is not only recreating, but He is obviously redesigning the planet and our bodies. It is true that there will not be marriage in heaven, but I am confident that His new design will bring far more joy and pleasure and possibly intimacy than we could ever dream of in this life. Many of the things that we count as pleasure now will seem boring when we walk in our new bodies. Who can imagine the pleasures that He is preparing for those who love Him?

When we arrive in our heavenly home, each one of us—even the most reserved—is going to jump for joy at the realization of being there. But at the same time, we will realize how much we gave up because we chose earthly things over heavenly during our short time on this earth. When we obey the Lord, we truly have no idea of the personal gain that it profits. And the converse is also true: when we disobey the Lord, we truly have no idea of how much we are giving up in eternity.

Real Real Estate

This is heaven, and I am so looking forward to living there with Christ and with others whom I love... my wife, who will no longer be my wife, but will certainly be a very special friend, my children, my family, my friends, and even my enemies, because we will be at peace and they will also become my special friends. And I look forward to seeing many people who I have heard of and admired, who helped me in my walk with Christ, and anyone else I knew as I walked on this old planet earth.

But I would also love to meet you and hear your story. It would be great to sit and visit with you and get to know you, perhaps over a cup of coffee, perhaps beside a warm fire on a cool evening. We will have time to get to know each other in the world to come!

I will never forget the times many years ago, when I would put my sons to bed at night. At one point, my eldest son was about five years old, and he and I had spent some time talking about heaven. I told him about the magnificent wall and the gates and the throne of God, and everything about the new earth and heaven, and he was so excited about it.

And I said to him, "Jesse, if life is pretty normal for us, I will probably die long before you, but that's okay. Because when we get to heaven and after we've settled in, let's plan to meet each other by the gate of Judah... and we'll talk about old times here on earth and we'll talk about the things we're going to do together for the next million years." And he was so excited, and he clenched his fists and waved his little arms and laughing said, "Ya! Daddy, Ya!" No matter what happens here on this earth, I have the peace and confidence that I will, someday, be reunited with those whom I love so dearly. I am so looking forward to meeting those I've loved in this world, and those who have loved me, and especially to meeting Jesus who made it possible for us to truly live.

Heaven is real estate. And the things that we have on this earth? Well, since you can't take it with you, that means that this earth, which we call "real estate" is not very real. But heaven is real real estate. Is your estate truly real estate? Believers in the Messiah have the ultimate hope—there is nothing on this planet that compares with the things that God has prepared for those who love Him. So, during your time in this world, live with your focus on eternity and with your hope in heaven. I will see you on the other side!

Chapter 17 – Reflecting on the Appointed Times

We have been on an amazing journey since the first chapter of this book, beginning from the time of creation and traveling to the re-creation of the heavens and the earth. We have seen that some of life's deepest questions are answered through an understanding of the Bible and the Appointed Times. Questions such as "Why does evil exist in our world?" "Why is there sickness, war, suffering, and injustice?" "Why do the innocent suffer?" "What happens when we die?" "Is there life after death?" "Who is God and what is He like?" Even though we may not have addressed these questions directly, you now have a framework from which to consider the eternal mysteries.

Indeed, the Appointed Times are shadows of things to come.[406] It is by observing the shadows that we realize the significance of the object that is casting them, while not being distracted by the mysterious and glorious aspects of their substance. Now that you are acquainted with the Messiah—the Christ—you, no doubt, understand the reason for the praise and honor and glory that is given to Him.

Israel is, indeed, a theater through which the entire world can view the plan of God from the beginning to the end. We see the people of Israel annually portraying the high points of the Messiah's work for all the world to see through the Appointed Times. The backdrop of the divine drama is the conflict between God's holiness and His love for sinful man. Because of His love, He devised a plan to send His Messiah to redeem and restore the lost race of men, so He could adopt them as His beloved children and dwell with them for all eternity. It is a beautiful story that has the epitome of a "*happily ever after*" storyline.

The Emphases of the Bible

To many people, the Bible seems to be a complicated book that addresses an unwieldy number of subjects. How can we know which parts of the Bible should be emphasized? Indeed, heresy, false teaching, and cults have arisen because people have incorrectly emphasized various parts of the Scriptures. It is like being obsessed with the door-handle of a beautiful automobile, rather than understanding and appreciating the vehicle in its entirety. Every word of God's Word is important and precious, but the Appointed Times teach the things that should be our priority, and all other aspects will naturally fall into place within that structure. God Himself has declared

406 *Colossians 2:16–17*

His priorities through the Appointed Times—His emphasis is on the Messiah and His works.

With this as our perspective, we now heed the Father's words to Peter, "This is My beloved Son, listen to Him!"[407] So, as children who desire to please and as disciples who desire to obey and grow, we now focus on the words of Jesus to conform our ways to His ways. His wisdom is the wisdom of God and it leads to life—abundant life, eternal life.

With Us from the Beginning

The *spring* Appointed Times teach about the purity of the Messiah, His death, burial, and resurrection, along with the giving of the Holy Spirit to those who believe in Him. The *fall* Appointed Times teach about the return of the Messiah, His atoning for sin, obtaining eternal redemption, and taking those who believe to the place that He has prepared. The prize for those who believe is to live as immortals in paradise in perfect harmony with God as their Father.

These themes were intimated through the Appointed Times 3,500 years ago, not long after creation. The very same themes were fulfilled by Jesus and affirmed by His apostles. The words of the New Testament are alive with the message of the Christ, and the apostles later summarized it into the concise words of the Apostles' Creed.[408]

During the early centuries of the church, copies of Scriptures and written literature were somewhat rare, since the printing press had not yet been invented. Since Christians did not have their own copies of the Bible, the apostles composed a brief statement that was short enough for people to memorize for the purpose of recalling the important aspects of the Faith—it is called the Apostles' Creed. It is not a coincidence that the Apostles' Creed teaches every key aspect of the Appointed Times. The Lord told us which things should be emphasized through Moses, and the apostles affirmed it through the Apostles' Creed. Refer to Figure 22 to see a diagram of the common themes in the Apostle's Creed and the Appointed Times.

---

407 *Matthew 17:5, Mark 9:7, Luke 9:35*

408 *The authorship of the Apostle's Creed is somewhat questionable, and it is certainly not considered to be inspired. Nonetheless, the substance of its teaching is contained, almost in its entirety, in the Nicene Creed, which was crafted at the first church Council of Nicaea which convened in AD 325.*

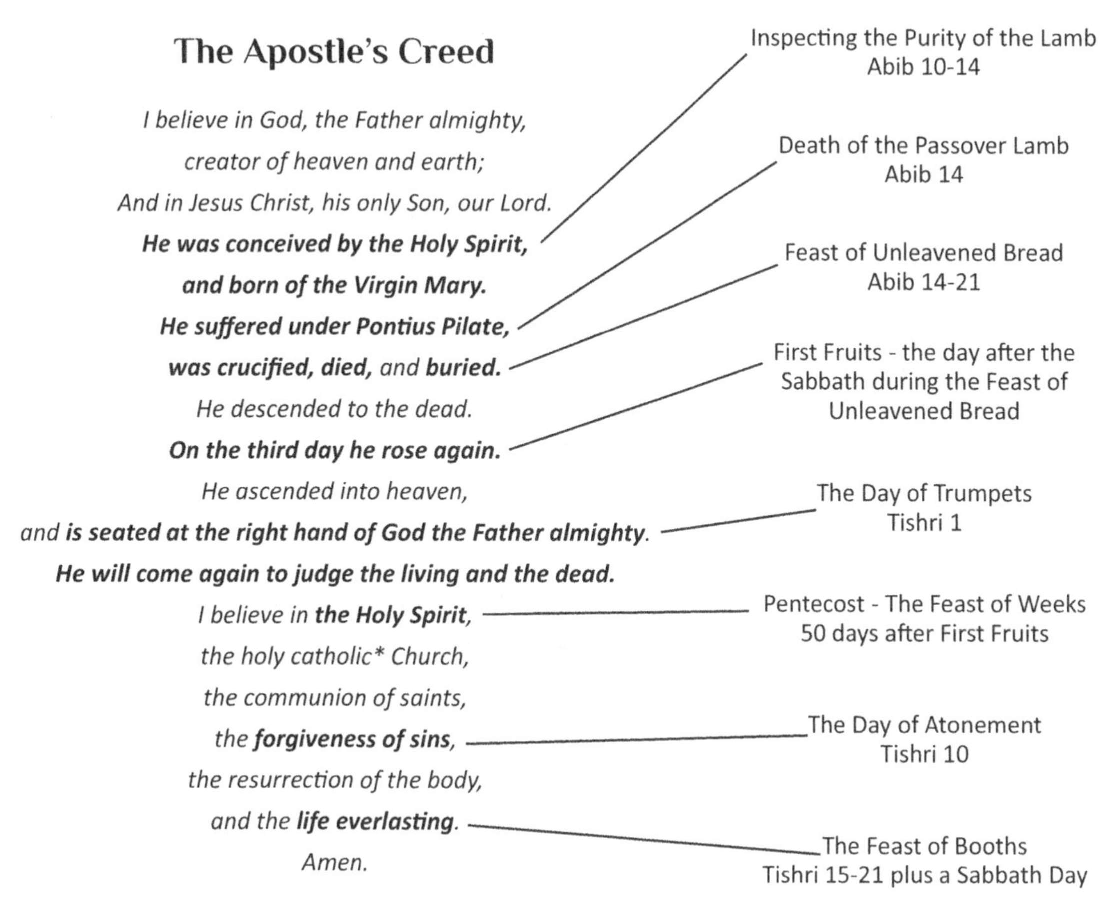

Figure 22 – The Apostle's Creed and the Appointed Times

This is the Christian Faith, and if you will, it is the Jewish Faith and the hope of all who believe—the Jewish prophecies were fulfilled by Jesus, their countryman, the Messiah of God. The Lord told Moses:

"I will raise up a prophet from among their countrymen like you,
and I will put My words in his mouth, and he shall speak to them all that I command him."

Deuteronomy 18:18

And Peter quoted the same words of Moses to the Jewish crowds in Jerusalem:

"Moses said,
'The Lord God will raise up for you a prophet like me from your brethren;
to Him you shall give heed to everything He says to you.'"

Acts 3:22

Messianic Magnitude

Did you notice the immensity and the magnitude of the fulfillments of the Appointed Times? The return of the Messiah profoundly impacted the heavens, the earth, the nations, and all humankind. The atonement of the Messiah cleansed even the most hideous sins of the repentant believer. Taking up residence involved creating a new planet and a city of enormous proportions, and life that never ends. Indeed, the magnitude of messianic events are unparalleled. Even the most fertile imaginations of science fiction and mythology come up short when compared to God's truth. Such are the Appointed Times. They reveal the truths of the Messiah with the magnificence of divinity, as they clearly point to Jesus as their fulfillment.

Seize the Prize!

No matter what your station in life, the things of God are deeply relevant to you—how you conduct yourself, how you treat others, how you honor God your maker. Everything that you say and do in this life has meaning since we must all give an account for every idle word and every action. Is your awareness of God merely academic, or is it an actual belief that results in introspection and aligning your ways with His?

If you say that you have trouble believing this message, then I recommend that you honestly explore it in depth, so you can see for yourself. There is nothing more worthy of your time and attention than investigating the promises of God and His Messiah. The hope of immortality and paradise are in the air, like the promise of a summer rain. Jesus told the crowds to seek the kingdom and seize it, because it is worth far more than anything we could ever own in this world.

"The kingdom of heaven is like a treasure hidden in the field,
which a man found and hid again;
and from joy over it he goes and sells all that he has and buys that field."

Matthew 13:44

"Again, the kingdom of heaven is like a merchant seeking fine pearls,
and upon finding one pearl of great value, he went and sold all that he had and bought it."

Matthew 13:45–46

Now you understand the reason for martyrs. They did not give their lives for a cause—they gave their lives for the prize... the ultimate prize. And now you understand the reason that Moses traded his enviable position as a prince in Egypt, along with his power and riches, for the infinitely greater eternal reward of living in paradise with the Messiah.

"By faith Moses, when he had grown up,
refused to be called the son of Pharaoh's daughter,
choosing rather to endure ill-treatment with the people of God
than to enjoy the passing pleasures of sin,
considering the reproach of Christ greater riches than the treasures of Egypt;
for he was looking to the reward."

Hebrews 11:24–26 (Emphasis added)

No one can rob you of the treasure of the Messiah—no one. Paul endured beatings, imprisonment, and martyrdom because he knew the prize of the Messiah could never be taken from him. The love of God is worth it all. Paul wrote:

"For I am convinced that neither death, nor life, nor angels,
nor principalities, nor things present, nor things to come, nor powers,
nor height, nor depth, nor any other created thing,
will be able to separate us from the love of God, which is in Christ Jesus our Lord."

Romans 8:38–39

How do we seize the prize of eternal life through the Messiah? It is by simply believing Him, that His atoning sacrifice will be reckoned to you for the forgiveness of your sin. Paul stated it very clearly:

"...if you confess with your mouth Jesus as Lord,
and believe in your heart that God raised Him from the dead,
you will be saved;
for with the heart a person believes, resulting in righteousness,
and with the mouth he confesses, resulting in salvation.
For the Scripture says,
'Whoever believes in Him will not be disappointed.'"

Romans 10:9–11

My recommendation to you? Sieze it!

Appendix A – Leviticus 23

1 The Lord spoke again to Moses, saying, 2 "Speak to the sons of Israel and say to them, **'The Lord's appointed times** which you shall proclaim as holy convocations—My appointed times are these:

The Sabbath Day

3 'For six days work may be done, but **on the seventh day** there is a sabbath of complete rest, a holy convocation. You shall not do any work; it is a sabbath to the Lord in all your dwellings.

Passover

4 'These are the appointed times of the Lord, holy convocations which you shall proclaim at the times appointed for them. 5 In the **first month, on the fourteenth day of the month at twilight** is **the Lord's Passover.**

The Feast of Unleavened Bread

6 'Then on the **fifteenth day of the same month** there is **the Feast of Unleavened Bread** to the Lord; for seven days you shall eat unleavened bread. 7 On the first day you shall have a holy convocation; you shall not do any laborious work. 8 But for seven days you shall present an offering by fire to the Lord. On the seventh day is a holy convocation; you shall not do any laborious work.'"

First Fruits

9 Then the Lord spoke to Moses, saying, 10 "Speak to the sons of Israel and say to them, 'When you enter the land which I am going to give to you and reap its harvest, then you shall bring in the sheaf of the **first fruits** of your harvest to the priest. 11 He shall wave the sheaf before the Lord for you to be accepted; **on the day after the sabbath** the priest shall wave it. 12 Now on the day when you wave the sheaf, you shall offer a male lamb one year old without defect for a burnt offering to the Lord. 13 Its grain offering shall then be two-tenths of an ephah of fine flour mixed with oil, an offering by fire to the Lord for a soothing aroma, with its drink offering, a fourth of a hin of wine. 14 Until this same day, until you have brought in the offering of your God, you shall eat neither bread nor roasted grain nor new growth. It is to be a perpetual statute throughout your generations in all your dwelling places.

The Feast of Weeks

15 'You shall also **count for yourselves from the day after the sabbath**, from the day when you brought in the sheaf of the wave offering; **there shall be seven complete sabbaths**. 16 **You shall count fifty days to the day after the seventh sabbath**; then you shall present a new grain offering to the Lord. 17 You shall bring in from your dwelling places two loaves of bread for a wave offering, made of two-tenths of an ephah; they shall be of a fine flour, baked with leaven as first fruits to the Lord. 18 Along with the bread you shall present seven one year old male lambs without defect, and a bull of the herd and two rams; they are to be a burnt offering to the Lord, with their grain offering and their drink offerings, an offering by fire of a soothing aroma to the Lord. 19 You shall also offer one male goat for a sin offering and two male lambs one year old for a sacrifice of peace offerings. 20 The priest shall then wave them with the bread of the first fruits for a wave offering with two lambs before the Lord; they are to be holy to the Lord for the priest. 21 On this same day you shall make a proclamation as well; you are to have a holy convocation. You shall do no laborious work. It is to be a perpetual statute in all your dwelling places throughout your generations.

22 'When you reap the harvest of your land, moreover, you shall not reap to the very corners of your field nor gather the gleaning of your harvest; you are to leave them for the needy and the alien. I am the Lord your God.'"

The Day of Trumpets

23 Again the Lord spoke to Moses, saying, 24 "Speak to the sons of Israel, saying, 'In the **seventh month on the first of the month** you shall have a rest, a reminder by **blowing of trumpets**, a holy convocation. 25 You shall not do any laborious work, but you shall present an offering by fire to the Lord.'"

The Day of Atonement

26 The Lord spoke to Moses, saying, 27 "**On exactly the tenth day of this seventh month** is the **day of atonement**; it shall be a holy convocation for you, and you shall humble your souls and present an offering by fire to the Lord. 28 You shall not do any work on this same day, for it is a day of atonement, to make atonement on your behalf before the Lord your God. 29 If there is any person who will not humble himself on this same day, he shall be cut off from his people. 30 As for any person who does any work on this same day, that person I will destroy from among his people. 31 You shall do no work at all. It is to be a perpetual statute throughout your generations in all your dwelling places. 32 It is to be a sabbath of complete rest to you, and you shall humble your souls; on the ninth of the month at evening, from evening until evening you shall keep your sabbath."

The Feast of Booths

33 Again the Lord spoke to Moses, saying, 34 "Speak to the sons of Israel, saying, '**On the fifteenth of this seventh month** is the **Feast of Booths** for seven days to the Lord. 35 On the first day is a holy convocation; you shall do no laborious work of any kind. 36 For seven days you shall present an offering by fire to the Lord. On the eighth day you shall have a holy convocation and present an offering by fire to the Lord; it is an assembly. You shall do no laborious work.

37 'These are the appointed times of the Lord which you shall proclaim as holy convocations, to present offerings by fire to the Lord—burnt offerings and grain offerings, sacrifices and drink offerings, each day's matter on its own day— 38 besides those of the sabbaths of the Lord, and besides your gifts and besides all your votive and freewill offerings, which you give to the Lord.

39 'On exactly the fifteenth day of the seventh month, when you have gathered in the crops of the land, you shall celebrate the feast of the Lord for seven days, with a rest on the first day and a rest on the eighth day. 40 Now on the first day you shall take for yourselves the foliage of beautiful trees, palm branches and boughs of leafy trees and willows of the brook, and you shall rejoice before the Lord your God for seven days. 41 You shall thus celebrate it as a feast to the Lord for seven days in the year. It shall be a perpetual statute throughout your generations; you shall celebrate it in the seventh month. 42 You shall live in booths for seven days; all the native-born in Israel shall live in booths, 43 so that your generations may know that I had the sons of Israel live in booths when I brought them out from the land of Egypt. I am the Lord your God.'" 44 So Moses declared to the sons of Israel the appointed times of the Lord.

Note: The emphases and section headings were added by the author

Appendix B - The Timing of First Fruits

In order to convey the importance of this question, please allow me to explain how the question, or rather, how the *dispute* evolved within the Jewish religious leadership. About 500 years before the time of Christ, after the Jews returned to Jerusalem from their exile in Babylon and rebuilt the temple, the responsibility for the maintenance of the temple and its services were assumed by priests who eventually divided into two closely related schools of thought: the Zadokites and the Baitusees[409]—the Zadokites later became known as the Sadducees. As you would expect, they were wholly committed to a strict, literal interpretation of the Torah (i.e., the Law), since they were responsible and accountable for overseeing the festivals and the Appointed Times. They wanted to get it right since they had paid such a high price for going astray, being exiled to a foreign land.

According to Rabbi Dr. Abraham Geiger, the Zadokites became the nobility and the elite of Israel, having both the hereditary dignity and the *perceived* attribute of holiness. But, as the Talmud and the book of Acts further explain, the Sadducees and the Baitusees did not believe in an afterlife with rewards or consequences, so their honorable priestly position degraded into a worldly way of life that became corrupt and was ultimately despised by the people of Israel. They surrounded themselves with pomp and flaunted their gold and silver of this world in order to spite those who believed in the hereafter.[410] The result was a corrupt religious aristocracy that was out of touch with the common citizens of Israel.

Predictably, a group of separatists arose in opposition to the Sadducees; this group eventually became known as the Pharisees. Rather than holding to a strict, literal interpretation of the Torah that would strengthen the position of the Sadducees, the Pharisees sought to appeal to the greater population of Israel and emphasized a *figurative* approach to interpreting the Law. Their driving philosophy came from a passage in the Second Book of Maccabees, which says, *"Unto all are given the heritage, the kingdom, the priesthood, and the sanctuary."*[411] Thus, they taught that everyone should be regarded as priestly and holy, not just the religious elite. So, the separatist Pharisees became the champions of the people by undermining the Sadducees' monopoly on religious authority and transferring religious privilege to the common believer.

---

409 (Rodkinson, The Babylonian Talmud 1903) – Volume 5 JURISPRUDENCE, TRACT ABOTH, Chapter I, p. 27 – The Sadducees derived their name from Zadok (i.e., the Zadokites), who was the leading priest during the reigns of Kings David and Solomon. See 1 Kings 1:32–39; the Baitusees derived their name from their founder, Baitus.

410 (Rodkinson, The Babylonian Talmud 1903) – Volume 5 JURISPRUDENCE, TRACT ABOTH, Chapter I, p. 27 – "...these disciples deviated from the path of the Torah... They surrounded themselves with pomp and the brilliancy of shining metals, gold and silver, not so much for the delight and pleasure which they derived from those things as to spite the Pharisees, who deprived themselves of enjoyment here, in order to inherit the world to come, which in their opinion was a mere delusion."

411 (Geiger 1865) – p 165 – 2 Maccabees 2:17

Despite the corruption of the Sadducees and Baitusees, we cannot simply discard all of their teachings. We must assess each teaching in light of the Scriptures. The Sadducees answered the *"which Sabbath"* question as the ***weekly*** **Sabbath** that occurs during the week-long Feast of Unleavened Bread, which means **that the Day of First Fruits will always be on Sunday**, the first day of the week. But the popularity of the Pharisees was strong, and using their influence, they were able to modify some of the administration of the Temple services, including the timing of the Appointed Times. Thus, we learn from Levi Rodkinson's comments "that the strife between the Pharisees and the Baitusees was amicably concluded by adopting the decree of the Pharisees..."[412] Rather than maintaining a literal interpretation of Leviticus 23, the Temple leadership gave way to popular opinion and adopted the position of the Pharisees on this issue. And why shouldn't they? After all, the Sadducees did not believe there would be any eternal consequences for their actions.

What was the position of the Pharisees regarding the "which Sabbath" question? Although it is well known and still in effect today, we find the answer in a footnote in Levi Rodkinson's English translation of the Babylonian Talmud:

"but the Pharisees... maintained that the passage implies that the counting must be commenced on the day following the first day of the festival..."

This means that First Fruits will always be observed on Abib 16, which is the day after first high Sabbath of Abib 15, at the beginning of the Feast of Unleavened Bread.

Using the Pharisees' interpretation, the Day of First Fruits could fall on any day of the week. The religious-political position of the Pharisees carried a lot of weight in Israel, since they were able to prescribe the interpretation of the Law of Moses as they saw fit. This may have been what Jesus was referring to when He told the crowds and His disciples, "The scribes and the Pharisees have seated themselves in the chair of Moses,"[413] meaning that they proclaimed themselves as the religious authority in Israel.

---

412 (Rodkinson, The Babylonian Talmud 1903) – Volume 4 Festivals Part III, TRACT TAANITH (FASTING), Chapter II, p. 44 – Rodkinson's footnote for this section clarifies the strife as "The Pharisees and Bathusees also disputed about the date when the feast of Pentecost was to be celebrated, the latter claiming that as it is written [Lev. xxiii. 15]: 'And ye shall count unto you, from the morrow after the Sabbath... seven complete weeks,' ***the day of Pentecost must necessarily fall on the first day of the week; but the Pharisees,*** *through R. Johanan ben Zakkai,* ***maintained that the passage implies that counting must be commenced on the day following the first day of the festival,*** *and therefore the feast of Pentecost would fall on the sixth day of the month of Sivan." (Emphasis added)*

413 Matthew 23:2

Appendix C – Judaism and the Fall Appointed Times

Before we explore the *fall* Appointed Times, it would be helpful if we explain the Jewish teachings of how these holy days fit together. This is not for the purpose of merging our interpretations, but for the purpose of comparison. It is of great importance that we clearly understand the differences between the Appointed Times holy days and the **non**-Appointed Times holy days.

To begin, you may have heard the term *Rosh Hashanah*, which is the name given to the first day of the Jewish civil year. Rosh Hashanah means *head of the year.* It is observed on Tishri 1, which is the same date of the Day of Trumpets, so we must be careful not to confuse the two. You should be aware that Rosh Hashanah is not an Appointed Time.

One of the prominent themes of Rosh Hashanah is repentance. According to tradition, God annually judges all creatures in the days between Rosh Hashanah and the Day of Atonement, so getting your life in order with God and with others is essential before the judgments begin and especially before they are finalized on the Day of Atonement. The Talmud teaches "On new year's day," three books (i.e., scrolls) are opened that determine how the judgment will unfold.

One of these scrolls records the names of those who are wholly wicked or evil. The names of these people are inscribed in this scroll on Rosh Hashanah and it is then closed and sealed on that same day. As the scroll is sealed, the fates of these people are also sealed and they are destined for destruction during the next year.

Another scroll records the names of those who are wholly good or righteous. Their names are inscribed in this scroll on Rosh Hashanah and it is also closed and sealed on that same day, and these people are destined to live throughout the next year.

But the third scroll is for the average class of people, those who are neither wholly wicked nor wholly good, and these hang in the balances during the ten days between Rosh Hashanah and the Day of Atonement. This scroll is called the Book of Life or the Book of the Living from Psalm 69:28. People seek to get their names inscribed in this scroll by proving themselves worthy through three acts:

- Prayer
- Acts of Charity and
- Repentance

One of the main emphases of Rosh Hashanah is to reconcile with people whom you have wronged during the past year and turn from your offending ways. The Talmud teaches that the

Day of Atonement provides forgiveness only for the sins that are committed against God, but it is up to each person to atone or make things right when they've sinned against another person.

The Book of Life remains open for ten days. Then, on the Day of Atonement, the Book of Life is closed and sealed. And according to the Talmud, if people have proven themselves worthy, they are inscribed for life for the next year – if not, they are inscribed for destruction. These ten days are known as the "**Days of Awe**" or the "**Days of Repentance**," and they are a solemn time in the life of Jewish people as they seek reconciliation with those whom they have wronged, and engage in prayer and acts of charity. It is a time of serious introspection of their actions during the previous year, reconciling with others with the hope of having their names inscribed in the Book of Life.

Now you should know that the people do not simply change their behavior and begin seeking reconciliation when Rosh Hashanah arrives on Tishri 1. They begin pursuing these acts for the entire month prior to Tishri, which is the month of Elul. The 30 days of Elul, plus the ten days between Rosh Hashanah and the Day of Atonement are referred to as the 40 Days of Repentance. The people seek to have their names inscribed in the Book of Life by proving themselves through observing these acts of piety. If successful, their names will be inscribed in this book and they will live through the upcoming year.

The Jewish people have a common greeting during this time of the year that reflects their sincerity and goodwill. You may hear someone say, "May your name be inscribed and sealed for another good year."

Now, it is interesting that only five days after the very solemn Day of Atonement on Tishri 10, we encounter the most joyous Appointed Time of all – the Feast of Booths. The Jewish people believe this Appointed Time is affirmation that they are the people of God, and they celebrate this feast with great joy. The command from the Lord repeatedly says to celebrate and rejoice!

This final Appointed Time seams together all of the *fall* Appointed Times, from the 30 days preceding the Day of Trumpets to the Day of Atonement and all the way to the Sabbath Day that concludes the Feast of Booths. It brings a special unity and meaning to the Law of Moses.

For our study, we will return to our investigation of the Appointed Times and examine the shadows of messianic events to come through the lens of the Law of Moses, the Psalms, Prophets, and the apostles, along with teaching directly from Jesus. We will encounter events of messianic magnitude that will literally shake the heavens and the earth, as we explore prophetic utterances that terrify and visions that entice us with the hope of new life, peace, and an eternal home with the Messiah.

Appendix D – Leviticus 16 – The Day of Atonement

1 Now the Lord spoke to Moses after the death of the two sons of Aaron, when they had approached the presence of the Lord and died. 2 The Lord said to Moses:

"Tell your brother Aaron that he shall not enter at any time into the holy place inside the veil, before the mercy seat which is on the ark, or he will die; for I will appear in the cloud over the mercy seat. 3 Aaron shall enter the holy place with this: with a bull for a sin offering and a ram for a burnt offering. 4 He shall put on the holy linen tunic, and the linen undergarments shall be next to his body, and he shall be girded with the linen sash and attired with the linen turban (these are holy garments). Then he shall bathe his body in water and put them on. 5 He shall take from the congregation of the sons of Israel two male goats for a sin offering and one ram for a burnt offering. 6 Then Aaron shall offer the bull for the sin offering which is for himself, that he may make atonement for himself and for his household. 7 He shall take the two goats and present them before the Lord at the doorway of the tent of meeting. 8 Aaron shall cast lots for the two goats, one lot for the Lord and the other lot for the scapegoat. 9 Then Aaron shall offer the goat on which the lot for the Lord fell, and make it a sin offering. 10 But the goat on which the lot for the scapegoat fell shall be presented alive before the Lord, to make atonement upon it, to send it into the wilderness as the scapegoat.

11 "Then Aaron shall offer the bull of the sin offering which is for himself and make atonement for himself and for his household, and he shall slaughter the bull of the sin offering which is for himself. 12 He shall take a firepan full of coals of fire from upon the altar before the Lord and two handfuls of finely ground sweet incense, and bring it inside the veil. 13 He shall put the incense on the fire before the Lord, that the cloud of incense may cover the mercy seat that is on the ark of the testimony, otherwise he will die. 14 Moreover, he shall take some of the blood of the bull and sprinkle it with his finger on the mercy seat on the east side; also in front of the mercy seat he shall sprinkle some of the blood with his finger seven times.

15 "Then he shall slaughter the goat of the sin offering which is for the people, and bring its blood inside the veil and do with its blood as he did with the blood of the bull, and sprinkle it on the mercy seat and in front of the mercy seat. 16 He shall make atonement for the holy place, because of the impurities of the sons of Israel and because of their transgressions in regard to all their sins; and thus he shall do for the tent of meeting which abides with them in the midst of their impurities. 17 When he goes in to make atonement in the holy place, no one shall be in the tent of meeting until he comes out, that he may make atonement for himself and for his household and for all the assembly of Israel. 18 Then he shall go out to the altar that is before the Lord and make atonement for it, and shall take some of the blood of the bull and of the

blood of the goat and put it on the horns of the altar on all sides. 19 With his finger he shall sprinkle some of the blood on it seven times and cleanse it, and from the impurities of the sons of Israel consecrate it.

20 "When he finishes atoning for the holy place and the tent of meeting and the altar, he shall offer the live goat. 21 Then Aaron shall lay both of his hands on the head of the live goat, and confess over it all the iniquities of the sons of Israel and all their transgressions in regard to all their sins; and he shall lay them on the head of the goat and send it away into the wilderness by the hand of a man who stands in readiness. 22 The goat shall bear on itself all their iniquities to a solitary land; and he shall release the goat in the wilderness.

23 "Then Aaron shall come into the tent of meeting and take off the linen garments which he put on when he went into the holy place, and shall leave them there. 24 He shall bathe his body with water in a holy place and put on his clothes, and come forth and offer his burnt offering and the burnt offering of the people and make atonement for himself and for the people. 25 Then he shall offer up in smoke the fat of the sin offering on the altar. 26 The one who released the goat as the scapegoat shall wash his clothes and bathe his body with water; then afterward he shall come into the camp. 27 But the bull of the sin offering and the goat of the sin offering, whose blood was brought in to make atonement in the holy place, shall be taken outside the camp, and they shall burn their hides, their flesh, and their refuse in the fire. 28 Then the one who burns them shall wash his clothes and bathe his body with water, then afterward he shall come into the camp.

29 "This shall be a permanent statute for you: in the seventh month, on the tenth day of the month, you shall humble your souls and not do any work, whether the native, or the alien who sojourns among you; 30 for it is on this day that atonement shall be made for you to cleanse you; you will be clean from all your sins before the Lord. 31 It is to be a sabbath of solemn rest for you, that you may humble your souls; it is a permanent statute. 32 So the priest who is anointed and ordained to serve as priest in his father's place shall make atonement: he shall thus put on the linen garments, the holy garments, 33 and make atonement for the holy sanctuary, and he shall make atonement for the tent of meeting and for the altar. He shall also make atonement for the priests and for all the people of the assembly. 34 Now you shall have this as a permanent statute, to make atonement for the sons of Israel for all their sins once every year." And just as the Lord had commanded Moses, so he did. ***[NASB]***

Appendix E – Appointed Times Quick Facts

Quick Facts about Passover

Name: Passover—also known as Pesach. It is important to know that the Scriptures sometimes use the names Passover and the Feast of Unleavened Bread synonymously. This can cause ambiguity in interpretation.
Leviticus 23 verse: 5
Date: Abib 14 (Note: Abib, which is also known as Nisan, is the first month of the Hebrew year. It occurs in the March-April timeframe of the Gregorian calendar)
High Sabbath Days: Abib 14 is not a Sabbath day; it is the day of preparation for the first day of the Feast of Unleavened Bread on Abib 15, which is a Sabbath day.
Shadow: The people were to kill a pure and spotless lamb and put its blood on the doorposts and lintel of their homes, so the destroyer would pass over their homes and not harm the firstborn of the household.
Messianic Substance: The substance of Passover was the death of Jesus, which occurred on Abib 14, at the same time the Passover lamb was killed, almost 1,500 years later. The lamb being set apart for inspection on Abib 10 corresponds to Jesus entering Jerusalem to be inspected by the religious leadership of Israel.
Historical: When the nation of Israel was enslaved by Pharaoh in the land of Egypt, the Lord inflicted ten plagues on the Egyptians for the purpose of convincing Pharaoh to release the Israelites. The message was not heeded after the first nine plagues, so the Lord determined to convince Pharaoh through the fateful tenth plague, which was taking the life of the firstborn of every household. The Israelites were protected from the plague by following the instructions of the Lord.
Things to watch for: There are *two key dates in Passover*. The first is Abib 10, when the lamb was set apart to be inspected for its purity as the Passover sacrifice. The second key date is Abib 14, on which the lamb was killed in the late afternoon and its blood was applied to the doorposts and lintel of each household. Note also that Passover is *not* a high Sabbath.
Related passages in the Pentateuch: Exodus 12:3–14, Exodus 12:21–51, Exodus 34:25, Numbers 9:2–14, Numbers 28:16, Numbers 33:3-4, Deuteronomy 16:1-6

The Feast of Unleavened Bread – Quick Facts

Name: The Feast of Unleavened Bread. It is important to know that the Scriptures sometimes use the names Passover and the Feast of Unleavened Bread synonymously. This can cause ambiguity in interpretation.
Leviticus 23 verses: 6–8
Dates: Abib 15 through Abib 21—a seven-day feast.
High Sabbath Days: The first and last days of the Feast of Unleavened Bread are **High Sabbath Days**. Thus, Abib 15 and 21 are high Sabbath days.
Shadow: The people of Israel were not allowed to eat leavened bread or anything that contained leaven (i.e., yeast) during this seven-day feast. During the early hours of Abib 15 (which is the evening of Abib 14), the people ate the Passover meal that they had prepared earlier that day. The meal consisted of the roasted lamb, unleavened bread, and bitter herbs. Future generations ate this same type of meal to commemorate the affliction of their ancestors as they journeyed into the wilderness.
Messianic Substance: The messianic substance is Jesus being placed in the tomb on Abib 15 (which is the evening of Abib 14), almost 1,500 years later. Jesus, who is the Lamb of God, tasted the bitterness of death as our Passover Lamb, while the people ate the Passover meal.
Historical: The feast commemorates the Israelites' difficult exodus from Egypt. They were required to eat unleavened bread, which is the bread of affliction. They left in haste during the night with the fear of Pharaoh and his armies pursuing and annihilating them.
Things to watch for: The Scriptures sometimes use the terms Passover and Unleavened Bread interchangeably, since the date of Passover is adjacent to the first day of the Feast of Unleavened Bread. Thus, it is sometimes difficult to determine which is being referenced, and great care must be exercised as we interpret these passages.
Related passages in the Pentateuch: Exodus 12:14–20, Exodus 13:6–10, Exodus 23:14–17, Numbers 9:2–14, Numbers 28:16–25, Numbers 33:3–4, Deuteronomy 16:1–8

First Fruits – Quick Facts

Name: First Fruits, First Fruits of the Barley Harvest
Leviticus 23 verses: 9–14
Timing: The first fruits of the barley harvest were offered on the Sunday (i.e., the day after the weekly Sabbath day) that occurs during the Feast of Unleavened Bread.
High Sabbath Days: First Fruits is not a high Sabbath day. It is the day on which the First Fruits offering was presented.
Shadow: The people were to offer a sheaf of their pre-harvested barley crop to the Lord. The sheaf was presented to the priest, who would wave or elevate it before the Lord, thus introducing the term wave offering.
Messianic Substance: The messianic substance is the resurrection of Jesus from the dead, which occurred almost 1,500 years after the Appointed Times were instituted. His resurrection also occurred on Sunday, probably around dawn, during the Feast of Unleavened Bread.
Historical: The Israelites arose alive from the sea at dawn on the first Sunday after they exited the city of Rameses of Egypt. The First Fruits offering was not required until the Israelites occupied the Promised Land and reaped the harvest of the land.
Things to watch for: The First Fruits sheaf was to be offered on the day after the Sabbath, so we must determine which Sabbath Moses was referencing. Was it the weekly Sabbath or the first high Sabbath of the Feast of Unleavened Bread? The answer is in the text!
Related passages in the Pentateuch: Exodus 23:14–19, Exodus 34:21–26, Leviticus 2:11–16

The Feast of Weeks - Quick Facts

Name: The Feast of Weeks was also known as Pentecost. Other names include the Counting of the Omer, the Feast of the Harvest, the Counting of the Sheaves, and First Fruits of the Wheat Harvest.
Leviticus 23 verses: 15–22
Timing: Observed exactly 50 days after First Fruits. It falls during the month of Sivan, which is the third month of the Hebrew calendar. This feast could occur anywhere between Sivan 4–13, depending on the date of First Fruits and the length of the previous lunar months (Abib and Iyar).
High Sabbath Days: The Feast of Weeks is the third high Sabbath day of the Jewish year.
Shadow: The Israelites were to celebrate a feast to the Lord and offer a first fruits offering of the *wheat* harvest. It is reasonable to believe that the Feast of Weeks was given by the Lord as a commemoration of the Law being given to Moses, although the Scriptures do not explicitly make that connection.
Messianic Substance: On the Day of Pentecost, almost 1,500 years later, the Holy Spirit descended on the believers in the upper room in Jerusalem, baptizing and indwelling them and sealing their salvation.
Historical: It is likely that the Law was given to Moses on Mount Sinai on this special day, fifty days after Israel arose alive from the sea. The Lord descended on the mountain as the nation of Israel was gathered at its base. The flames and smoke and the sound of the ram's horn terrified the people to the extent that Moses spoke to the Lord on their behalf.
Things to watch for: There is a beautiful irony between the Lord's meeting with the people at Mount Sinai versus His meeting with the people in the upper room in Jerusalem, almost 1,500 years later. The visitation at Sinai marked the terrifying chasm that existed between this holy God and the sinful people. The visitation in the upper room in Jerusalem, on the other hand, marked the loving adoption of the people by this holy God. The difference, of course, was the complete and utter reconciliation between God and man through the atonement of the Messiah.
Related passages in the Pentateuch: Exodus 23:14–17, Exodus 34:21–26, Numbers 28:26–31, Deuteronomy 16:9–12

The Day of Trumpets – Quick Facts

Name: The Day of Trumpets—also known as Yom Teruah. It occurs on the same day as Rosh Hashanah (The Head of the Year), although the two events are not related in the Scriptures.

Leviticus 23 verses: 23–25

Date: Tishri 1 *(Note: Tishri is the seventh month of the Hebrew year, which is in the September-October timeframe of the Gregorian calendar.)*

High Sabbath Days: According to the Bible, Tishri 1 is to be a Sabbath day—the people were not to do any laborious work. This is the fourth high Sabbath of the Appointed Times.

Shadow: The people were to have a rest—a Sabbath—a reminder by creating *teruah*, which is making noise by blowing trumpets and ram's horns (i.e., shofars), shouting, and singing.

Messianic Substance: On a predetermined day in the future, the Messiah will descend from heaven with a shout, with the voice of the archangel and with the trumpet of God. He will come as the conquering king, to ascend the throne of the universe and judge the living and the dead.

Historical: The Scriptures offer little or no historical parallel for the Day of Trumpets, as if to look forward to a great day to come. Psalms 47 and 98 connect teruah with the great king ascending His throne and bringing salvation to His people.

Things to watch for: Keep in mind that the name of this day is Yom Teruah in the original language of the Scriptures. Blowing trumpets is certainly a form of teruah, but many forms of creating sound or noise are also considered to be teruah. Also be aware that this day is a reminder, in which the teruah reminds the Lord of the people and their situations.

Related passages in the Pentateuch: Numbers 29:1–6

The Day of Atonement – Quick Facts

Name: The Day of Atonement—also known as Yom Kippur.
Leviticus 23 verses: 26–32
Date: Tishri 10
High Sabbath Days: Tishri 10 is to be a Sabbath day—it is the most sacred day of the year, and the people were not to do any work of any kind. This is the fifth high Sabbath of the Appointed Times.
Shadow: On this day, the high priest of Israel was to conduct a solemn ceremony in the tabernacle. Two goats were selected, one of which was selected by lot to be the Lord's, while the other was the scapegoat. On this day, the Lord's goat was slaughtered, and its blood was taken into the most holy place and sprinkled before the cherubim, which are on top of the ark of the covenant. After presenting the blood of the Lord's goat, the high priest conferred the sins of the entire nation of Israel onto the scapegoat, and it was set free in the wilderness. Through this ceremony, which is detailed in the 16th chapter of Leviticus, atonement was made for the nation of Israel.
Messianic Substance: The ceremony of the Day of Atonement foreshadows the Messiah entering the tabernacle of God in the heavenly places and, with His own blood, He obtained eternal redemption. The scapegoat is analogous to the people of the world, who are utterly sinful but were freed since the Lord's Messiah paid the ultimate price.
Historical: The Day of Atonement is not mentioned in any place in the Scriptures other than in the Law of Moses. Thus, we are not given a historical meaning for this day. The book of Hebrews, however, provides much detail about how this Appointed Time speaks of the work of Jesus making propitiation (i.e., atonement) with His own blood.
Things to watch for: A key component of the Day of Atonement ceremony is releasing the scapegoat into the wilderness, thus liberating it. However, many years after the passing of Moses, the Jewish leadership added their commentary to the law, teaching that the scapegoat is to be pushed off a cliff, to its death, believing it was given to a goat demon. Obviously, this teaching is not found in the Law of Moses, and it distorts the symbolism that was originally intended by the Lord.
Related passages in the Pentateuch: Leviticus 16 (the entire chapter), Numbers 29:7-11

The Feast of Booths – Quick Facts

Name: The Feast of Booths, the Feast of Tabernacles, Sukkot, the Feast of the Ingathering
Leviticus 23 verses: 33–36 & 39–43
Dates: Tishri 15–21, followed by an additional Sabbath day on the 22nd, after the conclusion of the feast.
High Sabbath Days: The first day of the Feast of Booths, Tishri 15, is a high Sabbath day, and the **day after the conclusion of the feast** is also a Sabbath day. Thus, Tishri 15 and 22 are high Sabbath days, which are the sixth and seventh high Sabbath days of the Appointed Times.
Shadow: The Israelites are to live in booths (i.e., temporary shelters) for seven days to commemorate their forefathers living in booths during their exodus from Egypt. Even though it remembers a somber time, the people were told to celebrate and rejoice before the Lord for seven days. They are to construct their booths in a festive manner, adorning them with the foliage of beautiful trees, palm branches, boughs of leafy trees, and willows of the brook. This is the most festive and joyous of the Appointed Times, as it also celebrates the completion of the fall harvest with an air of fullness and contentment.
Messianic Substance: Perhaps the greatest theme of the Feast of Booths is the idea of taking up residence. The people of Israel joyously took up residence in their festive booths, perhaps depicting the people of the Messiah joyously taking up residence in the eternal homes that He prepared for them in His Father's house. The Sabbath rest that occurs after the conclusion of the feast may foreshadow the never-ending Sabbath rest for the Lord's people after the conclusion of their time on this earth.
Historical: The Feast of Booths reminds the people of Israel that the Lord had the generation of the exodus live in booths when He brought them out of Egypt. The Scriptures mention the feast in several places, including 2 Chronicles 5:3, Nehemiah 9:14, and John 7:2.
Things to watch for: As you read about the Feast of Booths, take special note that the final Sabbath day takes place *after* the conclusion of the feast, rather than during the seven-day feast.
Related passages in the Pentateuch: Numbers 29:12-38, Deuteronomy 16:13–15, Deuteronomy 31:10–13

TRACKING TIME IN ISRAEL

by Don McCluskey

Tracking Time In Israel

by: Donald McCluskey

www.TheAppointedTimes.com
Rev. 0122216-01

Contents

Introduction – For Signs and for Seasons

How often have you marveled at the rising or setting sun as it set the sky ablaze with color? Have you ever beheld the beauty of a full or crescent moon and felt there must be some sort of meaning in this lesser light? These are some of the most common, yet magnificent events that bless our planet each day, and I am here to tell you that there is indeed some significance to be found these heavenly events.

I am certainly not suggesting astrology, but these lights and luminaries were placed in the heavens by the Creator to give light and to act as signs, so people could know the seasons, days, and years of our planet. These heavenly lights were created so mankind could know when to plant, harvest, conduct business, and even worship. In the account of creation, we read:

Then God said,
"Let there be lights in the expanse of the heavens to separate the day from the night, and let them be for signs, and for seasons, and for days and years;"

Genesis 1:14

One of the keys to interpreting the Scriptures is found in understanding how these lights were used by the ancient Israelites to track time. For example, when did a day begin and end? At what time of the year did the months of the Bible occur? What determined when a month began and ended? What is the meaning of twilight? What is a watch in the night? What is meant by the biblical references to hours, such as the third hour, the sixth hour, or ninth hour? These are excellent questions and knowing the answers can greatly enhance our understanding of God's Word.

Since precise time-measuring devices were not available in the ancient world, civilizations relied on observations of the sun, moon, and stars to track time. Our modern days end and begin at midnight, which is a point in the nighttime that can be precisely known only with the aid of an electronic or mechanical clock. But since ancient civilizations, including the nation of Israel, did not have such devices, they used the setting of the sun as their indicator of a new day.

The Israelites also tracked their months in a very different way than we do with our modern calendar. The Hebrew months are determined by observing the phases of the moon. Their months begin when the fine edge of the crescent new moon is first observed. From that date, the days are counted from sunset to sunset until the next crescent new moon is observed. Since the Hebrew calendar relies on both the moon and the sun, it is called a lunisolar calendar.

Since tracking time involves much more than a knowledge of days and months, we have created this reference guide, which contains the details of ancient Israel's calendaring system in concise form to assist you in understanding the message of God's Word.

The Hebrew Calendar

The calendar that was used by the ancient Israelites, also known as the Hebrew calendar, is still in use today in Jewish and Messianic circles. The details of this calendar are relatively easy to learn – many Jewish people learned it when they were children. It is fun and interesting and you can enjoy the pleasure of moon-watching while gaining an awareness of when significant days and events of the Bible begin and end.

Once again, I must emphasize that this is a study of astronomy—it is not astrology. Astrology is a form of divination, seeking hidden knowledge from sources other than God, such as spirits, speaking with the dead, and idol worship, all of which are abominations to God.[1] Astronomy is, among other things, the study of the heavenly bodies and how God set them in beautiful, predictable motion that we can use to track time. He declared that the lights of the heavens, the sun, moon, and the stars, were created for giving light, for signs, seasons, days, and years,[2] so it is perfectly acceptable for us to observe the lights of the heavens for this purpose.

In this reference guide, we will explore the ancient Hebrew concepts of

Day

Daytime

Nighttime

Twilight

Week

Sabbath

High Sabbath

Month

New Moon

Year

1 *Isaiah 47:13 "Let now the astrologers, those who prophesy by the stars, those who predict by the new moons, stand up and save you from what will come upon you."*

2 *Genesis 1:14–18*

The Appointed Times

Every student of the Bible would benefit by becoming familiar with the Appointed Times, also known as the Jewish holy days, which are recorded in chronological order in the 23rd chapter of Leviticus. We frequently refer to the Appointed Times in this guide since they provide many examples of timing in the Bible, but of greater importance, these special days reveal profound insights about the person and work of the Messiah.[3]

Day

The Hebrew day **begins** at sundown

God called the light day, and the darkness He called night. And there was evening and there was morning, one day.

Genesis 1:5

You might think it strange that the day would begin when the sun goes down; perhaps it would be easier to think of the day ending at sundown. Either way, the end of a day and the beginning of the next day occur simultaneously, at the same instant in time. It is important, however, to make sure that everyone in the community agrees about when the change-of-day occurs. Since digital and mechanical clocks did not exist during the time of Moses, the sunset was used as the indicator of the change of day.

3 *If you would like to learn more about the Appointed Times, I enthusiastically refer you to our book, The Messiah Beyond a Shadow of Doubt, which explores how the Appointed Times are shadows of things to come, but their substance is actually about the Messiah.*

Why did the Israelites choose sundown instead of sunrise? It was because of the wording in Genesis 1:5 (see above). Notice that evening was mentioned first, and then morning. Thus, the ancient Israelites considered a day to be from sunset to sunset. When the sun set, both the day and the date changed. This concept will be of great importance when you study Passover, since the lamb was killed on the afternoon of the 14th, and it was eaten after the sun had set. It would have been the same day from our modern perspective, but for the Israelites it was the next day, since the date changed to the 15th when the sun set.

This little piece of information is able to shed light on other Bible passages and increase your overall understanding of the Scriptures. For example, you may be familiar with the following account in the life of Jesus:

And when evening had come, ***after the sun had set,***
they began bringing to Him all who were
ill and those who were demon-possessed.

Mark 1:32 (Emphasis added)

The paragraph that precedes this verse makes it clear that it was the Sabbath day (before the sun had set), which meant that the people were not allowed to do any labor, such as walking long distances or carrying heavy loads, including carrying their sick loved ones. But this verse explicitly says, "when evening had come, after the sun had set," which ushered in the next day. Suddenly, it was Sunday, the first day of the week, even though it would seem like Saturday night to you and me. The Sabbath Day had ended, along with its restrictions against work, so the people were allowed to walk long distances and bring their sick friends and loved-ones to Jesus.

By knowing the Hebrew time-keeping methods, we understand that the people were waiting for the sun to set. It was like watching the clock – they were watching the sun as it set, anticipating the moment they could take their sick to Jesus. They did not have to wait for midnight for the Sabbath to end – they went to Jesus immediately after the sun had set.

Caveat

I must mention one caveat within the naming convention that can mislead readers. Even though the calendar day begins at sundown, the evening portion of a day was sometimes referred to with the same date as the daytime.

For example, in Exodus 12:18, the Passover lamb was killed in the afternoon of Abib 14, but the evening of the same day is referred to as "the fourteenth day of the month at evening." This can be confusing since the calendar date had actually changed to Abib 15 at sundown. The same type of date reference can be seen regarding the Day of Atonement in Leviticus 23:32, which says, "on the ninth of the month at evening, from evening until evening you shall keep your sabbath." In reality, the date had changed to Tishri 10 at sundown, but the evening is referred to as the evening of the ninth. For the most part, however, the Scriptures are consistent about the day and date changing at sundown.

The Days are Numbered

As you read the Bible, you will notice that the Hebrew days do not have names such as Sunday, Monday, or Tuesday. Instead, they use ordinals (i.e. numbers or ordered items) to refer to their days, such as "the first day of the week," "the second day of the week," and so on. The counting begins with Sunday, which is the first day of the week. The only day that was named is the Sabbath Day, which is the seventh day. For ease of understanding, however, we will in most cases, use our familiar names of weekdays.[4]

4 *The names of the weekdays vary widely from country to country. In this guide, however, we will use the more common names: Sunday, Monday, Tuesday, Wednesday, Thursday, Friday, and Saturday.*

Daytime

In our modern world, the day is divided evenly into 24 hours. But in the ancient world, the daytime or *daylight* was divided into **twelve equal parts**, beginning at sunrise and ending at sundown. The twelve parts were called hours, and were called by their ordinal names, such as the first hour, the second hour, and so on.

Daytime was divided into twelve equal parts, beginning at sunrise and ending at sundown.

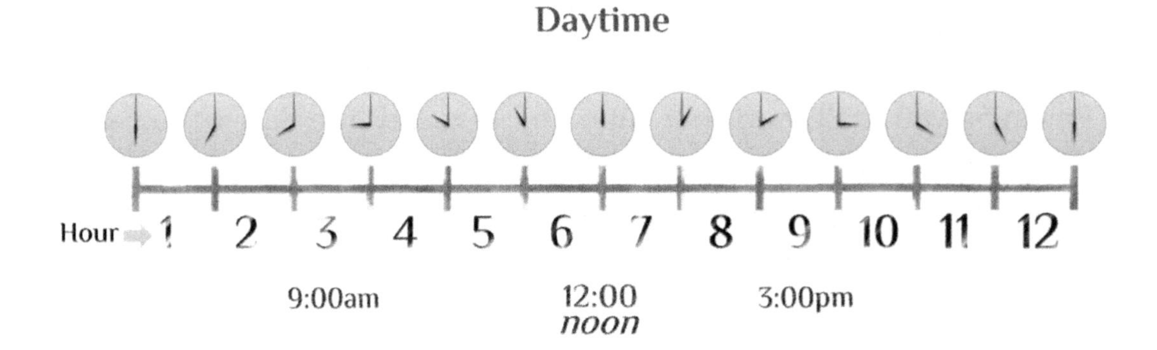

The following table compares modern times-of-day to the Biblical hours:

Biblical Hour	**Approximate 24-Hour Clock**	**Approximate 12-hour Clock**
First	6:00-7:00	6:00am – 7:00am
Second	7:00-8:00	7:00am – 8:00am
Third	8:00-9:00	8:00am – 9:00am
Fourth	9:00-10:00	9:00am – 10:00am
Fifth	10:00-11:00	10:00am – 11:00am
Sixth	11:00-12:00	11:00am – 12:00pm
Seventh	12:00-13:00	12:00pm – 1:00pm
Eighth	13:00-14:00	1:00pm – 2:00pm
Ninth	14:00-15:00	2:00pm – 3:00pm
Tenth	15:00-16:00	3:00pm – 4:00pm
Eleventh	16:00-17:00	4:00pm – 5:00pm
Twelfth	17:00-18:00	5:00pm – 6:00pm

You may be thinking that the length of an hour would be dependent on the time of year and the latitude of the country, and you would be correct. The summertime hours in Israel, for example, are very long when compared to its wintertime hours since the duration of daylight in June is several hours longer than the duration of daylight in December. Because of this, the duration of an hour in June is relatively long when compared to an hour in the winter. The hours were probably tracked by shadows on some type of sundial.

To see a practical application of biblical hours, I recommend that you read Jesus' parable of the *Laborers in the Vineyard* (Matthew 20:1–16). In addition to mentioning "early in the morning," Jesus refers to the third, sixth, ninth, and eleventh hours, which are important for understanding the point of the parable.

Other examples of biblical hours have been provided below:

- While Jesus was on the cross, darkness fell over the land from the sixth hour to the ninth hour. Matthew 27:45
- Jesus invited two of John's disciples at the tenth hour. John 1:39
- Jesus encountered the Samaritan woman at Jacob's well at the sixth hour. John 4:6
- On the day of Pentecost, the apostles addressed the crowds in their own languages at the third hour. Acts 2:15
- Cornelius recounted that during the sixth hour, a man stood before him in shining garments. Acts 10:9

Twilight

Twilight is an important timing concept when studying the Appointed Times. Moses gave the following instructions about the Passover lamb to the people:

"You shall keep it until the fourteenth day of the same month, then the whole assembly of the congregation of Israel is to kill it at ***twilight****."*

Exodus 12:6 (Emphasis added)

Twilight- Literally "Between the Two Evenings" (Exodus 12:6)

In the above passage, twilight literally means ***between the two evenings***. In our modern world, twilight refers to the time after the sun has set, while the sky is still illuminated with soft, diffused light. Twilight can also refer to the morning twilight, which occurs before the sun rises and the atmosphere is illuminated with the soft, diffused light of the sun.

For lack of a better term, many modern Bible translations use the term "twilight" to translate Moses' words *between the two evenings*, while some translations simply refer to it as "evening." It is interesting that Moses was the only biblical writer who used this phrase; it is found in Exodus, Leviticus, and Numbers.

The obvious question, of course, is what are the two evenings? It seems strange that the issue has not been settled, especially since scholars have been wrestling with it for almost 3,500 years. The question has puzzled students of God's Word for thousands of years. So, for your benefit, I will list the four most popular views and then explain which I believe is the most likely option.

Four Views of "between the two evenings"

1. **Between sundown and complete darkness**

   » It is unlikely that this view is valid, because it would actually be the next day if the sun had already set. This is important in the case of Passover, since the people were required to sacrifice the Passover lamb on the 14th. If the sun had already set, then the date would have become the 15th, meaning they had missed their window for completing the task.

2. **Between sundown at the beginning of the day and sundown at the end of the day**

   » It is unlikely that this view is valid, because it would include the entire 24-hour day, so there is really no purpose in stipulating a time, since it could be anytime of the day.

3. **The time between noon and sundown**

   » This view holds some possibility since the beginning of the first evening can be determined by increasing shadow length due to the declining sun.

4. **Between the time of the evening sacrifice and sundown.** The evening sacrifice was offered at the 9th hour, which is 3:00pm by our modern timing. The people would have sacrificed the Passover lamb between 3:00pm and sundown.

   » This view is the most plausible for several reasons that are explained below.

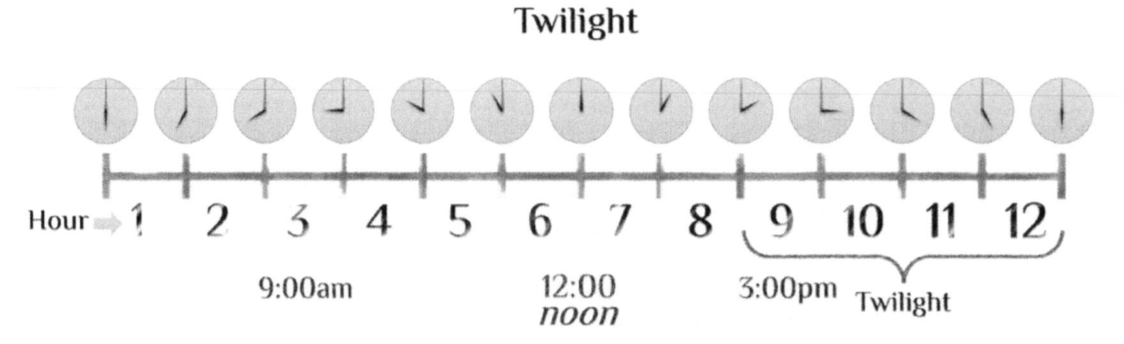

Between the 9th hour and Sundown

Twilight – Between the 9th Hour and Sundown

As we try to understand the meaning of *two evenings*, we can safely assume that the second of the two evenings is the end of the day, which is indicated by sundown. So, now the question is **what is the first evening?** The 29th chapter of Exodus holds some interesting clues that relate to this mystery. Let's look into this chapter to see what we can learn.

In Exodus 29:38–42, Moses explains the Lord's command to offer a one-year-old male lamb in the morning and *evening* of each day as a continual burnt offering throughout all of Israel's generations. In this passage, he uses the same phrase, "between the two evenings." So, we can infer that this daily offering is presented in the morning and later in the day, which is called *evening*. As history revealed, the Jewish community interpreted the timing of the sacrifice to be soon after sunrise and, in a similar way, the evening sacrifice was offered shortly before sunset.

With a little more investigation, we find that the Jewish priests, during the second temple period[5], were committed to offering the evening sacrifice **at the ninth hour of each day**, even if it resulted in their own physical harm or death. Josephus, the first-century historian, recorded how the Jewish priests faithfully continued their temple service even during the Roman siege of Jerusalem. Josephus related the following account of the situation:

"[A]nyone may hence learn how very great piety we exercise towards God, and the observance of his laws, since the priests were not at all hindered from their sacred ministrations, by their fear during this siege, but did still twice each day, in the morning and about the ninth hour, offer their sacrifices on the altar; nor did they omit those sacrifices, if any melancholy

5 *The second temple period began in 597 BC and ended in 70 AD, when the Romans destroyed the temple.*

accident happened, by the stones that were thrown among them." [6]

From Josephus' record, we learn that the Jewish priests in the first century understood that *between the two evenings* meant to **begin at the ninth hour (3:00pm)**.

The between the two evenings concept gives some latitude in the timing of the priestly responsibilities, since the sacrifice could legitimately be offered anytime between the ninth hour and sundown. So for our understanding, we will consider *twilight* or *between the two evenings* as the time period between the ninth hour and the end-of-day, which is at sunset.

Twilight or Between the Two Evenings

Begins at the ninth hour of the day (3:00pm)

and

Ends at sunset

6 *(Josephus 1994) The Antiquities of the Jews, Book 14, Chapter 4, 3 (65) (Emphasis added).*

Nighttime

In the ancient world, nighttime was divided into **four equal parts**, beginning at sunset and ending at sunrise. Each part was called a *watch*, not like the watch that we wear on our wrists, but referring to guards *watching* over the city.

Nighttime was divided into four equal parts, beginning at sundown and ending at sunrise.

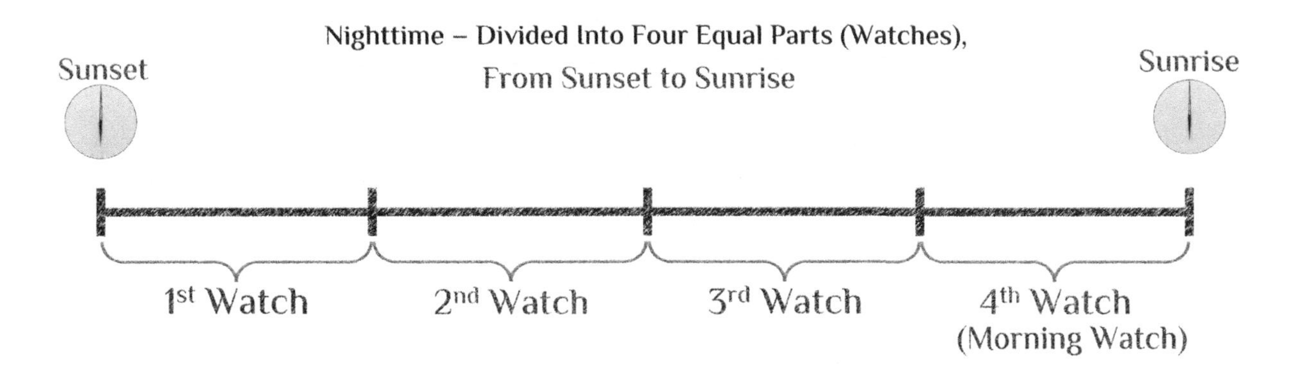

The first watch began at sunset and continued for approximately one fourth of the nighttime; it was followed by the second, third, and finally by the fourth watch. The fourth watch was sometimes called the *morning* watch, since the watchmen literally watched for the rising of the sun, which ended their shift. The shifts may have been timed with sand-clocks or water-clocks, but little is known about how the ancients tracked time during the hours of darkness.

The Scriptures mention the watches of the night in various ways. Consider the following verses to see if they make more sense to you now:

For a thousand years in Your sight
Are like yesterday when it passes by,
Or ***as a watch in the night****.*

Psalm 90:4 (Emphasis added)

At the ***morning watch****, the LORD looked down on the army of the Egyptians through the pillar of fire and cloud and brought the army of the Egyptians into confusion.*

Exodus 14:24 (Emphasis added)

When I remember You on my bed,
I meditate on You ***in the night watches,***

Psalm 63:6 (Emphasis added)

My eyes anticipate ***the night watches,***
That I may meditate on Your word.

Psalm 119:148 (Emphasis added)

And in ***the fourth watch*** *of the night He came to them, walking on the sea.*

Matthew 14:25 (Emphasis added)

Whether he comes in the second watch, or even in the third,
and finds them so, blessed are those slaves.

Luke 12:38 (Emphasis added)

Other passages include: Judges 7:19, 1 Samuel 11:11, 1 Chronicles 9:27, and Psalm 130:6.

Note: There is some evidence that only three watches were used during certain periods of Israel's history, but the concept of dividing the nighttime hours into equal segments or watches remains the same.

Midnight

Midnight is another important timing element that we find in the story of Israel's exodus from Egypt. The Hebrew word for midnight means half or mid. Since the ancients were not able to precisely track hours and minutes during darkness, they estimated the halfway point of the night, although it was probably not exactly at 12:00 midnight as it is defined in our modern world.

Week

Our modern world's concept of the seven-day week probably originated from ancient Israel's unbending commitment to observing the Sabbath on the seventh day of every week. Other civilizations had the concept of a seven-day week, but their weeks were not consistently seven days long. The ancient Babylonian calendar, for example, implemented a seven-day week by dividing the 29.5-day lunar month into four segments of seven days. But since the lunar month is slightly longer than 28 days, the fourth week of their month had to be stretched from seven days to eight.

It was not so with the Jewish people. For them, the Sabbath day occurred every seventh day, and the day after the Sabbath was always the first day of the next week. Thus, the word sabbath was sometimes used to refer to a seven-day period of time,[7] which we would call a week. The fact that a week could overlap from one month into the next was not an issue for them just as it is not an issue in our modern world.

7 Leviticus 23:15 provides an example of the word sabbath referring to a period of seven days, or one week: "You shall also count for yourselves from the day after the sabbath, from the day when you brought in the sheaf of the wave offering; there shall be seven complete sabbaths." Also, Leviticus 25:8 uses sabbath synonymously with seven, but in this case it refers to seven years.

The Hebrew language has a word for week, but it does not necessarily mean seven *days*; it refers to a *set of seven*, such as seven years or seven of anything.

The Sabbath Day

He ceased from His labor and was refreshed...

"Remember the Sabbath day, to keep it holy.
Six days you shall labor, and do all your work,
but the seventh day is a Sabbath to the Lord your God.

...

For in six days the Lord made heaven and earth,
the sea, and all that is in them, and rested on the seventh day;
Therefore the Lord blessed the Sabbath day and made it holy.

Exodus 20:8-11

Sabbath is more than just a timing word. More importantly, it is the first Appointed Time that is mentioned in Leviticus 23,[8] indicating its importance in the sight of God and in the life of Israel. Once again, it is observed on the seventh day of every week, which is Saturday. Based on what we have learned about days, the Sabbath begins at sundown on the sixth day and ends at sundown on the seventh day. Or stated differently, the Sabbath begins at sundown on Friday and ends at sundown on Saturday evening. Since the Sabbath occurs on the seventh day of every week, we sometimes refer to it as the weekly Sabbath in order to avoid confusion with great or high Sabbaths, which we will explore in a later section.

The Sabbath is the commemoration of the Lord's rest from His work after completing the six days of creation[9] and is intended to be a day of rest for everyone. The Hebrew word for Sabbath is *shabbat* and is based on the Hebrew word that means "and He rested," *shabath*, referring to God resting after His work of creation.[10] Resting from our labors is the essence of the Sabbath. It was given as a blessing from God so we can be refreshed

8 *Leviticus 23:2–3*

9 *Exodus 20:11 – "For in six days the Lord made the heavens and the earth, the sea and all that is in them, and rested on the seventh day; therefore the Lord blessed the sabbath day and made it holy."*

10 *Genesis 2:2 – "By the seventh day God completed His work which He had done, and He rested on the seventh day from all His work which He had done."*

as He was refreshed when He ceased from His labor.[11]

The Sabbath day was not just a commemoration. It is one of the hallmarks of God's covenant with Israel, to the extent that they would forever be known as God's people through their keeping the commandments regarding the Sabbath.[12] Every Israelite is required to rest on the weekly Sabbath, including the head of the household, the entire family, the slaves/ servants, guests, and even the animals that belong to the household. The penalty for failing to keep the Sabbath was extremely severe, so the entire nation dutifully obeyed this command.

If someone were to ask you, "Which day is the Sabbath?" how would you respond? The Israelites observe the Sabbath as the seventh day of the week, which is Saturday.

"If because of the sabbath, you turn your foot
From doing your own pleasure on My holy day,
And call the sabbath a delight, the holy day of the Lord honorable,
And honor it, desisting from your own ways,
From seeking your own pleasure
And speaking your own word,

Then you will take delight in the Lord,
And I will make you ride on the heights of the earth;
And I will feed you with the heritage of Jacob your father,
For the mouth of the Lord has spoken."

Isaiah 58:13–14

11 *Exodus 31:17 – "It is a sign between Me and the sons of Israel forever; for in six days the Lord made heaven and earth, but on the seventh day He ceased from labor, and was refreshed."*

12 *Exodus 31:16–17a – "So the sons of Israel shall observe the sabbath, to celebrate the sabbath throughout their generations as a perpetual covenant. It is a sign between Me and the sons of Israel forever..."*

The origin of the Sabbath rest is very interesting. The Scriptures taught it as the way of the Lord even before the He gave His Law to Moses (see Exodus 16:22–30). According to the creation accounts in Genesis chapters 1 and 2, God rested on the seventh day, and even though the accounts do not contain an explicit command for mankind to rest, they offer a subtle, refreshing appeal for us to rest after our labors. What does your day of rest look like?

The Day of Preparation

The day *before* a Sabbath Day is referred to as *a day of preparation.* Shopping, chores, and laborious activities were completed on the day of preparation since work was forbidden on the Sabbath. Meals were prepared and clothes were cleaned and pressed in advance of the seventh day to assure that everyone could rest from their work on the Sabbath.

This is also the case with great or high Sabbaths, which are addressed in a later section. For example, the 14th day of Abib (the first month of the Hebrew religious calendar) is Passover and is also referred to as *the day of preparation* for the first high Sabbath, which is the Feast of Unleavened Bread on the 15th day of Abib. Preparation for this high Sabbath may be done on the 14th, but not on the 15th, since it is a high Sabbath, a day of rest.

A Sabbath Day's Journey

All travel had to be completed before the sun went down on a day of preparation, whether it was a journey to visit the sick or commuting to and from work. Riding an animal instead of walking did not release a person from the requirement for rest since forcing the animal to work as a beast of burden also violated the Sabbath.[13] Simply stated, God forbade all labor for both animals and humans on Sabbath Days.

The Talmud[14] places a limit on the maximum distance a person can travel on foot on the Sabbath day[15] — anything beyond that distance is considered to be labor and a violation of the Sabbath. This maximum distance is referred to as a *"Sabbath day's journey"* and was defined as 2,000 normal steps or 2,000 cubits, which is approximately 0.6 miles or 0.9 kilometers. It is interesting that the Talmud does not place a limit on how far a person could walk within a walled city.

Great or High Sabbaths

In addition to the weekly Sabbaths, **seven special Sabbaths were established by the Lord in His Appointed Times in Leviticus 23**. We refer to these Sabbaths as great or high Sabbaths, but for convenience we will simply refer to them as *high* Sabbaths.

The *high* Sabbath terminology is not common in the Scriptures, but it is certainly there. John 19:31, for example, refers to the first day of the Feast of Unleavened Bread as a high Sabbath, thus differentiating it from

13 *Deuteronomy 5:12–14*

14 *The Talmud is the compilation of the Jewish oral laws that were recorded in written form after the destruction of the Temple in A.D. 70. The purpose of the Talmud was to provide information about how the laws and commands of Moses were to be carried out. Although it is not considered to be inspired, the Talmud provides extremely valuable insights about how Judaism was lived out through the centuries.*

15 *(Rodkinson, The Babylonian Talmud 1916) Book 4, TRACT BETZAH, Chapter II, p. 31*

a *weekly* Sabbath. The underlying Greek word is *megas* (μέγας), from which we get the prefix *meg* or *mega*. Even in our modern world, when something is said to be mega, you know it's big or special. The term carries multiple meanings, all of which suggest something of great magnitude or magnificence.

Why would the Lord require a day of rest as part of His Appointed Times? Simply stated, I believe it is a way of telling us to honor the Lord by stopping, pausing, and considering what is being taught by this Appointed Time. We will explore the timing and substance of each high Sabbath in detail in our book *The Messiah Beyond a Shadow of Doubt*.

The seven high Sabbaths are listed in their annual order in the following table:

The Seven High Sabbaths

	#	Sabbath
Easy!	1	1st Day of Unleavened Bread – 15th day of 1st moon
	2	7th Day of Unleavened Bread – 21st day of 1st moon
	3	Feast of Weeks (50 Days after First Fruits)
	4	Day of Trumpets – 1st day of 7th moon
	5	Day of Atonement – 10th day of 7th moon
Easy!	6	1st Day of Feast of Booths – 15th day of 7th moon
	7	8th Day after the Feast of Booths begins – 22nd day of 7th moon

Since the high Sabbaths are found throughout the Scriptures, it would be worth your time to memorize them – it's really quite simple! Just remember that the first and last Appointed Times in Leviticus 23 are week-long feasts, and both begin and end with a high Sabbath— that makes it **Easy!** to remember. So, you now already know four of the seven high Sabbath Days, which makes it easier to memorize the remaining three high Sabbaths that occur in between them.

Notice that Passover is not listed in the table above because it is not a high Sabbath. As we've already discussed, Passover, which is always on Abib 14, is a day of preparation, or more specifically, the day of preparation for the first high Sabbath Day of the Feast of Unleavened Bread. It is a day of preparation because the Israelites prepare for the next day, Abib 15, which is the first day of the Feast of Unleavened Bread.

A word of caution: The terminology may be a little confusing at times. Even though Abib 14 is the date of the Lord's Passover,[16] the actual "pass over" event did not occur until midnight of Abib 15, when the destroyer *passed* over the homes that had the blood of the lamb on the doorposts and lintel.[17] We must also be careful as we study, because the Scriptures sometimes use the terms *Passover* and *The Feast of Unleavened Bread* interchangeably. Furthermore, the day before a *weekly* Sabbath is also called a day of preparation, so, it is important to give close attention to the context of a passage in order to know which type of Sabbath is being discussed.

High Sabbaths Occur Throughout the Scriptures

As you read through the Bible, you will begin to recognize the Appointed Times as they are mentioned, but they are sometimes

16 *Leviticus 23:5 – "In the first month, on the fourteenth day of the month at twilight is the Lord's Passover."*

17 *Exodus 12:23b – "...the Lord will pass over the door and will not allow the destroyer to come in to your houses to smite you."*

mentioned by their dates, rather than by their names so, knowing their dates and the names will add color and precision to your understanding of the Bible.

Month

When the Lord conveyed His Appointed Times to Moses, He was very specific about the months in which they were to be observed. The spring Appointed Times begin in the month of Abib, the first month of the year, while the *fall* Appointed Times are observed during the month of Tishri, which is the seventh month of the year. In the following figure, the months of the Hebrew calendar are positioned next to the more familiar months of the Gregorian calendar[18] to help you visualize how the calendars relate to each other.

Comparison of the Gregorian and Hebrew Months

(Alternate names are in parentheses)

Gregorian	Hebrew
January	
	Sh'vat
February	
	Adar
March	
	Abib (Nisan)
April	
	Iyar (Zif)
May	
	Sivan
June	
	Tammuz
July	
	Av
August	
	Elul
September	
	Tishri (Ethaninm)
October	
	Cheshvan (Bul)
November	
	Kislev
December	
	Tevet

18 The Gregorian calendar is the most widely used calendar in the world. It was implemented by Pope Gregory XIII in October of 1582. Before that time, the Julian calendar was in use in the western world since 46 BC, but due to its inaccuracies, the dates for the holy days had become unreliable.

Notice that the months of the Hebrew calendar seem to occur in-between the months of the Gregorian calendar. Passover and the resurrection of Christ, for example, are always observed in the March-April timeframe of the Gregorian calendar, since the Scriptures teach that they occurred during the Hebrew month of Abib. Likewise, the Day of Atonement is always observed in the September-October timeframe during the Hebrew month of Tishri.

The months of the Gregorian calendar will always occur during the same seasons of the year since they are based on earth's position as it revolves around the sun. The Hebrew months, on the other hand, do not begin on a fixed day of the solar year, which is the reason the dates of the Appointed Times shift from year to year on the Gregorian calendar. The Hebrew months begin on varying dates of the solar year since they are determined by the phases of the moon, which are not in sync with the solar year.

The duration of a lunar month is 29 days, 12 hours, and 44 minutes[19], which is roughly 29.5 days. That means that, after 12 lunar months, there are about 11 days remaining in the solar year.[20] Because of this, the Hebrew months will not occur on the same Gregorian dates from year to year — they would occur approximately 11 days earlier in the following year if an adjustment is not made.

---

19 *Based on the synodic month*

20 *29.5 days x 12 months = 354 days, which is 11 days less than the 365 days of the solar*

Does the Hebrew Year Always Contain Twelve Months?

Since the solar and lunar years differ in length, a special intercalary month,[21] called **Adar** II, is inserted into the Hebrew calendar immediately *before* the month of Adar during certain years. If this correction is not made, then the Appointed Times and other events on the calendar would occur at different seasons each year. For example, it would be possible that Passover could occur in the fall or in the summer, or any other time of the year, rather than during the early spring months, as did the first Passover during the exodus from Egypt. Without the adjustment of the intercalary month, the required grain offerings would not be available for the people since the dates of their worship might not coincide with the timing of their harvests.

Because of this additional intercalary month, some years on the Hebrew calendar contain 13 months. The intercalary month is a concept that is similar to the leap year in the Gregorian calendar, which inserts an extra day in February every four years. This technique assures that the spring Appointed Times will always occur in the springtime, rather than sliding throughout the seasons of the solar year. Likewise, it assures that the fall Appointed Times will always be in the autumn, in the September-October timeframe.

The intercalary month is not randomly inserted into the Hebrew calendar. It is inserted in specific years that are predetermined by a lunar-solar cycle that is known as the Metonic Cycle. The Metonic Cycle repeats every 19 years and identifies years 3, 6, 8, 11, 14, 17, and 19 as years that must have an additional month in order to synchronize the Hebrew calendar with the solar seasons. You can research the Metonic Cycle to learn more about this phenomenon.

21 *Intercalary month refers to an additional month that is added to the year during certain years. It is similar to an additional day (i.e., February 29th) that is added to the Gregorian calendar during a leap year.*

New Moon, New Month

Jewish New Moon
Courtesy of NASA

The Hebrew months begin with the appearance of the new moon. The Jewish leaders, therefore, carefully tracked the moon throughout its various phases. Even though they were able to calculate the date of the new moon, their rule was to rely on the testimony of witnesses who actually observed it.

Witnesses were examined by the Council in a large court in Jerusalem called Beth Ya'azeq. Once the Council was satisfied that the witnesses' testimonies were true, they would then consecrate the new moon and proclaim throughout the land that a new month had begun.[22]

The methods of proclaiming the new moon varied throughout Israel's history. In Numbers 10:1–2, the Lord instructed Moses to "Make yourself two trumpets of silver, of hammered work." The trumpets were designated for multiple uses, but in verse 10, we are told that they should also be used to proclaim the first days of the months.

22 *(Rodkinson, The Babylonian Talmud 1916) Book 2, TRACT ROSH HASHANA, FESTIVALS PART 1, "NEW YEAR" – Chapter II, p. 45-46*

"Also in the day of your gladness and in your appointed feasts, and on the first days of your months..."

Numbers 10:10

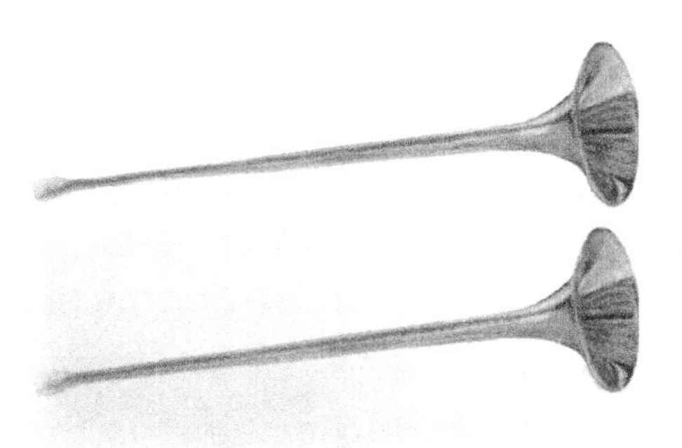

Trumpets were eventually replaced by the lighting of signal bonfires[23] and later by sending messengers throughout the land.

23 *(Rodkinson, The Babylonian Talmud 1916) Book 2, TRACT ROSH HASHANA, FESTIVALS PART 1, "NEW YEAR" – Chapter II, p. 42*

The Silver-Edge Moon - A New Month

What does a Jewish new moon look like? Although the Israelites could have chosen any phase of the moon to indicate a new month, they chose the phase when the illumination from the sun begins to appear on the edge of the moon. This phase is informally known as the Silver Edge moon, shown in the left-hand side of Figure 23.[24] You should know that the phase when the moon has no illumination, and is completely dark, is also called a new moon, but it is the astronomical new moon shown in the right-hand side of Figure 23. The astronomical new moon is used by modern astronomers, but it is not the same as the Jewish new moon – be careful not to confuse them!

The Silver Edge – 1st Day The Jewish New Moon

– A new month has begun! –

Astronomical New Moon A new month will soon be here!

Figure 23

Remember, an astronomical new moon does not signal a new month in Judaism—the new month is signaled only by the appearance of the new silver edge moon.

24 *The moon phases that are pictured are from the northern hemisphere. Moon phases in the southern hemisphere appear to be the opposite or mirror image, since the north and the south view the moon upside-down from each other.*

The Phases of the Moon

You may be wondering what causes the moon's phases. Having a basic understanding of the phases of the moon will give insight into the approximate day of the month of the lunar calendar, when the Appointed Times begin and end, and whether we are in the first or latter half of the current month.

With the exception of an eclipse, half of the moon is always illuminated by the sun, but from our perspective on earth, we are only able to see a portion of that illumination. When the earth is directly between the sun and the moon, the moon appears to be fully illuminated, but as the moon circles around the earth in its 29 ½ day orbit, we are not able to see the fully illuminated hemisphere—we can only see a portion of it until it becomes like a narrow sliver. When the moon is directly between the earth and the sun, we are unable to see any of its illuminated hemisphere, and it appears to be completely dark. This is the reason for the astronomical new moon, which is shown in the lower right-hand corner of the image below.

Moon Phases

The Moon Phases image shows some of the phases of the moon that appear after the silver edge new moon. The Hebrew month, of course, begins when the silver edge (*upper left-hand corner of the Moon Phases image*) occurs after the astronomical new moon (*pictured in the lower right-hand corner of the Moon Phases image*).

At times, the moon seems to be so close that you might think you could hit it with a stone. But it is actually much farther than it appears. The following is a scale image of the relative size of the earth, the moon, and the distance between them, which averages 238,900 miles or 384,472 kilometers.

Year

If someone were to ask, "When does the Jewish year begin?" the correct response would be, "Which year do you mean?" You may have heard that the Jewish new year is observed on Rosh Hashana, which falls on Tishri 1 in the September-October timeframe. But, just before the exodus from Egypt, the Lord told Moses and Aaron that Abib (aka. Aviv or Nisan) shall be the beginning of months,[25] which falls during the March-April timeframe. Both of these dates mark the beginning of years on the Jewish calendar. Rosh Hashana, which means head of the year, marks the beginning of the civil year, while the first day of Abib marks the beginning of the year for religious observances. Jewish law also has two additional dates which mark the beginning of years, meaning that Judaism has four new year observances.

25 *Exodus 13:4, 23:15, 34:18 and Deuteronomy 16:1*

According to the Talmud,[26]

> *"The first of Abib or Nisan is the new* **year for kings and for festivals, which includes the Appointed Times.**
>
> *The first of Elul is the new year* **for the tithing of animals.**
>
> *The first of Tishri is the new year* **for years, which included Sabbatical years, Jubilee years, and for the planting and for vegetables.**
>
> *The first of Shevat is the new year* **for trees** *(Note: The House of Hillel considers the fifteenth of Shevat to be the new year for trees)."*

The additional years can be likened to fiscal years or academic years, which provide a convenience for accounting and school activities. Josephus, the first-century Jewish historian, wrote that Tishri 1 was actually the original new-year date for buying and selling, so Moses preserved that as the original order of the months. But Moses said that Nisan (i.e., Abib) should be the first month for their festivals because God brought them out of Egypt in that month. "So that this month began the year as to all the solemnities they observed to honor God."[27]

26 *(Rodkinson, The Babylonian Talmud 1916) Book 2, TRACT ROSH HASHANA, FESTIVALS PART 1, "NEW YEAR" – Chapter I, p1: "MISHNA I.: There are four New Year days, viz.: The first of Nissan is New Year for (the ascension of) Kings and for (the regular rotation of) festivals; the first of Elul is New Year for the cattle-tithe, but according to R. Eliezer and R. Simeon, it is on the first of Tishri. The first of Tishri is New Year's day, for ordinary years, and for sabbatic years and jubilees; and also for the planting of trees and for herbs. On the first day of Shebhat is the New Year for trees, according to the school of Shammai; but the school of Hillel says it is on the fifteenth of the same month."*

27 *(Josephus 1994) The Antiquities of the Jews, Book 1, Chapter 3, 3 (81)*

When does the month of Abib begin? As a general rule of thumb,[28] it begins when the first new moon (i.e., the silver edge) is observed that occurs after the spring equinox (in the northern hemisphere[29]). Two equinoxes occur during each solar year—one in the spring (i.e., the vernal equinox) and one in the fall (i.e., the autumnal equinox). The word equinox is derived from a Latin term that means equal night, referring to specific days during the solar year when the amount of daylight is almost the same as the amount of darkness.

The Original Meaning of Abib

The Hebrew word "Abib" originally referred to green ears of grain, rather than to a month. It was synonymous with springtime. Thus, the lunar month in which the barley ears were green but not fully ripe for harvest became known as the month of Abib. The first fruits offering of Leviticus 23:9–14 consisted of a sheaf of barley that was abib—that is, the grain had matured to a head, but it was still green and not fully ripe. Using this original meaning of abib, the start of a year could have been delayed for a month in the event of a long winter.

Regardless of how the month of Abib was determined, it was the first month of the year for religious observances. But the Hebrew calendar was later refined so that the new year, beginning with Abib, was based on soli-lunar (i.e., sun and moon) events that are described by the Metonic cycle. After the Babylonian exile, the month of Abib became known as Nisan, so the two names are synonymous.

---

28 This is a general rule of thumb, but you should be aware that many variables factor into the determination of the beginning of months and years. The eastern and western churches use different criteria for determining these dates.

29 Although the equinox occurs on the same day in the northern and southern hemispheres, the names are different, since the beginning of springtime in the northern hemisphere is the beginning of autumn in the southern hemisphere. Thus, the month of Abib is based on the vernal equinox in the northern hemisphere.

Summary

You will find that having an understanding of the ancient Hebrew calendaring system can reveal insights into how the Appointed Times and various events of the Scriptures fit together. But you will also find that having this knowledge will unlock clues that can explain other parts of the Scriptures, as well. I hope this information will become second nature to you, so you will not have to refer to this guide. But until then, may it be a valuable resource for you as you study the Bible.

Bibliography

Josephus, F. (1994). *The Works of Josephus*. (W. Whiston, Trans.) Peabody, Massachusets, USA: Hendrickson Publishers, Inc.

Rodkinson, M. L. (1903). *The Babylonian Talmud* (English Edition ed.). (M. L. Rodkinson, Ed., & M. L. Rodkinson, Trans.) New York: New Talmud Publishing Society.

Rodkinson, M. L. (1916). *The Babylonian Talmud* (Vol. 2). Boston, USA: New Talmud Publishing Society.

Glossary

Word/Phrase	Definition
Abib, Aviv, Nisan	Names of the first month of the Jewish year. Versions of the Bible may use different names, but Abib is the most common (see Exodus 13:4). The Lord said that "This month shall be the beginning of months for you" (Exodus 12:2). The month of Abib begins with the first *silver* edge moon that occurs after the vernal equinox in the northern hemisphere.
Anoint	The act of pouring oil over the head of a chosen individual to signify that this person has been set apart by the Lord to fill a special role or office. Anointing was a very important rite in ancient Israel for the purpose of consecrating priests and kings. The anointing was administered by prophets or priests.
Anointed One	An individual who has been anointed (see *Anoint*, above)
Apocalypse	1) A prophetic revelation, especially concerning a cataclysm in which the forces of good permanently triumph over the forces of evil. (*def. N 3. dictionary.com/browse/apocalypse.*) 2) "Apocalypse" is often used as a synonym for the book of Revelation, the last book in the Bible.
Apocalyptic Event	A cataclysmic event that was prophesied in the Apocalypse or an event of apocalyptic magnitude.
Astronomical New Moon	The astronomical term for the moon phase when the sun, moon, and earth align, with the moon directly in between the earth and the sun. In this phase, the moon has no visible illumination from the earth. Be careful that you do not confuse the astronomical new moon with the Jewish new moon which is the Silver Edge.
Chronology	The sequential order in which past events occur. (*def. N 1. dictionary.com/browse/chronology.*)
Christ	Christ means anointed one, as one who is anointed with oil. Please refer to the definition of anoint in this glossary. Christ and Messiah both mean anointed one - Christ is the Greek word and Messiah is the Hebrew word.

Convocation	A gathering of the people for a holy purpose; a sacred meeting or worship service. Convocations involved teaching, worship, and giving praise to God.
Crescent New Moon	The first visible illumination of the moon that follows an astronomical new moon. A crescent new moon appears as an illuminated crescent, which is also called a *silver* edge.
Cut Off	(Hebrew: Kareth) "means not necessarily physical dissolution but extinction of the soul and its denial of a share in the world to come." – (Ehrman 1965) Volume 1
Day of Preparation	The day that precedes a Sabbath day. Its purpose is to make preparations for meals and activities that are not allowed to be performed on a Sabbath day, since they consist of routine work or labor.
Eschatological or Eschatology	This term refers to events of the *last* days of this world—events that are still in the future.
Gospel	The term means "good news," specifically, the good news that forgiveness, adoption, resurrection, and eternal life are available to mankind because of the completed work of the Messiah/ Christ.
Great Sabbath – also known as a High Sabbath	The term is used in John 19:31 to differentiate between a *weekly* Sabbath and a *great* or *high* Sabbath. The underlying Greek word is megas - μέγας. The Great or High Sabbaths are listed in chronological order in Leviticus 23.
Hebrew	Generally synonymous with Israelite or to describe people who speak the Hebrew language.
Hebrew Bible aka. Hebrew Scriptures	Used synonymously with *Old Testament*.
High Sabbath	Refer to *Great Sabbath.*
Israel – the man	The younger twin son of Isaac, and grandson of Abraham. His birth name was Jacob. He was given the name of Israel after wrestling with an angel for an entire night (Genesis 32:28).
Israel – the nation	The descendants of Jacob (aka. Israel), who were eventually forged into a nation during their bondage of slavery in Egypt.
Israelite (i.e., Named from Jacob)	Any person who traces their lineage back to Israel, the son of Isaac and grandson of Abraham.
Jew, Jewish	A descendant of Israel.

Law of Moses	The first five books of the Bible, also called the Pentateuch.
Lunar Calendar	A calendar that is based on the phases of the moon.
Lunisolar Calendar	A calendar that is based on a combination of moon phases as they relate to the sun. Israel's calendar is a lunisolar calendar.
Messiah	Messiah means anointed one, as one who is anointed with oil. Please refer to the definition of anoint in this glossary. Messiah and Christ both mean anointed one - Messiah is the Hebrew word and Christ is the Greek word.
New Moon	A new moon, per the Hebrew calendar, is defined as the phase of the moon with the first visible illumination that follows an astronomical new moon and Silver Edge moon. See also: *Crescent Moon*.
Sabbath	Sabbath means "rest" and is taken from the creation account in Genesis, which says, "He rested." The term describes a day in which no work is to be done—a complete rest from work. The word can refer to a weekly Sabbath or to a great or high Sabbath.
Pentateuch	The first five books of the Bible, Genesis, Exodus, Leviticus, Numbers, and Deuteronomy—all were written by Moses.
Progressive Revelation	Certain subjects of the Scriptures were introduced briefly, and somewhat cryptically, but they were developed as the revelation of the entire Bible unfolded, progressively revealing new information about a subject. Thus, the term *Progressive Revelation*.
Ram's Horn	An ancient musical horn that was made from a ram's horn. It was used for signaling and for ceremonial purposes. A ram's horn is also called a *shofar*.
Rapture	The word rapture is often used to describe the Greek word harpazō - ἁρπάζω in 1 Thessalonians 4:17. The term *rapture* is taken from the Latin Vulgate translation of the Bible, wherein harpazō is rendered as *rapiemur*. Rapture refers to the Messianic event of snatching or rapturing the righteous from the earth and uniting them with the Messiah forevermore.
Sanhedrin	An assembly of 71 judges or leaders, which constituted the religious and civic leadership of ancient Israel.
Shofar	An ancient musical horn that was made from a ram's horn. It was used for signaling and for ceremonial purposes.

Silver Edge Moon	The phase of the moon in which the first visible illumination **follows** an astronomical new moon. A silver edge moon appears as an illuminated crescent. The silver edge moon signifies the beginning of a new month on the Jewish calendar.
Sukkah	A temporary dwelling or shelter, typically made from easily obtainable organic materials, including the foliage of trees, palm branches, and boughs of leafy trees and willows of the brook. This type of shelter was the lodging as the Israelites sojourned in the wilderness after their exodus from Egypt.
Sukkot	Plural form of sukkah
Synoptic Gospels	Synoptic Gospels refer to the three gospels, Matthew, Mark, and Luke, which *look alike* or are *similar* in their message, while the gospel of John conveys the good news (i.e., gospel) of Christ from a different perspective. The gospels tend to be grouped as the synoptic gospels versus John's gospel. Despite their different perspectives, a careful study of all four gospels will show that they complement and harmonize with each other, rather than contradict.
Talmud	The Talmud (Hebrew for "study") is one of the central works of the Jewish people. It is the record of rabbinic teachings that spans a period of about six hundred years, beginning in the first century C.E. and continuing through the sixth and seventh centuries C.E. The rabbinic teachings of the Talmud explain in great detail how the commandments of the Torah are to be carried out. (Isaacs 2003) – Introduction, Page ix
Torah	The Hebrew term for *Law or the Law of Moses.* Generally considered to be the first five books of the Bible, but it can also refer to the entire body of the Hebrew Scriptures aka. the Old Testament.
Weekly Sabbath	Every seventh day of the week, which is Saturday, is considered to be the *weekly* Sabbath, although it is usually referred to simply as the Sabbath. The term *weekly Sabbath* is sometimes used to distinguish it from a *great* or *high* Sabbath.

Bibliography

Albright W. F., Mann, C. S. 1971. The Anchor Bible - Matthew - A New Translation with Introduction and Commentary. Vol. 26. New York, New York: Doubleday.

Bard, Mitchell G. 2016. Days of Awe - Asseret Yimei T'Shuva. January. Accessed May 2019. https://www.jewishvirtuallibrary.org.

Bullinger, E.W. 2012 - First Published in 1898. Figures of Speech Used in the Bible. New York, New York: Cosimo Classics.

Byers, Gary A. 2008. "New Evidence From Egypt on the Location of the Exodus Sea Crossing, Part 2." Bible and Spade (Associates for Biblical Research) 19: 14-22.

Cohen, Shaye. 2006. From the Maccabees to the Mishna. Louisville, Kentucky: Westminster John Knox Press.

Ehrman, Arnost Zvi. 1965. The Talmud with English translation and commentary. Vol. 1. LEOR: El-Am - HOZA'A. https://books.google.com/books?id=9DXRswEACAAJ.

Freedman, David Noel. 2000. *Eerdmans Dictionary of the Bible*. Grand Rapids, Michigan: William B. Eerdmans Publishing Co.

Geiger, Abraham. 1865. Judaism and Its History. Translated by Maurice Mayer. New York, New York: New York M. Thalmessinger.

Hutchins, Robert Maynard, Editor in Chief, ed. 1952, 1989. Great Books of the Western World. 31st. Vol. 6. 54 vols. Chicago, Illinois: William Benton, Publisher.

Isaacs, Ronald H. 2003. A Taste of Text - An Introduction to the Talmud and Midrash. New York, New York: UAHC Press.

Josephus, Flavius. 1994. The Works of Josephus. Translated by William Whiston. Peabody, Massachusets: Hendrickson Publishers, Inc.

Lewis, C.S. 1977. The Weight of Glory. Grand Rapids, Michigan: William B. Eerdmans Publishing Company.

Mounce, William D. 2006. Mounce's Complete Expository Dictionary of Old & New Testament Words. Grand Rapids, Michigan: Zondervan.

Neusner, J. 2011. The Babylonian Talmud: A Translation and Commentary. Peabody, MA: Hendrickson Publishers.

Philo. 1993. The Works of Philo. Translated by C.D. Yonge. Peabody, Massachussets: Hendrickson Publishers, Inc.

Rodkinson, Michael L. 1903. The Babylonian Talmud. English Edition. Edited by Michael L. Rodkinson. Translated by Michael L. Rodkinson. New York: New Talmud Publishing Society.

—. 1916. The Babylonian Talmud. Vol. 2. Boston: New Talmud Publishing Society.

Swanson, James A. 1997. Dictionary of Biblical Languages with Semantic Domains: Hebrew (Old Testament). Logos Research Systems, Inc. Oak Harbor.

The Encyclopaedia Britannica. 2016. "https://www.britannica.com/topic/pharaoh." https://www.britannica.com. Edited by The Editors of Encyclopaedia Britannica. July 04. Accessed November 27, 2018. https://www.britannica.com/topic/pharaoh.

The Episcopal Church. 1979. Book of Common Prayer, The. New York, New York: The Church Hymnal Corporation.

The Lockman Foundation. 1995. The New American Standard Bible Updated Edition. La Habra, CA: The Lockman Foundation.

Unger, Merrill F. 1957, 1961, 1962, 1982. Unger's Bible Dictionary. Chicago, Illinois: Moody Press.

Vine, W.E. 1981. Vine's Expository Dictionary of Old and New Testament Words. Edited by F.F. Bruce. Iowa Falls, Iowa: World Bible Publishers.

Wilson, John A. 1969. "Egyptian Historical Texts." In Egyptian Historical Texts, by John A. Wilson, edited by James B. Pritchard, 227–64 in Ancient Near Eastern Texts Relating to the Old Testament. Princeton : Princeton University.

Wood, Bryant G. 2009. "Recent Research on the Date and Setting of the Exodus." Bible and Spade Magazine (Fall 2009). http://www.biblearchaeology.org/.

About the Author & Illustrator:

Donald McCluskey

is the president of Ancient Words Ministries, an organization that specializes in teaching the Bible and Bible study techniques to church leaders in remote parts of the world. With a love for studying and teaching, he excels at explaining complex concepts in ways that are enlightening and enjoyable for learners.

He and his wife, Jill, live in the heart of Texas and recently celebrated their 40th wedding anniversary. They have two sons, a daughter-in-law, and the first of many grandchildren.

Mr. McCluskey holds degrees in Biblical Studies, Electronic Engineering Tech, Computer Science, and Telecommunications. Just for fun, he enjoys family, friends, music, and road trips.

www.AncientWords.us

Kate Orr

is an award-winning artist from Indianapolis, Indiana. Recently featured in Southwest Art Magazine's "21 Under 31" Article, Kate has displayed her work in exhibitions regionally and with the National Scholastic Art Competition and Allied Artists of America in New York City. Primarily working in charcoal and oils, she strives to capture the reflection of God in His Creation. People have always been her favorite subject, and she has been drawing portraits her whole life, most often of her brother and four sisters. Kate's portraits have been described as "expressive and sensitive." When she's not painting or drawing, Kate enjoys spending time with her family, dancing, and trying new experiences.

KateOrrFineArt.wixsite.com/katenorrfineart

Other Books by Donald McCluskey

Principles of Bible Study © 2015 – ISBN 978-0-9966758-0-2

Tracking Time in Israel © 2020 – ISBN 978-0-9966758-3-3

Made in the USA
Middletown, DE
04 February 2023